Colonel Benjamin Stephenson and the History of Early Illinois

Colonel Benjamin Stephenson and the History of Early Illinois

Sidney G. Denny

with a Foreword from Jason Stacy

Southern Illinois University Press

Carbondale

Southern Illinois University Press
siupress.com

Printed in the United States of America

First printed May 2025.

Cover illustration: Portrait of Colonel Benjamin Stephenson. Unidentified artist, ca. 1800, watercolor on ivory, sight size 2-7/8 × 2-1/8 in. (7.2 × 5.3 cm) oval, Smithsonian American Art Museum, museum purchase, 1976.56

ISBN 978-0-8093-7015-3 (paperback)

ISBN 978-0-8093-7016-0 (ebook)

This book has been catalogued with The Library of Congress.

Printed on recycled paper ♻

CONTENTS

ILLUSTRATIONS

Figures

Tables

FOREWORD

From the outset, Sid Denny was one of the people who saw the potential in restoring the Colonel Benjamin Stephenson House. After restoration, he served on the board for 12 years and was instrumental in supporting the living museum it became. But perhaps Sid's greatest act of friendship was the recording of the House's early history and connecting it to the broader history of Illinois and the United States. In 2009, he began to write what eventually became a decade's worth of short historical articles for the House's newsletter, the *Spectator*. These articles covered topics as wide ranging as Indigenous Illinois before white settlement, the events that led to Stephenson's arrival, and the very bricks with which the house was built. While the Stephenson House is a living history museum, Sid's articles kept the history of Benjamin Stephenson alive.

When Sid passed away in 2023, this history was largely lost. I first thought to collect his newsletter articles as a resource for visitors to the Benjamin Stephenson House. I also hoped to save them for posterity. However, in early 2024, RoxAnn Raisner, director of the House, discovered Sid's unpublished manuscript that told the history of Benjamin Stephenson in book form. And while it included much of the material from the newsletters, it also provided a thoroughgoing history that connected early Illinois history to the history of westward settlement and, before that, the American Revolution itself. This is the book you're now holding.

Much of *Colonel Benjamin Stephenson and the History of Early Illinois* is drawn from contemporaneous primary sources. It traces Stephenson from his childhood in 18th-century Pennsylvania to his experiences on the Illinois frontier and, finally, to his last residence, which is now a museum of his life and times in Edwardsville. I believe it is a proper testament to Sid's work as a historian of early

Illinois. It is also a fitting testament to his friendship for the House he helped restore.

My thanks go to Jane Denny and the Friends of the Colonel Benjamin Stephenson House Board for supporting this project. And special thanks to Jessica Guldner for her help editing the manuscript and building the index.

Jason Stacy
Edwardsville, Illinois
2024

Colonel Benjamin Stephenson and the History of Early Illinois

CHAPTER ONE

Revolution's Child

In the early summer of 1778, nine-year-old Benjamin Stephenson, and most of the other scattered residents of the Manor of Maske, York County, Pennsylvania, anxiously awaited news of the latest developments in the war with Great Britain. The previous year had brought news of countless disasters. The costly defeat at Long Island, in August of 1776, had resulted in the capture of Ben's uncle, Thomas Reed, who remained a prisoner of the British for nine months before being exchanged. Shortly after the Battle of Long Island came news of the abandonment of New York City and the loss of Fort Washington. At Fort Washington almost an entire battalion of York County soldiers had been killed or captured, including the commanding colonel, all of the officers, and most of the sergeants and other lower ranks. The loss of New York City and the surrender of Fort Washington were followed by the retreat of George Washington's army all through New York and New Jersey.

In early September had come the news of another defeat at Brandywine in which a number of soldiers from York County and the Manor of Maske had been killed, wounded, or captured. Only a few days later had come more terrible news of the "massacre" at Paoli. At Paoli a detachment of soldiers of the Pennsylvania line, including units of the 11th Pennsylvania, had been left behind to act as a rear guard for Washington's retreating army. The 11th Pennsylvania had been recruited from Philadelphia and four neighboring counties including York County. The detachment had been surprised by a dawn attack by the British. One York County survivor of the attack later wrote:

> the annals of the age cannot produce such a scene of butchery. All was confusion. The enemy was among us . . . The enemy rushed on with fixed bayonets, and made use of them as they intended. Our loss: Col. Grier, Capt. Wilson, and Lieut. Irvine, and sixty-one non-commissioned officers and privates killed–just half of the men we had . . . I went to see the wounded. The scene was shocking. The poor men groaning under their wounds, which were all by stabs of bayonets and cuts of light horsemen's swords. (Bates, 1992, p. 35)

Rumors had begun to circulate that the British had bayoneted those who were trying to surrender and that the battle had been a massacre. In fact, 71 had surrendered, and there never was a massacre. Nevertheless, most believed that the British had instituted an order of "no quarter," and fears of future massacres grew.

Finally, by the end of September 1777, Philadelphia had been occupied, and the Continental Congress had fled to York, only 100 miles from Philadelphia and only 40 miles from the Manor of Maske. It seemed as if the winter of 1777 and 1778 saw nothing but one disaster after another. The bad news had been relieved only by Washington's victories at Trenton and Princeton. But those victories had provided merely a short respite from the almost endless stream of bad news. Just when it seemed that the news could not get worse, things became even more depressing when reports of the suffering of the army at Valley Forge were received. The army had gone into winter camp in mid-December 1777, and by February more than 2,500 members of the army had died of starvation, disease, or exposure. Now, in late June of 1778, rumors of another battle had begun to trickle into the settlements.

Almost every rumor or bit of reliable news was greeted with mounting anxiety. Most of it had been negative, and Benjamin Stephenson, like many other residents of the Manor of Maske, had a personal stake in the outcome of the revolution. His father, maternal grandfather, and all seven of his maternal uncles, as well as his uncle by marriage, were members of the local militia, and several of them had later transferred to the regular Continental Army.

Before the war, Ben's maternal grandfather, James Reed, had served as the colonel of the local county militia. James had immigrated to America around 1728 and probably married Margaret Floyd sometime in the early 1730s. In August 1738, he filed a claim for 900 acres of land in the area that was called the Marsh Creek settlement. Most of the area was drained by Marsh Creek and a number of its tributaries. The area east of Reed's claim later became the Manor of Maske. James and Margaret Reed had nine children. Thomas and James R. were the first two sons. Ben's mother, Mary, was the older daughter. Following Mary's birth were Sarah, Benjamin J., John, Joseph, Samuel, and William. When the local militia regiments were formed, all seven of the Reed sons, son-in-law James Stephenson, and William McKesson, the husband of Ben's aunt Sarah, all joined James Stephenson's regiment (Sampson, 1922).

When news of Lexington arrived, Thomas Reed, the oldest son, immediately journeyed to Boston to enlist as a private. He was captured in Washington's defeat at Long Island, held prisoner for nine months, and was ultimately exchanged. James, the second son, was a captain in the militia and later served as a lieutenant in a regular army regiment of the Pennsylvania line. Benjamin Reed was the third son to serve in the revolution, first as an ensign of the 3rd Company of the 5th Battalion of militia. Later he became a lieutenant of the 1st Company of the 2nd Battalion. The remaining sons all served as officers in the militia (Riley, 1999). According to family legend, Margaret Reed, true to her Scots-Irish heritage, blessed her sons before they went off to war "and told them never to come back to her with a bullet in the back" (Sampson, 1922).

Margaret Reed's blessing and admonition to her sons were typical of the attitudes and historical roots of the Scots-Irish residents who made up the largest portion of the population of the Manor of Maske. The Scots-Irish were a fractious, bellicose bunch. The old adage "Hell hath no fury like a woman scorned" would apply equally well to any Scots-Irishman scorned. They were descendants of the warlike clans of Scotland. Most had grown up listening to the heroic and tragic stories of the fierce highland clans led by

"Braveheart," William Wallace. Their warlike propensities were whetted by their Presbyterian beliefs, which spurned ritual and rejected almost all hierarchical authority. A war against one of the most powerful hierarchical authorities in the world, the king of England, was a war against the perfect enemy.

The residents of the Manor of Maske had followed the news of the continuing troubles in Massachusetts. They had heard about the Boston Massacre, followed by a string of ever more restrictive acts of the English Parliament. These included the Sugar Act, the Currency Act, the Quartering Act, and the Stamp Act. All of these acts were attempts by the British to defray the cost of maintaining the colonies and to contain the revolutionary furor in Boston. For the residents of the Manor of Maske, the idea of an act like the Quartering Act, which required the residents of Boston to quarter British soldiers in their own homes, would have been anathema. The news of the Boston Tea Party was greeted by the residents of the manor with celebrations and lots of drinks that were stronger than tea. Thus, when news of Lexington and Concord finally made its way to the Manor of Maske, many of the residents could not wait to come to the aid of their beleaguered Massachusetts colleagues. When Lexington and Concord took place, Benjamin Stephenson was almost six years old. When the news of the Declaration of Independence came just over a year later, the news was greeted with rejoicing. Ben was just four days short of his seventh birthday, and the Fourth of July became a focal point of celebration throughout the rest of his life.

The Scots-Irish, from whom Ben descended, had come to the New World in the early 1700s. They were not Irish at all. They were originally from Scotland. When the English occupied Ireland in the early 1600s, they confiscated the estates of Irish landowners. King James I encouraged his Scottish subjects to emigrate to Ireland and take over the confiscated lands. Since the Scottish clans were known as fierce warriors and their Presbyterian beliefs were opposed to Irish Catholicism, James I saw the Scots-Irish as the perfect answer to his Irish problem.

Unfortunately for the Scots-Irish, King James I died, and Charles I came to the throne in 1625. He tried to force Scots-Irish Presbyterians to adhere to the Church of England. "At the same time the native Irish rose to expel the Scotch and succeeded in killing a few thousand of them" (Prowell, 1907, p. 121). Faced with both religious persecution and the hostility of the native Irish, many of the Scots-Irish emigrated to America. From 1700 to 1740, thousands of families left Ireland. Those who stayed were clustered around Ulster and became "Ulstermen." Even today, they remain hostile to the native Irish.

When the Scots-Irish arrived in America, they tended to shun the cities and to gravitate toward the frontier. Many of them made their way into the mountains of the Carolinas and Virginia, but the largest group of them settled in Pennsylvania. The Quaker beliefs of William Penn and his tolerance of other religions, coupled with the promise of thousands of acres of cheap land, made Pennsylvania an irresistible attraction.

The Province of Pennsylvania (Penn's forest) was founded in 1681 when King Charles II granted 40,000 square miles of land to Admiral Sir William Penn in order to pay off a debt. The grant was given to the admiral's son, also named William Penn. The younger Penn sailed to the New World in 1682 and induced a number of people to emigrate by offering land for 40 shillings per 100 acres or 5,000 acres for 100 pounds. Following the negotiation of a treaty with the Leni Lenape tribe (also known as the Delaware), a site was selected for the town of Philadelphia. Over the next few years, immigration increased substantially owing to the ready availability of cheap land. All of the land that William Penn granted to anyone during his lifetime was located east of the Susquehanna River. Penn eventually returned to England, encountered financial problems, and ended up in debtors' prison. He died in 1718, and his widow, Hannah, took over the estate until she died in 1726. Penn's three sons, John, Thomas, and Richard, became the proprietors of Pennsylvania.

The provincial land office, which served the Penns, was located in Philadelphia, and those who desired to acquire land purchased it under what was called "common terms." Under common terms in 1732, the price for 100 acres of land was 15 pounds and 10 shillings. "At three shillings a bushel, one would have needed something over 100 bushels of wheat to pay for 100 acres of land" (Glatfelter

& Weaner, 1992, p. 6). Up until 1736–1739, almost all of the land sales were located east of the Susquehanna River, which runs north to south from New York through eastern Pennsylvania and into Maryland before emptying into Chesapeake Bay. The lack of sales west of the river was the result of two problems.

The Penns had always made it a rule to establish ownership through treaties with the Native Americans. Only in 1736 had they reached agreement to purchase lands west of the Susquehanna with five of the tribes belonging to the Iroquois Confederation (the Onondaga, Seneca, Oneida, Tuscarora, and Cayuga tribes). The second problem was conflicting claims of ownership over all of the southern part of Pennsylvania. A strip of land along the southern border of the colony was claimed by both Pennsylvania and the Colony of Maryland. Maryland was selling land to settlers in an area the Penns considered part of the Pennsylvania Colony. This dispute was finally settled in 1739 when the current border between Maryland and Pennsylvania was established and surveyed.

When the two problems of Native ownership and the Maryland border dispute were finally settled, the Penns thought they could begin to sell land west of the river. The original 1681 charter allowed the Penns to sell land in two ways. Land could be sold by common terms, under which all land was sold for a common set price. But the Penns could also create a "manor" and operate under rules much more favorable to them. The manor concept allowed the proprietors to select sites for manors, which could be the choicest, and therefore most expensive, available lands. The rules stipulated that land designated a manor had to be surveyed before a property could be sold or soon thereafter. Finally, in a manor, the Penns could institute special courts and other restrictions that favored them. However, neither the special courts, nor the special restrictions, were ever instituted. For the Penns, the advantage of the manor concept was that land could be leased on an annual basis, meaning that the people who worked the land were tenants rather than owners and could be coerced by those who owned it. If the Penns did sell the land, they could charge a higher price. By the time William Penn died, he had already established 11 of these manors, and some sources suggest that the Penns ultimately created 44 manors, while one source says they created around 80 of them (Glatfelter & Weaner, 1992, p. 7).

One of the largest of the manors was the Manor of Maske. It was created in 1741 and encompassed 43,500 acres (Glatfelter & Weaner, 1992, p. ix). It was located in York County, just west of the Susquehanna River, and extended almost nine miles north from the newly created border with Maryland. The manor was an almost perfect rectangle, nine miles north to south, six miles east to west. With the creation of the manor, the Penns believed they had solved all of the problems with the Natives and the Marylanders, and they could begin surveying the land and preparing it for sale. However, the Penns had unwittingly sowed the seeds of discord in 1729 and were about to reap what they had sown.

The problem started in 1729 during the period of the border dispute between Maryland and Pennsylvania. The Colony of Maryland had sold warrants for land to a number of settlers. Pennsylvania believed that the land was really in Pennsylvania and the sales were illegal. To stop such sales and remove those who had already settled, the governor of Pennsylvania sent officials to remove the settlers. The officials were forcefully resisted, however, and additional attempts to remove the settlers were equally unsuccessful. Finally, in 1729, the governor sent word to the Penns that he needed "some fighting men" to enforce his intentions. In response, the Penns sent 140 families from Ulster, led by Captain Hance Hamilton. The families immediately moved to the area, which later became the Manor of Maske, and took up residence on lands that they believed they had earned. Between 1729 and 1741, a number of additional Scots-Irish families moved into the area. Some of them, like Ben's maternal grandfather, James Reed, had purchased warrants for the land at common terms. Reed ended up with a farm of about 900 acres.

Reed's farm was just west of the western boundary of the Manor of Maske. Most of the Scots-Irish immigrants who settled in Pennsylvania during the 1720s and 1730s had never bothered to purchase land; they simply moved into areas that were unoccupied and squatted on land of their own choice. Since the area of eastern Pennsylvania between Philadelphia and the Susquehanna

River was already settled, the new immigrants moved west of the Susquehanna and squatted there. Thus, by the time the Penns got around to establishing the Manor of Maske, the area was already populated by hundreds of Scots-Irish settlers. Some of them had come with Hance Hamilton, and some like James Reed, who lived west of the manor, had purchased their land. A large number of them had simply squatted on the land and begun the work of improving their farms and trying to develop some level of economic security.

One of the provisions of the manor concept was that the land had to be surveyed before, or shortly after, it was sold. By 1741, when the manor had been created, the seeds of discord had sprouted into a potential revolution. In order to start land sales, the Penn brothers ordered a survey of the Manor of Maske and also ordered the removal of squatters to commence. The surveyors were met with immediate resistance. The settlers there had a long history of being pushed off their former lands in the Old World, by the English in Scotland and later by the English and Irish in Ireland. Furthermore, their Presbyterian beliefs spurned most hierarchical authority. Consequently, they were determined not to move again, and even those, like James Reed, who had paid for their land did not trust the surveyors. The fighting qualities of the Scots-Irish who had come with Hance Hamilton were greatly admired in 1729 when fighters were needed. Those same qualities in 1741, though, posed a huge potential problem when they were threatened with eviction.

In May 1741, deputy surveyor Zachary Butcher was ordered to start the survey of the manor. In a letter dated June 17, 1741, Butcher informed the governor that he had intended to "lay out the Mannor at Marsh Creek" two weeks before but encountered trouble when he tried:

> the inhabitants are got into such Terms, that it is as much a man's life is worth to go amongst them, for they gather'd together in Companies and go in Arms every Time they Expect I am any where near there about, with full resolution to kill or cripple me, or any other person, who shall attempt to Lay out a mannor here. If the honorable Proprietor should

> think fit such assistance, as shall withstand such unreasonable creatures, I shall be ready and willing to prosecute the same with my upmost Endeavor. (Glatfelter & Weaner, 1992, pp. 7, 10)

The Quaker Penn brothers were reluctant to use force to expel the squatters and instead went on with the sale of other lands outside the limits of the Manor of Maske.

In the meantime, additional families moved into the manor and squatted. Sporadic attempts to survey all or part of the manor continued and were unsuccessful. In 1754, one surveyor wrote to a local magistrate:

> if I were to ask Information of any of the Inhabitants they would immediately suspect my Intentions and probably use me ill, or brake some of my Instruments, as they did to you and Mr. Parsons formerly and to Mr. Armor lately. (Glatfelter & Weaner, 1992, p. 11)

The Penn brothers displayed great forbearance with the situation. Though they were legally permitted to do so, they made no move to eject the squatters and gave up all attempts to conduct surveys. They may have been moved by the hope that "if you ignore a problem, it will go away." As so happened, it didn't. The impasse dragged on for almost a quarter of a century.

To some degree, the Penn brothers' patience with the settlers probably derived from the fact that, other than their opposition to the surveyors, the Scots-Irish settlers were model citizens. They paid their taxes, voted in elections, willingly joined the militia, helped protect both themselves and their neighbors from the Natives, settled disputes in the county courts rather than by the use of force, and were profoundly religious. Most were such good citizens that they served in a number of county offices, including tax collector, constable, and even overseer of the poor. Hance Hamilton and Robert McPherson were elected as sheriffs of York County (Glatfelter & Weaner, 1992, p. 11). Of course, the settlers remained model citizens only as long as they were left alone by the authorities.

Consequently, the situation remained unresolved, and the longer it persisted, the worse it could get. Finally, in 1763, John Penn, grandson of William Penn, was appointed governor. One of the first things he did was move to end the standoff between the government and the settlers of the Manor of Maske:

> On March 18, 1765, Governor John Penn wrote a letter directing James Agnew (1711–1770) and Robert McPherson (1730–1789), two of the leaders of the Marsh Creek settlement who were acting on behalf of their friends and neighbors, to prepare a list of the holders of real estate within what the community believed would be the eventual actual limits of the manor. In each case they were asked to give the month and year of the first settlement of the tract. In return for allowing the survey of the manor to proceed, the residents on tracts settled before June 18, 1741 [the date of the manor warrant], were promised that they could purchase their land on the common terms. In the language of the warrant of the time, these terms were as follows: "at the Rate of Fifteen Pounds, Ten Shillings, current Money of this Province, for every Hundred Acres; and also . . . the yearly Quitrent of One Halfpenny Sterling for every Acre thereof." (Glatfelter & Weaner, 1992, p. 13)

The notion of *quitrent* is unfamiliar to modern Americans. It is sometimes called a tax, but in fact, it is quite different. The closest thing to quitrent in America might be the sale of mineral rights. It is possible to sell land and retain the mineral rights on the land. In the case of quitrent, the person who sold the land retained the right to use the land for special purposes unless an annual quitrent fee was paid. In the 1740s, quitrent was only a halfpenny per acre but was due every year.

The Agnew and McPherson list provides the names of 157 heads of household holding land and of three churches owning land (the lower, middle, and upper Marsh Creek Presbyterian churches). There is no way of knowing how many people lived in the Manor of Maske by the time of the American Revolution. The first census in America did not occur until 1790. The 157 heads of families on the 1765 Agnew and McPherson list is the only data for making any kind of population estimate. In the 1700s, families were certainly larger than they are today. The Reed family included two parents and nine children. Ben's family included two parents and seven children. If Ben's family was average, the 157 families would yield a manor population of just over 1,400. If the average family were as large as the Reed family of 11, then the 157 families would yield a population of just over 1,700. Because the Manor of Maske was nine miles long and six miles wide, comprising 43,500 acres, population density was low and families were scattered over a large area.

In addition to the names of landowners, the list has the dates when the land had first been claimed. Included are the names of most of Benjamin Stephenson's maternal relatives and many Stephenson family friends. Ben's maternal grandfather, James Reed, entered his land in August 1738. James Reed is on the list even though his tract was not located in the Manor of Maske. The Reed land was about one mile west of the western boundary of the manor. The reason for the anomaly is that the Agnew and McPherson list was created prior to the official survey and included all properties thought to belong to the manor before the survey. The name William Stephenson (listed as Stevenson), probably Ben's paternal grandfather, appears beside a date of 1741. The records are not complete enough to prove that the William Stevenson on the list is the father of James Stephenson and, therefore, Ben's grandfather. The case for believing that William Stevenson is Ben's grandfather rests on there being only two Stevensons listed for the Manor of Maske. William and Samuel Stevenson owned adjoining farms only a half mile apart and only a mile or so from the middle Marsh Creek Church. James and Mary (Reed) Stephenson named their first son William. The name William is not a common ancestral name among the Reeds and most probably comes from the ancestral line of James Stephenson. Furthermore, the name Samuel does not appear in any subsequent generations of Ben's family. From this evidence, it appears that William Stevenson (Stephenson) was the father of James. William and Samuel could have been unrelated, but they were more likely to be cousins or brothers. If they were brothers, then Samuel was the uncle of Ben's father, James.

William, Thomas, and John Boyd appear on the list with dates of initial occupation of 1740 and 1741. The Reeds, Stephensons, and Boyds would stay closely allied through the next several generations. Others on the list include Samuel Gettys, who occupied land south of the Reeds and north and east of the Stephensons and Boyds in 1741. Gettys gave his name to the little settlement that grew to occupy the rocky lands making up the north central part of the Manor of Maske. Gettys's land included places that six score and two years later would become consecrated ground in American history: the Devil's Den, Culp's Hill, Little Round Top, Cemetery Ridge, and other landmarks of the Battle of Gettysburg.

More than likely, Benjamin Stephenson's father, James, was the son of William Stephenson of the 1841 Maske land deed. Ben's parents, James Stephenson and Mary Reed, the oldest daughter of Colonel James Reed, were married in 1763 at the Manor of Maske and settled on a farm within it. They had seven children: William (1763–1821), James (1764–1833), Benjamin, Margaret (ca. 1767), Sarah (1771–1821), Isabelle (1777–1855), and Maria (1779–1857). Benjamin Stephenson was born on July 8, 1769.

The marriage of Mary Reed and James Stephenson coincided with the end of the French and Indian War. Early in the war, the Quaker leaders of Pennsylvania opposed the organization of a militia, which would have been in conflict with their pacifist beliefs. Fortunately for those who lived on the frontier, Benjamin Franklin, concerned with the safety of Philadelphia, led an effort to organize militia-like units to protect the settlers. The Scots-Irish settlers in Pennsylvania, including those of the Manor of Maske, led by settlers like James Reed, enthusiastically organized for the defense of the frontier.

The war was a brutal small-unit conflict between the settlers and the Natives, punctuated by battles where British regulars and American militia fought against French regular troops and their Native allies. The largest of these battles was the disastrous defeat of General Edward Braddock's army near Fort Duquesne. Most of the Native raids and Braddock's defeat took place near the western frontier along the Allegheny, Monongahela, and Ohio Rivers. Fighting raged along the rivers both north and south of modern Pittsburgh. York County and the Manor of Maske were too far east to be greatly threatened by the Natives. Militia groups east of the mountains, like those at the Manor of Maske, were kept ready but dealt with only sporadic attacks. The French and Indian War ended with the signing of the Treaty of Paris in 1763. It ended with a British and American victory and the French cession of the eastern half of the Louisiana Territory to the British. This half of the Louisiana Territory included all of the land between the Ohio and Mississippi Rivers. The area eventually became the Northwest Territory, and it included all of the future state of Illinois.

British victory in the war had secured British claims to a huge territory in the Americas, but it left the British deeply in debt. Over the next six years, the British Parliament took a series of actions intended to recoup the cost of defending the crown's American colonies by shifting the cost of their defense to the colonists. The acts of Parliament, and the never-ending arrogance of the British, led to ever-mounting anger among the colonists and eventually to the Declaration of Independence and the revolution.

Benjamin Stephenson was a child of the American Revolution. All of his early life was dominated by it. He was born shortly before the Boston Massacre; he was old enough to remember the news of Lexington and Concord; and he celebrated his seventh birthday only four days after the Declaration of Independence was signed.

By the early summer of 1778, nine-year-old Ben comprehended the tragedy of the Battles of Brandywine and Paoli and the terrible winter encampment at Valley Forge, where many of his neighbors, friends, and relatives had suffered greatly. Then, in late June, word arrived that a new battle had been fought at Monmouth, Pennsylvania. The news brought joy since the Continental Army, freshly retrained by Friedrich Wilhelm von Steuben, had defeated the British forces. The British had abandoned Philadelphia and were in retreat toward New York. This good news was tempered, though, by the fact that the heaviest fighting had involved several Pennsylvania regiments, notably the locally recruited 11th Pennsylvania, which had suffered many casualties, plus deaths from heatstroke. The losses in the 11th were so severe that the regiment was absorbed into the 10th Pennsylvania Regiment and ceased to exist.

The events of the war, Ben's experiences, and the experiences of his relatives and friends had a profound effect on him and influenced his behavior throughout the rest of his life. Like many of his generation, he was intensely patriotic. Many of those who grew up during the revolution, as well as veterans of the revolution, shared a number of core ideas and qualities that shaped their lives. Most had almost unbounded optimism and a willingness to explore new places and have new experiences. Most, like Benjamin Stephenson, had a strong belief in the value of public service. Furthermore, many believed that the desire for national freedom was universal. (It later came as a shock, therefore, to Ben and most of his generation when the Canadians refused to join the American cause in the War of 1812.) Ben shared several other of his generation's less positive views as well: a deep distrust of the English and a strong fear and loathing of Native Americans. For Ben, those feelings were confirmed some 30 years later during the War of 1812.

Unknown that summer to Benjamin Stephenson and the residents of the Manor of Maske, the Battle of Monmouth and the British retreat from Philadelphia marked a turning point in the revolution. The war dragged on for three more years until the British surrendered at Yorktown in October 1781. By 1783, when the Treaty of Paris formally ended the war, Ben's father, James, had become a successful farmer. The 1783 tax roll records a 170-acre farm, 6 cattle, 6 horses, and 13 sheep. The tax roll also indicates that there was one house and one outbuilding. His entire holding was valued at 394 British pounds, 15 shillings, and 6 pence. The yearly tax was 8 pounds, 4 shillings, and 6 pence. In 1783 the English pound was worth slightly less than five American dollars. Thus, James Stephenson's holding in 1783 was worth almost $2,000, which today would be equal to about $44,500.

Thus, one generation after some Scots-Irish emigrated to America, a second-generation farmer like James had become a substantial landowner. At the age of 14, Ben was a member of a comfortable and respected family and was nearly ready to embark on a new stage of his life.

CHAPTER TWO
Ambition

In late 1789 Samuel Reed, the younger brother of Mary Reed Stephenson, moved to Martinsburg in Berkeley County, Virginia, now West Virginia, where he opened a law office. Samuel was the fifth of the seven sons of James Reed and Margaret Floyd. His two oldest brothers, Thomas and James R., had already begun successful legal careers in Pennsylvania. Evidence suggests that Samuel must have quickly established a good reputation and a thriving law practice. In the days before the establishment of most banks, almost all business was transacted with cash, and Samuel's wife, Anna Kennedy Reed, recalled that he frequently came home from appearances in various courts with his saddlebags bulging with money (Sampson, 1922). He was not only a success as a lawyer, but he also became a valued member of the growing Martinsburg settlement. He was active in the militia and was called up as a colonel during the Whiskey Rebellion.

Soon after Samuel Reed moved to Martinsburg, James Stephenson Jr., the second son of James Stephenson and Mary Reed Stephenson, also moved to Martinsburg. The move must have occurred before the 1790 census because that census shows only eight people, two parents and six children, in the James Stephenson household in Pennsylvania. James Jr.'s motive for moving almost certainly was his desire to read the law with his uncle Samuel. In the 1700s, most prospective lawyers did not go to law school but rather "read the law" under the supervision of a practicing lawyer. Moving to Martinsburg to study law under Samuel Reed's guidance thus made sense.

James was probably the family member who was closest to Benjamin Stephenson. He was the respected older brother, and he and Benjamin maintained contact throughout the rest of their lives. Though separated by considerable distances after the early 1800s, their careers followed almost identical paths. They both became high-ranking officers with local militia groups, and both had successful political careers. James and Benjamin served in the United States Congress in the House of Representatives, although their terms did not overlap.

While it is not clear when and why the rest of the Stephenson family moved from the Manor of Maske to the area of Martinsburg, the move must have been completed in the early 1790s. There were probably several factors behind the decision to move. By that time, James and his uncle Samuel were established in Martinsburg and probably had reported favorably on the prospects for success in the area. It is also likely that the ongoing legal hassles over land ownership in the Manor of Maske became extremely irritating to a number of the settlers. Despite the resolution of the disputed border between Pennsylvania and Maryland and the resulting agreement to survey the land, problems persisted.

Earlier, Maryland had granted two large tracts of land in what was now Pennsylvania. These were called Digge's Choice and Carroll's Delight. Claims on Digge's Choice had been settled in favor of the residents of the Manor of Maske fairly early on. The leaders of the Maryland faction residing in Digge's Choice had been arrested and tried. Carroll's Delight was initially not thought to be a problem since it occupied 5,000 acres just east of the Manor of Maske and was separated from the manor by a narrow strip of land. However, in the later 1780s, some of the residents in Carroll's Delight began to claim that their lands included a portion of the Manor of Maske and that those of the manor occupying it were thus trespassing. Finally, in 1789, a petition was presented to the Supreme Council of Pennsylvania, asking for a resurvey of Carroll's Delight (Bates, 1886, p. 277). The James Stephenson farm was located in the portion of the manor claimed by the residents of Carroll's Delight.

After enduring 40 years of uncertainty over who owned the land, the Carroll's Delight claims were the last straw for some residents of the Manor of Maske. The Stephenson family could well have been ready to move to Martinsburg, and the Carroll's Delight controversy simply spurred them on. Strangely, there is no evidence of the sale of their land. The 1788 tax record shows that the family paid taxes on 170 acres of land, and the value of James Stephenson's total holdings was 394 pounds, 15 shillings, and 6 pence. The land must have been sold, and the records just did not survive. It is almost inconceivable that James would have walked away from his farm without getting any money for it to buy land elsewhere.

Whatever the case, the Stephenson family moved to a new farm about eight miles south of Martinsburg sometime in the early 1790s. The oldest son, William, took his inheritance early and lived on his own property in Berkeley County. In the following years, William is almost never mentioned and seems not to have had much influence on his little brother Ben. On the 1798 tax record, William has a house tax of $262 and no enslaved persons. He was clearly not wealthy at the time. William left Martinsburg and is recorded in Grainger County, Tennessee, in 1810. Ben never mentions William in any extant record. James Stephenson Jr. had become fairly well to do by 1798. The tax record shows him with a house tax of $1,890 and shows that he owned two enslaved persons. James was already embarking on a legal career, which left Benjamin Stephenson as the only male available to work the new farm other than his aging father. For five or six years after the move, there is a frustrating lack of information about Ben in any of the sources covering the Martinsburg area. This is probably consistent with the suggestion that Ben was heavily involved in helping on the family farm.

While there is little information about Ben, there is substantial information about his older brother James. James had joined the militia just after his move to Martinsburg to study law. In the fall of 1791, he took part in an expedition commanded by General Arthur St. Clair. The expedition aimed to put an end to Native American opposition to American settlement on the west bank of the Ohio River and the rest of the fertile Ohio region.

James was appointed captain in command of a rifle company. After a series of long delays, St. Clair moved his army from Pennsylvania and Virginia down the Ohio River by flatboat, all the way to Fort Washington at Cincinnati. From Fort Washington the expedition set out in pursuit of the elusive Natives. The army ran into difficulties at every turn. As the weeks dragged on, they were troubled by a lack of supplies, bad weather, increasing desertions, and difficulties in caring for the growing numbers of camp followers. The camp followers included wives and children of some of the soldiers as well as "girl friends" and "women of easy virtue." Even worse than these problems was the fact that the army seemed never to be able to catch up with the Natives. Unfortunately for the army, it was the Natives who caught up to them.

In early November, the army had reached the Wabash River near the modern border between Ohio and Indiana. At dawn on the morning of November 4, 1791, a large number of Native Americans, representing multiple tribes, attacked St. Clair's camp. The attack overwhelmed the sentries and overran the camp. It was a total disaster. By noon the battle was over, and the remnant of St. Clair's army was in retreat. The battlefield was littered with the bodies of over 800 soldiers and camp followers. Only 48 of St. Clair's soldiers escaped unwounded. James escaped and seems to have been among those unwounded or only slightly wounded. The defeat at the Wabash was the worst defeat the American army ever suffered at the hands of Native Americans. James was fortunate to escape with his life and return to Martinsburg.

Undaunted, he got married the following May to Ann Cunningham, the daughter of a successful landowner whose ancestors had, for many years, lived along Mill Creek. The Cunninghams lived only a couple of miles from the elder James Stephenson's farm. Ann's great-grandfather had built a stone bridge over Mill Creek in 1757 and also a large stone building, which Ann Cunningham Stephenson inherited. The building eventually became known as the "Old Stone Tavern" and later as the "Stephenson Tavern."

The tavern was an extremely valuable property. The 1798 Berkeley County house tax valued it at $1,890, which made it one of the most valuable buildings in Berkeley County at that time. It occupied part of a 200-acre tract that also housed two distilleries. Halfway between Martinsburg and Winchester and close to four roads, the tavern was a popular stopping place. It was within 100 yards of a grist mill and within a mile of a cooper shop and two blacksmith shops, and water ran only 200 yards from the door. Because the deed for the Cunningham land and the tavern was fairly old and not entirely clear, James sold the land to his brother Ben for one dollar. Ben then sold it back to James to establish the legitimacy of the deed. In 1819 James sold the stone tavern and the 200 acres for $13,350. The tavern still stands and is part of the Mill Creek Historic District (Wood, n.d.).

James Stephenson's military service did not end with the St. Clair expedition. Beginning in 1791, substantial unrest began to develop along the frontier in Pennsylvania and Virginia and in a number of other areas farther south. The unrest, and the resulting Whiskey Rebellion, was sparked by the imposition of a federal tax on distilleries. The tax was the brainchild of Alexander Hamilton, U.S. secretary of the treasury. The tax was intended to raise money to fund the federal government's assumption of the Revolutionary War debts of the states. The assumption was opposed by Thomas Jefferson, who argued that Virginia had already repaid most of its debts and that assumption would create more federal power than was desirable. Jefferson and Hamilton finally worked out a deal by which Jefferson dropped his opposition to assumption and Hamilton agreed to back the location of the nation's capital along the Potomac River in Virginia. After the agreement, the tax was imposed, and the unrest spread. There were sporadic acts of violence and large demonstrations, which frequently threatened to get out of control. Finally in 1794, reacting to the arrival of a U.S. marshal assigned to deal with the distillers who had failed to pay the tax, a mob of almost 500 armed men assembled. The mob descended on the home of General John Neville, the tax inspector, and badly damaged it.

In early 1794, the widespread unrest was becoming increasingly violent, so President George Washington put out an order to the governors of Virginia, Pennsylvania, Maryland, and New Jersey to call out the militia. Eventually a militia army of 13,000 was assembled, and President Washington assumed command. Samuel Reed served as a colonel commanding a regiment, and James Stephenson, promoted to the rank of major in the militia, became a brigade inspector. When the militia army assembled in Pennsylvania, George Washington returned to the capital, Philadelphia, since Congress was in session. The command of the army then went to "Light Horse" Harry Lee of Virginia, who had been a hero of the revolution. "Light Horse" Harry was the father of General Robert E. Lee. Because of his service, James became well known to both Lee and President Washington. Faced with an overwhelming force numbering 13,000 soldiers, protestors of the tax on distilleries backed down. No military action was ever taken against them, and few were ever arrested and convicted of any crime. Those who were convicted were all pardoned, and the Whiskey Rebellion was at an end. The military career of James Stephenson was also at an end. He never again served in the army or the militia.

James went on to have a distinguished career as a lawyer and public servant. When Jefferson County was created by the division of Berkeley County, James moved to Charles Town, the county seat of the newly created Jefferson County. James served a term as county commissioner. He also became a judge and served in the Virginia House of Delegates from 1800 to 1802. He eventually served three terms in the United States House of Representatives. He was first elected in 1803 for a two-year term. He was elected again in 1809. After his second term, he remained out of politics until 1822 when Thomas Swearingen, the serving representative, died. James was elected to serve the remaining year of Swearingen's term and the following two-year term, from 1822 to 1825.

Although there is not much personal information about James, it does appear that he inherited a fiery temper from his Scots-Irish ancestors. In his later years he was involved in a duel with the aging General William Darke. The two old men got into a bitter argument and, as a result, scheduled a duel. Both were veterans of the St. Clair expedition. Darke had been a colonel in St. Clair's army and was credited with saving the remnant by mounting a counterattack that momentarily stopped the Natives. The delay allowed the surviving soldiers to retreat. Darke, described as a man "of gigantic proportions," had led the counterattack armed with only a huge sword. He wielded the sword with such force that one account of the attack says he cleaved the skull of one of the Natives and almost severed his head with one stroke.

When James Stephenson and William Darke arrived at the site selected for their duel, the two men who were designated their seconds collected the swords of Stephenson and Darke. The seconds then began announcing the rules for the duel. As they did, the seconds remarked the disparity of size between the two men and their weapons. James was a small man and had brought a rapier, a light and slender fencing sword. Darke, "of gigantic proportions," had brought along the huge broadsword he had wielded during the St. Clair expedition. The two seconds were so amused by the contrast that they became convulsed with laughter. When Darke and Stephenson realized what was so funny, they too began to laugh uncontrollably. They canceled the duel and remained friends for the rest of their lives (Aler, 1888, p. 127).

While James Stephenson was beginning to develop into one of Berkeley County's most respected young men during the 1790s, his younger brother Ben seems to have labored in anonymity. That historical anonymity began to change, though, in the late 1790s and early 1800s. One cause of the change in his fortunes came when he married Lucy Swearingen, the daughter of Van Swearingen. Though the date they married is uncertain, it most likely occurred in 1799. Two years later, on October 26, 1801, a second change in Ben's fortunes occurred when Berkeley County was divided into two counties: Berkeley and Jefferson.

The newly created Jefferson County had its county seat in Charles Town. In September 1801, Governor James Monroe had appointed a number of justices of the peace and a sheriff for the new county. Among the justices were General Darke, Daniel Morgan, and Joseph Swearingen. Governor Monroe appointed William Little as sheriff. Little served until 1803, when Joseph Swearingen became sheriff. After being sworn in to office, the new justices of the peace and the sheriff appointed four deputy sheriffs: Cyrus Sanders, William Little Jr., John Sanders, and Benjamin Stephenson. Joseph Swearingen, one of the justices, was appointed one of the two county commissioners. Samuel Reed was admitted to the bar as one of the practicing attorneys of the new county (Bushong, 1941, pp. 65–67).

Prominent among the leading figures in the early history of Jefferson County were a number of members of the Swearingen family in Virginia. The Swearingens were wealthy and well respected. When Ben married Lucy Swearingen, he created an alliance with the Swearingen family, which became one of the two greatest influences on his later life.

Lucy Swearingen Stephenson was the daughter of Van Swearingen Jr., also known as "Indian Van." Indian Van was a legendary, almost mythical, figure on the frontiers of Pennsylvania and Virginia. The Swearingens had come to America in the 1600s when Gerret VanSwearingen emigrated from Beemesterdam, near Amsterdam, Netherlands, in 1636. Subsequent generations dropped the Van prefix and called themselves Swearingen. Van became the first name of numerous male descendants down the line. "Indian Van" was born in 1734, the son of Thomas Swearingen III. Thomas was one of the many fifth-generation Swearingens in the American colonies. He established a ferry across the Potomac River near

Portrait of Lucy Swearingen Stephenson. Karen Campe Mateyka, "Stephenson, Lucy, née Swearingen (1788–1850)," *Madison Historical: The Online Encyclopedia and Digital Archive for Madison County, Illinois*, last modified February 19, 2019. Photo by Roxann Raisner. https://madison-historical.siue.edu/encyclopedia/stephenson-lucy-nee-swearingen/

Shepherdstown, Virginia (now West Virginia), in 1734. According to family lore, General Braddock and George Washington used the ferry in 1755 to cross the Potomac on their way to attack Fort Duquesne in Pittsburgh. As related in chapter 1, the Braddock expedition was a disaster and Braddock was killed. Braddock's defeat was one of the earliest battles of the French and Indian War.

Van's father, Thomas III, died when Van was 17. The young Van Swearingen joined the colonial army as a subaltern. The term *subaltern* was used by the British army to designate any commissioned officer below the rank of captain. Van Swearingen was likely a teenager when he entered the French and Indian War. By the time the war ended with the Treaty of Paris in 1763, Van was 29 years old and had already earned a reputation as a fierce and intelligent fighter (Bell & Zinsser, 1990). In 1769 Van and his brother, Thomas IV, both applied for grants of land in Westmoreland County, Pennsylvania. The land was on the banks of the Monongahela River north of Pittsburgh, where the Monongahela and Allegheny Rivers join to form the Ohio River. When the French and Indian War concluded, the French withdrew from the Ohio River area and all of France's former territory. Their Native allies did not. The numerous tribes that inhabited the vast area west of the Ohio River had no intention of ceding their lands to the American colonists. Beginning almost immediately after the Treaty of Paris, the Natives began to attack the settlers on the Ohio and Pennsylvania frontier. Local militia units and disorganized groups of settlers attempted to defend the frontier from regular raids by small parties of Natives. Along the loop of the Allegheny River, the local militia was led by Van Swearingen. For almost 10 years, he was continually responding to Native attacks and proved to be extremely fearless and effective.

During the decade after the end of the French and Indian War, Van nursed a growing dissatisfaction with the British. He thought his service had been ignored by the king as he had never received any advantage from anyone in England. His feelings were strikingly similar to those of George Washington. Washington felt that he had served with distinction in the French and Indian War and was repaid by being denied a commission in the British army.

Van, feeling ignored, had no hesitation in joining the fight against England at the beginning of the revolution. Shortly before the war, Van had commanded a militia company called the Military Associators. It was formed to defend Westmoreland County, Pennsylvania, against the Natives who were increasingly allied with the British. Shortly after Lexington and Concord, the two battalions of militia that made up the 8th Pennsylvania Regiment were formed in Westmoreland County. The first battalion carried the "Gadsden Flag," the famous yellow flag featuring a coiled rattlesnake and the words "Don't Tread on Me." The flag never appeared on any battlefield during the war despite its historical fame. In December 1776, the two battalions of the 8th Pennsylvania were ordered to New Jersey to join George Washington's retreating army. Van was a captain commanding one of the companies in the second battalion. Author Carl Baldwin (1986) says that the best fighting men in the second battalion "were in a company organized earlier for frontier duty by Capt. Swearingen, a former Virginian and noted Indian fighter" (p. 17). Most of the men in the 8th objected to the order to join Washington's army since they had joined to protect their families against the Natives. By joining Washington's army in New Jersey and Pennsylvania, they would be leaving the frontier undefended. Furthermore, they argued, they were not prepared for a winter march over some of the toughest mountain terrain in America at the worst time of the year (Baldwin, 1986). They petitioned Congress to rescind the order but were rebuffed. Consequently, the 8th eventually departed on January 6, 1777.

On the march, the men had no tents and slept between rows of large bonfires. They traversed the Allegheny Mountains, climbing frozen mountain slopes and sliding down the other side. All the streams were frozen, and they had to chop through the ice to find drinking water. By the time they reached Philadelphia, "many men had died along the way and many others were ill with fever and severe sore throats. The men were in rags, but supplies were limited. Not all received heavy overcoats and boots" (Baldwin, 1986, p. 28). Van Swearingen and the surviving men of the 8th reached Trenton, New Jersey, on February 14, 1777. They had covered almost 500 miles, including some 150 miles traversing the Alleghenies.

They then settled in a winter camp at Valley Forge. By the spring, the official report of the 8th tallied the attrition: of the 684 men who had originally left the frontier, 126 had deserted, 51 had died, 36 were prisoners of war, 14 were missing in action, and 15 had been discharged (Baldwin, 1986, p. 33).

In June, the best marksmen in the 8th were selected from all of the companies of the regiment and sent to join the unit known as "Morgan's Rifles." Van Swearingen went as a company commander. The riflemen from the 8th were joined by sharpshooters from the 1st Pennsylvania, a number from Maryland, and 163 from Virginia. They joined the unit, which was commanded by Daniel Morgan, a rough-hewn Virginian and a general who later became famous at the Battle of Cowpens. Long after Van Swearingen served under him, Morgan was ordered south to join General Nathaniel Green in his attempts to defeat Lord Cornwallis. The Battle of Cowpens involved a number of units, commanded by Morgan, against units commanded by Banastre Tarleton. Tarleton was the cavalry officer who had become the British officer most hated by the Americans. He had earned a reputation for extreme cruelty on the battlefield and was known to have killed a number of Americans who had tried to surrender. Morgan defeated Tarleton's army at Cowpens. The climactic battle of the movie *The Patriot* is a recreation of Cowpens.

In June 1777, Van Swearingen and the riflemen from the 8th became part of Morgan's Rifles and were ordered to join the army of General Horatio Gates. "While on this assignment on September 19, 1777, near Bemis Heights, N.Y., Swearingen was wounded and, with a number of others, taken prisoner by Indian elements of a British-Indian force which raided Morgan's camp at Stillwater" (Trussell, 1977, p. 104). Before the Natives could kill Swearingen, he

> was rescued by Gen. Fraser's bat man . . . who took him before the General. The latter interrogated him concerning the numbers of the American army, but got no answer other than that it was commanded by Gens. Gates and Arnold. He then threatened to hang him. "You may, if you please" said Van Swearingen. Fraser then went off, leaving him in the care

> of Sergt. Dunbar, who consigned him to Lt. Auburey, who ordered him to be placed among the other prisoners, with directions not to be ill treated. Swearingen, after Burgoyne's army was removed to Virginia, made especial exertions to have Dunbar and Auburey exchanged. (Linn & Egle, 1880, p. 647)

In the Battle of Saratoga on October 7, 1777, General Simon Fraser was mortally wounded by one of Morgan's riflemen. When Burgoyne's army surrendered after the Battle of Saratoga, Van Swearingen was released from captivity. On August 10, 1779, he resigned from the army and returned home.

He had sold his land along the Monongahela in 1776, just before the 8th Pennsylvania departed for New Jersey. While he was still serving in the army, he purchased 800 acres of land in Strabane Township, in what became Washington County, Pennsylvania. The land was in a disputed area claimed by both Pennsylvania and Virginia. The land he bought was, at the time of his purchase, thought to be in Yohogania County, Virginia. Van's brother Andrew purchased land nearby. Van resumed his role as a militia leader in Washington County and also served a term as the first sheriff from 1781 to 1783. During his relatively short stay in Washington County, he again met George Washington. Van rode with Washington from Canonsburg to Monongahela. They had met twice before, the first time being when Van was a teenager and Braddock and Washington had used his father's ferry to cross the Potomac. They met again at Valley Forge, and Washington later wrote a letter approving Van's resignation from the army. While they could not be called friends, they were clearly acquaintances.

In early 1785, Van sold his land in Washington County and moved to what was then Ohio County, Virginia (now Brooke County, West Virginia). He settled near Wellsburg and purchased land from the Coxes. He also began the construction of Cox's Fort.

Over the years, Van married three times. The names of his first two wives are unknown. He was first married in 1765. His second marriage was in 1774. After the revolution, he married his third wife, Eleanor Virgin, on May 3, 1786. His marriage to Eleanor was not without some controversy. Van had something of a reputation with the ladies. He had fathered a child, Sarah Brown, with Nancy Brown out of wedlock before being twice married . Long after Van's death, his third wife, Eleanor, applied for a military pension. In the application, she appended a deposition from William Darby, who attested to Van's military record. In addition, his deposition states:

> Captain Van Swearingen who was a Captain in Morgan's Rifle Corps who married Eleanor or Nelly Virgin as she was generally called and known by in the said County That she had three brothers Rezin Virgin, John Virgin, and Brice Virgin That she was the particular protection of Rezin Virgin; and that when Capt. Van Swearingen applied to Rezin Virgin for his sister Nelly aforesaid as his intended wife, Rezin Virgin observed that he had no objection to the marriage, but that he must not ill treat his sister Nelly, if he did, he must abide the consequences . . . That Capt. Van Swearingen was long Sheriff of Washington County and that at the time of the event he the affiant heard all those circumstances stated and they made a vivid impression on his mind He farther declares that Capt. Van Swearingen was something of a libertine and had an illegitimate child by Miss Brown who was living there at the time and it was on account of his libertine issue that Rezin Virgin made the threat that he did. (Whyte, 1997, p. 74)

Van Swearingen had eight children including Sarah Brown, the illegitimate daughter of Nancy Brown. Drusilla Swearingen was born about 1769. In 1784, Drusilla married Samuel Brady. Brady was a militia officer who had served in the revolution as a captain. He was also a brilliant ranger who served as a scout after the revolution. He was employed as a scout against the Natives, and he frequently ventured across the Ohio River all alone and spent weeks in hostile territory gathering intelligence on Native intentions. On two different occasions, he was captured by the Shawnee, and each time he escaped. Brady was almost as legendary as Van Swearingen along the Ohio frontier. Drusilla was courted by a number of people. She not only was the daughter of a wealthy and powerful father, but she was also, by the standards of the day, highly educated. Van had sent her to Philadelphia for a year to further her education. Since there were no public schools at the time, Drusilla was probably sent to a private subscription school.

Van's third child was Thomas. Thomas was a name that appears over and over in generation after generation of Swearingens. This Thomas was born about 1771. In 1787, at the age of 16, he disappeared. According to one source, he and three others were engaged in digging ginseng roots when they were attacked by Natives (Eckert, 1995, p. 519). According to Van Swearingen, Thomas was captured or killed while hunting for meat. In several letters, Van discussed the disappearance of Thomas. In a letter to Colonel Richard Butler, who had served as a colonel of the 8th Pennsylvania in the revolution, Van states:

> On Sunday evening last my son Thomas Swearingen was taken prisoner by the Indians, ten miles up Cross Creek west of Ohio . . . he was hunting for meat for a party of strangers, three of which was found dead, two escaped . . . he had lent his gun that day to one of the party to hunt, and was without arms and I think was in a waste cabin by himself when he was taken . . . he may be dead, but the parties have not yet found him. If you think it is best that a message should be sent to the Indian chiefs or others in that county that may have it in their power to be of service trying to save his life . . . if you have faith in me please to employ an Indian or white man that may answer the purpose and I will pay to the utmost farthing your contract with them, I am not well or I should have come to you myself . . . I hope to have a line from you by the bearer. I spoke to a gentleman from Morgan Town which informed me a few days ago a party of Indians was overtaken by a party of our people bearing off a number of horses from the inhabitants . . . Two Indians was killed and one white man, and the horses brought back. I am under many feeling apprehensions concerning my son, and hope that you will do everything in your power and you will

> forever oblige. Your most respectful, Obed. Servt. (Whyte, 1997, pp. 84–85)

Four months later, in December 1787, Van wrote a letter to his cousin Josiah Swearingen:

> My son Thomas is still missing and I can hear nothing from him. A great deal of search has been made for his bones in vain. The messenger that went into the nations to inquire after him has not yet returned. I am on a ugly frontier and lost my best gun when Dave Cox was killed. If I have any tenant that could be credited for a gun or two that is good with small bore, as maybe they can be payed in barter I wish you to send them to me . . . I should not ask such a unreasonable favor but I expect to be shut up or be after the Indians all next season and want to be well armed . . . The Indians is constantly doing mischief and I expect a desperate war. The Indian Nations have sent a late letter to the Indian agent informing that they will not give any part of their land up to Congress except they lose it by the sword, and I believe they are backed up by the British and their friends in the Canada and Detroit countries. Give my most respectful compliments to my good old uncle Van and to all the family. (Everson, 2004, p. 73)

The second letter seems to indicate that Richard Butler had responded to Van's first letter by sending a messenger into Native territory to inquire about Thomas. No trace of Thomas was ever found, and he was presumably killed by Natives.

The fourth child was Elzey Swearingen, born about 1773. The fifth child was Zachariah Swearingen, born about 1775. The first four legitimate children were the children of Van's first two wives. In 1786 he married Eleanor and had three more children. Lucy Swearingen, the future wife of Benjamin Stephenson, was born in either 1786 or 1788. Karel L. Whyte, the meticulous Swearingen family genealogist who did exhaustive research, lists Lucy as the first child of the marriage of Van and Eleanor Virgin and gives a date of 1786 for the birth. Van and Eleanor Virgin had two additional children: Vann Swearingen Jr. was born in 1787; Thomas Swearingen was born around 1791. Thomas was the second son of the same name. The first was the Thomas who was killed by Natives. Whyte's skill at genealogy makes it tempting to accept the date of 1786 for Lucy's birth. However, Lucy's obituary, written in 1850 by the local newspaper editor, John Halderman, says that Lucy was born in a fort near Wheeling, Virginia, on December 6, 1788. While there is little data for deciding between the two dates, an additional piece of information might be considered. In his will, discussed below, Van stipulates that his children should receive their bequests at the age of 18 for girls and 21 for boys. Lucy and Benjamin Stephenson began selling the land that Lucy inherited in 1806. She would have been 18 in 1806 if she was born in 1788, as the obituary states. In addition to all of the information already discussed, there is one final piece to add. The 1850 census, completed before Lucy's death, records her year of birth as 1786. So, the mystery remains.

Van Swearingen died on December 2, 1793, at the age of 51. His long and detailed will makes extensive bequests to his wife, Eleanor Virgin, and to his children. The will also mentions a number of enslaved persons and instructions for their future. Lucy Swearingen is mentioned a number of times. The main bequest includes the following:

> Item, I give and bequeath to my said Daughter Lucy Swearingen, the remainder of that tract of Land whereon I now live . . . to her and her Heirs and assigns forever—I also give and bequeath to my said Daughter Lucy, one Feather bed, also, the sum of fifty pounds lawful money, or a small Negro girl to that value to her, and to her Heirs and assigns forever, to be furnished to her by Executor hereafter mentioned, out of my estate.

The will provided "the sum of 100 pounds lawful money of Pennsylvania" to Sarah Brown, the daughter of Nancy Brown. Additionally, the will made provisions for all of the enslaved persons. As part of Zachariah's bequest, he was to receive "one negro boy by the name of Jesse." Drusilla Brady received

> one negro girl by the name of Pheby, to her and her heirs forever–nevertheless it is my will that in the case the said Negro girl should be offered for sale, or taken from her Drusilla or her Heirs by any means whatsoever, the said Negro shall revert to my other children.

To his wife, Eleanor, he bequeathed

> one negro girl by the name of Ester, and her daughter Win, during her natural life, and at her decease the said Negro Ester to be set free–but the said Negro Win, with all the offspring of the said Negro Ester (if any more) to equally be divided between her the said Eleanor Swearingen's three children afore named.

Son Vann was bequeathed

> one mulatto boy by the name of Isaak, generally known as by the name of Toby who is to become free at the age of 28. I also give my son Thomas, one Negro boy, by the name of Samuel.

Van's will also provided that

> my Negro woman Win, be set free by my Executors. It is also my Will that Negro Bill, son of Win, be not sold out of my family–to be either hired out by my Executors, or disposed to some of my Children.

Van authorized his executors "to sell, lease, rent, or dispose all of his buildings, improvement, Lots, millseats, etc." and to divide the proceeds of all sales equally among his children.

One of the final items in the will specified that the children would receive their "legacies . . . at such time as they shall, if boys, arrive at the Age of Twenty one years, if girls, at the Age Eighteen years." The will further states:

> profits and advantages arising from the rents or interests of the said Legacies shall be more than sufficient for the support and education of my three Children Vann–Thomas–and Lucy, that then the surplus to be considered as part of my Estate.

In closing, Van named Isaac Leet, Andrew Swearingen, Joseph Swearingen, and William Dodd the executors of his estate.

In a codicil to the will, he specified that his wife, Eleanor, should receive "the rents, issues and profits" from his "plantation" until she remarried. The codicil went on to state:

> and further, I do give and bequeath unto my Wife Eleanor Swearingen and equal share with my Children–Ellzy Swearingen, Zachariah Swearingen, Drusilla Brady, Vann Swearingen, Thomas Swearingen and Lucy Swearingen of all monies and profits arising from the sale of my Land in Washington county and the other property devised by said Will to be sold and devised and to remove all that may arise either in my Will or in the Codicil as to the person I mean by my wife Eleanor–I do hereby declare that whenever I have mentioned my Eleanor, in my said Will or this Codicil–I do thereby mean Eleanor Swearingen, formerly Eleanor Virgin, who has lived with me many years past as a faithful and loving wife.

Given the large number of properties, enslaved persons, and other items that Van had accumulated over his incredibly adventurous and profitable lifetime, Lucy and her brothers and sisters were, when they reached the age of 21 for the boys or 18 for the girls, destined to become fairly wealthy. It also meant that when Benjamin Stephenson married Lucy Stephenson, he stood to become a fairly wealthy husband.

There is no clear record of the marriage of Benjamin Stephenson and Lucy Swearingen. Various sources cite three different dates for the marriage. The earliest mention of Benjamin Stephenson and Lucy Swearingen Stephenson as man and wife is in the April 1799 court record of Augusta County, Virginia, where Ben is recorded as the husband of Lucy Swearingen. In the court records for the case of *Van Swearingen v. Braham Shepard*, the following is included: "Orators are, viz. Ellzey Swearingen, Van Swearingen, Thomas Swearingen, Benjamin Stephenson and Lucy, his wife, late Swearingen, heirs and devisees of Van Swearingen Jr." Karel Whyte, the genealogist who wrote a voluminous book on Swearingen genealogy, gives a marriage date of circa 1805. The 1805 date is the least likely of the three dates for the marriage, since Julia Stephenson, the oldest child of Ben and Lucy, was born in 1803. The third suggested date for the marriage is found in Lucy's obituary. In the obituary, Halderman (1850) states that "in November, 1803 she was united by Marriage to Col. Benjamin Stephenson, with whom she emigrated to Illinois, and settled in Kaskaskia, in the year 1809." The problem with the 1803 date for the marriage is the fact that Julia was born in 1803 even before the November marriage date. In addition to the court record that mentions Benjamin Stephenson and Lucy Stephenson as man and wife, there is also a record of a marriage recorded in Ohio County, Virginia. The record is almost impossible to read, and the names are obscured. The transcription reads:

> I do hereby certify that on the 7th day of September 1799 the rites of Marriage were solemnized by me in Wheeling between—Gad and Swearingen in pursuance of a license from the Clerk of Ohio county to me directed. Given under my hand—Jos. Doddridge. A Copy Teste Moses Chapline C. O. C.

The problem with this record is that it is dated a month after Ben and Lucy are mentioned as man and wife in the court record. The most likely date of their marriage is 1799. Benjamin Stephenson was 30 years old at that time. If Lucy was born in 1786, she was 13. If she was born in 1788 as her obituary states, she was just short of her 11th birthday.

The second mystery surrounding the marriage of Lucy Swearingen and Benjamin Stephenson is how the two met in the first place. Lucy grew up in Wellsburg, Ohio County, in the extreme northwest part of what is now West Virginia. Ben and his family had moved to the area around Martinsburg in the extreme northeast part of what is now West Virginia. The two areas are almost 200 miles apart. At a time when most people rarely traveled more than 20 miles from home, the distance between the two was considerable. Because there is no documented explanation, we may never know exactly what happened. There is no record that Ben ever traveled to Ohio County before the marriage, and he would not have had any reason to do so. However, there are some interesting but inconclusive clues that suggest Lucy might have traveled to the area around Martinsburg.

When Lucy's father, Van, settled in Wellsburg, he was only a few miles from Fort Henry, which was situated on the banks of the Ohio River. A small settlement grew up around Fort Henry, which became Wheeling, West Virginia. Andrew Swearingen built Fort Henry and was one of Van's younger brothers. Van was the leader of the local militia and came to Andrew's rescue during several Native attacks on Fort Henry. Van and Andrew became close friends as well as being brothers. Andrew became one of the executors of Van's will and was charged with providing for Lucy's education out of the funds of the estate. In 1798 Lucy's mother was remarried to John Newhouse. Court records confirm the date, as she sold land in 1798 and signed her name as "Eleanor Swearingen, ne Newhouse." Van's original will provided that Eleanor Virgin would get all of the proceeds from the Swearingen farm until she might remarry. In the event that she did remarry, the proceeds would then be divided among the children. Thus, Lucy was about to come into a substantial amount of money. Had she stayed with her mother, that money could have come under the control of John Newhouse.

Furthermore, Lucy's education had not yet been funded out of the estate. There was scant opportunity for education on the frontier. It is possible that Andrew, an executor of the will, decided that the best way to protect Lucy's inheritance, and provide her an education, would be to send her to live with his younger brother Joseph Swearingen, in Shepherdstown, Berkeley County, Virginia. Joseph was wealthy. He had received a 4,000-acre grant for his Revolutionary War service. He had just completed the building, a plantation house called Bellevue, and had only one child of his own. While such speculation about his sending Lucy to live with Joseph Swearingen is without any proof, there is one more fact that might support the scenario. Joseph Swearingen's only child was another in a long line of children named Thomas. Thomas was an only child born in 1784. He was only two to four years older than Lucy, depending on which date is taken for Lucy's birth. Thomas married Julia Lane in July 1802. Julia became was one of Lucy's best friends, and Ben and Lucy named their first child Julia. These close friendships lend some support to the speculation that Lucy was living with Joseph.

In 1914, a new courthouse in Stephenson County, Illinois, was dedicated in Freeport, Illinois. The county, created in 1837, had been named for Benjamin Stephenson. The committee that suggested the name for the county at the time it was created had originally decided to name it after James Stephenson, the son of Lucy and Benjamin Stephenson. After researching the life of James and

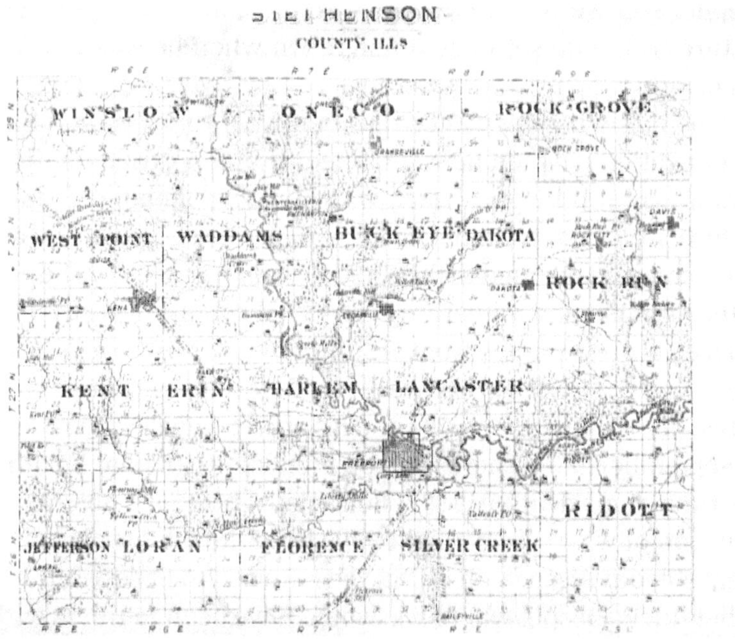

Map of Stephenson County, Illinois. *The History of Stephenson County, Illinois* [. . .], compiled by M. H. Tilden (Chicago: Western Historical Co., 1880). https://www.loc.gov/item/rc01002091/

becoming familiar with Ben's life, the committee decided that Benjamin Stephenson was much more important to the history of the state than his son James. Thus, the county was named after Benjamin Stephenson.

When the dedication ceremony of 1914 was held, Miss Virginia Freeman arrived with a picture of Benjamin Stephenson to be hung in the courthouse. The *Freeport Daily Bulletin* of June 4, 1914, reported that "the picture of Col. Stephenson, showing him dressed as the men were a century ago, was secured from a direct descendant of Colonel Benjamin Stephenson, his great granddaughter Miss Virginia Winchester Freeman of Chicago." The paper also reported that the picture was "copied from the only known picture extant, and which shows him in the flower of his youth, the dashing pioneer of early Illinois days." The paper said there were faded oil paintings of Ben and "his wife Lucy Van Swearingen to whom he was married in 1803" (another reference to the marriage taking place at late as 1803). According to the paper, "the portrait of Col. Stephenson we present today is taken from a tintype, a copied picture from one set in gold and taken when he was in Cuba for his health."

This is the only evidence that Ben went to Cuba, and there is no indication of when he went. The original portrait, a miniature in watercolor on ivory, which was photographed to produce the picture presented to Stephenson County, was eventually located in California and donated to the Smithsonian Institution. The curator of the Smithsonian miniature portrait collection suggested that the portrait probably dates from around 1800 based on Ben's clothing. If Ben went to Cuba for his health around 1800, it had to have been between his marriage in 1799 and his appointment as deputy sheriff in September 1801. There is no other evidence of poor health until the time of his death in 1822. Ben's departure for Cuba raises the question of where Lucy might have lived during his absence. The most obvious suggestion is that she returned to Bellevue, the home of her uncle Joseph, where she would have been reunited with her cousin and close friend Thomas Swearingen.

When Ben returned to America, probably sometime in 1801, he was appointed deputy sheriff of Jefferson County. It is probably no accident that his uncle, James Reed; his brother, James Stephenson; and uncles, Joseph Swearingen and Andrew Swearingen, were all leading citizens of the county. In fact, Joseph Swearingen, Lucy's de facto guardian, was one of the new justices of the peace who helped the new sheriff appoint his deputies. Today we associate the role of a deputy sheriff with the pursuit and apprehension of those who break the law. In the early 1800s, that was neither the only duty nor even the main duty of a sheriff or his deputies. More significant than arresting miscreants was the duty of assessing property, collecting property taxes and other taxes, and arresting those who evaded their taxes. Like the evil sheriff of Nottingham in the stories of Robin Hood, a 19th-century American sheriff spent more time on assessments, taxes, and tax collections than anything else. Along with the power of the role came a valuable education in real estate law. The education would have included the art of estimating the value of any piece of property. Benjamin Stephenson seems to have learned this lesson well. Over the next several years, he bought and sold multiple properties. His interest in property became a professional pursuit and determined his economic future.

The success of Ben and his brother James became a real advantage to the rest of the Stephenson family and their closest friends. Many years earlier in the Manor of Maske, the Stephensons and Reeds had developed a strong relationship with several families of Boyds who also lived in the manor. The older generations of the Boyds served with the Stephensons and Reeds during both the French and Indian War and the Revolutionary War. The bond between the three families had strengthened over the years. There is some controversy, however, over the origin of the specific line of the Boyd family that became closely allied with the Stephensons and Reeds.

It is likely they descended from the William Boyd who came to the Marsh Creek settlement, or the Manor of Maske, with Hance Hamilton in the 1720s. William, the first of the Boyds in the Manor of Maske, had several young children. William had been accompanied to America by Thomas and John Boyd. Thomas was probably William's brother while John seems to have been William's oldest son. William's younger son, Samuel, married Mary Beckett. They had two sons: Samuel, who was born in 1775, and John, who was born in 1776. Mary Beckett Boyd died in July 1789 when her young sons were 13 and 14 years old. Their father, Samuel, died only five months later, leaving the two teenage sons in the care of a relative. Their parents had left money to care for the two boys, but the relative "abused the trust." The two Boyd boys seem to have been left penniless to fend for themselves.

Soon after the Stephensons and James Reed moved to Martinsburg, the two Boyd teenagers seem to have followed and ended up near the Stephenson family farm. Samuel married Mary Reed "Maria" Stephenson in 1798. Shortly before or just after the wedding, Samuel and his brother moved to Middletown, later renamed Gerardstown, and opened a store. Samuel was the owner and John was the clerk. Middletown was south of Martinsburg, only a few miles from Darkestown and the Stephenson farm. Given the fact that the two boys had been destitute when they moved to Virginia, it is probable that Ben's father or Ben's brother James had loaned the money to Samuel to open the store. In 1803, John Boyd married Isabella, another of Ben's sisters. Ben, the newly financially secure deputy sheriff, provided the 50 pounds for the bond to secure John and Isabella's marriage. Samuel and Maria were the grandparents of Isabelle (Belle) Boyd, the charming courtesan and the courageous, or notorious (depending on whose side you were on), Confederate spy during the Civil War.

Following his appointment as deputy sheriff, Ben and Lucy moved to Harpers Ferry, Virginia. Although Harpers Ferry occupies a famous place in American history, it was hardly imposing in the early 1800s. For Ben and Lucy, its location was probably the most significant advantage. The little town was located only seven miles from Charles Town, which was the county seat and the town where Ben's brother James had settled. Since Ben seems to have continued serving as a deputy sheriff, it is probable that his duties included working in the Harpers Ferry vicinity. When Ben and Lucy moved there, Harpers Ferry was a new town. It had only been established in the late 1790s when President Thomas Jefferson had chosen it as the site for one of two United States armories. The Springfield Armory had been in existence for many years and was a growing concern. By contrast, Harpers Ferry was open farmland in the 1790s.

By 1800, the armory had been built in Harpers Ferry and was engaged in manufacturing and storing arms. It was never a huge operation, however. The federal law that authorized the establishment of the armory had limited its employment to only 100 workers. Thus, the town did not grow rapidly, and Ben and Lucy were probably a welcome addition to the population. On November 28, 1803, Julia Eleanor Stephenson was born at Harpers Ferry. Ben and Lucy's first child, Julia Eleanor was likely named after Lucy's' best friend, Julia Lane, and Lucy's mother, Eleanor Virgin Swearingen. In the following year, Ben continued his penchant for speculating in land. He purchased a portion of a lot for one dollar in Charles Town. The purchase price of a single dollar suggests that the lot had been sold at a tax sale and that Ben, as a deputy sheriff, was in a good position to know about the sale and to take advantage of the opportunity.

On September 8, 1804, Ben's father, James, died at the age of 64. His will had been written in August of the same year. In the will he gave his sorrel mare and his hogs, all the wheat in the barn, his household and kitchen furniture, and 105 pounds in cash to his wife. Son James received 40 pounds in cash. Son William got 10 shillings and James's clothing. Daughter Margaret, like William, got 10 shillings. Both William and Margaret had taken their portion of the holdings before James died. Ben was given a wagon and all the gear associated with it as well as 100 pounds in cash. James also made provision for a woman, Catherine McThomas, who would receive five pounds in cash when her term of indenture ended. The rest of the estate was to be divided between Ben and his three younger sisters, Sarah Kennedy, Isabella Boyd, and Maria Boyd. The will was recorded in February of 1805.

Between February 1805 and March 1806, Ben purchased a number of properties. In February he and his friend Daniel Morgan purchased 266 acres of land plus a house, enslaved persons, and tools for one dollar. Once again, the price would indicate that he had taken advantage of a tax sale to purchase a property at so advantageous a price. In May, Ben, acting in the capacity of deputy sheriff, and Daniel Morgan, acting in his capacity of justice of the peace, were appointed commissioners responsible for the sale of land through default by the owner in Shepherdstown. In this case they merely supervised the sale without buying the land. Ben also purchased 12 acres of land in Berkeley County for $480, which he and Lucy sold three months later for $420. Then, in March 1806, Ben purchased a town lot in Smithfield, Jefferson County, for $306.

The constant buying and selling of land was a major feature of the rest of Ben's life. He became a speculator and frequently gambled on land purchases. While his speculations sometimes ended in a loss, he seems to have been good at selecting the right investment. As a result, he and Lucy were beginning to build a decent nest egg. In 1806, things became considerably better. Ben must have resigned his position as deputy, because he and Lucy left Jefferson County. In 1806, Lucy seems to have reached her 18th birthday, which meant that she was now eligible to inherit the items left to her in Van Swearingen's will. Ben and Lucy moved to Brooke County, Virginia, in the spring of that year. Brooke County was the site where Van's will was administered. Lucy had been given one-third of the farm where she grew up, and shortly after the move, she and Ben sold her third of the land to John Newhouse, Lucy's stepfather. They sold the 280 acres for $200.

During their year in Brooke County, Ben and Lucy celebrated two important developments. James W. Stephenson, Ben and Lucy's oldest son, was born early in the summer of 1806. Throughout August, Ben fulfilled his civic duties by serving on three separate juries despite the fact that he had been a resident of the county for only five or six months. The second important event of the year was the sale of the most expensive piece of land that Lucy had inherited. She and Ben sold 150 acres of land for $3,000. The other item in Van's will was the provision that Lucy would receive "the sum of fifty pounds lawful money, or a small Negro girl of that value." Lucy exercised her right to choose an enslaved female named Win. Win was the daughter of the enslaved person Ester, who had been willed to Eleanor Virgin Swearingen. Lucy and Win had grown up together, it seems, and had established a relationship that lasted through the 1820s.

Ben and Lucy set off down the Ohio River in the spring of 1807 with their two young children and hopes of an even better life in Kentucky. In 1807 Kentucky had been a state for only 15 years. It was still thinly populated, despite Daniel Boone's complaint in 1799 that the young state already had too many people and too many lawyers living there when he left it for Missouri.

Ben and Lucy were not venturing into unknown territory. Eleanor Virgin, Lucy's mother, and her new husband, John Newhouse, had already left in 1804 for Kentucky, where they settled near her brother Reason, or "Rezin." Additionally, Lucy's favorite cousin, attorney Thomas Van Swearingen, married Julia Lane in July of 1803 in Nelson County, Kentucky. Thomas had established a law practice there, although he came too late to be one of the lawyers blamed for Daniel Boone's departure! Thus, Lucy's mother and her favorite cousin and his wife, who had now become a close friend of Lucy's, were already in Kentucky. In addition, a number of other Swearingens had settled in Kentucky in the 1780s. All of them were related to Lucy in one way or another. One of the earliest settlers in Kentucky, a friend of Daniel Boone, was a nephew of Indian Van. He was also named Van Swearingen. This Van Swearingen had joined St. Clair's army and was killed during St. Clair's defeat. His younger brothers had taken over the ownership of his land and were still living in Kentucky. Lucy's second cousin, Eleanor Swearingen, who grew up in Shepherdstown, had married Thomas Worthington and moved to Chillicothe, Ohio. Chillicothe was close to the Ohio River and the Kentucky border. Eleanor's husband, Thomas Worthington, became a two-term U.S. senator and was governor of Ohio from 1814 to 1818.

Ben and Lucy settled in Logan County, Kentucky, late in 1807. They still had business to settle in Virginia. In August, Ben sold the lot in Smithfield, which he had purchased in March of 1806 for $360, to his brother James for $500. He also brought suit in Brooke County in November 1807 against a William Pumphrey for trespass. Ben lost the suit against Pumphrey and was ordered to pay court costs. With his business in Virginia done, Ben began busily working on a variety of activities in Kentucky. Shortly after his arrival, Ben acquired several parcels of land. One was in Henderson

County. He also purchased two parcels of land in Logan County. One of these was on the Old Whippoorwill River where Ben and Lucy lived. The land on the Old Whippoorwill was assessed at $3,000 in the Logan County tax list in 1807. The second parcel in Logan County was assessed at $1,200. The couple also owned a parcel of land in Henderson County near the Ohio River assessed at a value of $495. The tax list for Logan County also indicates that the family included one male over 21 years (Ben), two "blacks" over age 15, five "blacks" under age 16, and six horses. In 1808, a second tax list shows that Ben had acquired two additional parcels of land in Logan County assessed at $200 and $400 and had one less horse. The property on the Ohio River in Henderson County had increased in value from $495 to $1,195.

Also in 1808, there is one curious entry in the Logan County records: "John Reed of Logan County, Kentucky appoints Benj. Stephenson of that county as his lawful attorney for management of property and certificate assignment." The entry is the only record anywhere asserting that Benjamin Stephenson was a lawyer. Most likely the entry is in error, and Ben was simply acting as a legal agent for the management of the land. While Ben and Lucy were prospering with Ben's land speculation and farming in Logan County, they became the parents of a second daughter. Elvira Amanda Stephenson was born in Russellville in Logan County on March 23, 1809 (Freeman, 1881). The fact that their daughter was named Elvira indicates that the second most important event in Ben's life had already happened: he had become a friend and political ally of Ninian Edwards.

The Stephensons' second daughter, Elvira, was named after Elvira Lane Edwards, the wife of Ninian Edwards. Elvira Edwards was one of Lucy Stephenson's most significant lifelong friends. Elvira was the sister of Julia Lane, who had married Lucy's favorite cousin, Thomas Swearingen. Julia Lane and Thomas Swearingen were married in Kentucky in 1803. Elvira Lane and Ninian Edwards were married at the Lane family home in Montgomery County, Maryland, also in 1803. Montgomery County, where the Lane sisters and Ninian Edwards grew up, was just across the Potomac River from Harpers Ferry and Charles Town, Virginia, and not far from Shepherdstown, Virginia, where Thomas Swearingen lived and where Lucy had stayed with her uncle Joseph, Thomas's father. Lucy had probably become acquainted with both of the Lane sisters while she was living in Harpers Ferry and her cousin Thomas was courting Julia. Through Julia, she almost certainly became acquainted with Elvira.

Ninian Edwards, the husband of Elvira Lane Edwards, was one of the most successful politicians of the early 19th century. He was the son of Benjamin Edwards, a very wealthy and successful farmer. Benjamin Edwards was a self-made man. He had no formal education but was self-taught and extraordinarily well read. He became a wealthy farmer by establishing a plantation known as Mount Pleasant in Montgomery County. He was well respected throughout Maryland. He was a delegate to the convention of the state of Maryland that ratified the United States Constitution. He also served in the state legislature as a representative of Montgomery County and was later elected to the United States Congress as a representative of his district. He established an enormous library and acquired land, not only in Maryland but also in Kentucky.

His son, Ninian Edwards, was born in 1775. Ninian, unlike his father, received a formal education. He started out as a student in a school taught by an Episcopal minister, the Reverend James Hunt, where he received the beginnings of a classical education. Reverend Hunt died in 1788, and the school closed. Ninian was only 13 at the time, and his education was incomplete. One of the other students in the school was an orphan, William Wirt, who had lived with Reverend Hunt after his mother's death. During his seven years living with Hunt, he had unfettered access to Hunt's extensive library. By the age of 15, when Hunt died, Wirt was already highly educated and extremely well read, but he had no money and no place to live.

Benjamin Edwards hired Wirt as a tutor for Ninian and his other children, and Wirt lived with the Edwards family. Once again, Wirt had access to an extensive library, and he and Ninian took full advantage of the opportunity. Wirt stayed with the Edwards family for nearly two years until Ninian was sent away to school at Dickinson College in Carlisle, Pennsylvania. Wirt went on to acquire a law degree and eventually became the attorney general of the United States in 1817. He was the longest-serving attorney general in the history of the United States, finally leaving office 12 years later in 1829. In 1832, he became a candidate for president but carried only one state. Throughout his lifetime, Wirt remained one of Ninian Edwards's closest friends. Until the end of Ninian's life, they exchanged long letters about everything from farming to politics.

Ninian eventually withdrew from Dickinson College to study law. According to his son, Ninian Wirt Edwards, who was also his biographer, Ninian was required to study history as well as law during his legal education. Having already been well educated in history, he decided to spend the time he was given to study history in studying medicine instead. While he never practiced medicine, he remained interested in medicine for the rest of his life (Edwards, 1870, p. 14). In the mid-1790s, his father sent him to Nelson County, Kentucky, to prepare a farm that his father had recently purchased and to acquire homes and farms for other members of the family. Ninian, still a teenager, wealthy and unattached, with no parental supervision around, took advantage of his situation to "sow his wild oats." His son, Ninian Wirt Edwards, writing about this period of his father's life, says:

> Thus sent forth upon the theatre of a new world, surrounded by companions whose pleasures and pursuits were in sensual indulgencies it is not surprising that this inexperienced youth . . . should have given away to excesses and indiscretions, till the hopes of his friends . . . had withered. (Edwards, 1870, pp. 14–15)

Despite his seeming dissipation, Ninian was elected a representative of Nelson County and reelected for a second term during this period. Furthermore, he completed his legal education and apparently left his life of "excesses and indiscretions" behind, as he was admitted to the Kentucky bar in 1798.

He then moved to Logan County, near Russellville, and began to practice law in Kentucky and Tennessee. During this period, he became friends with a number of other young lawyers, including Henry Clay and Felix Grundy. In the next decade "he filled in succession, the offices of Presiding Judge of the General Court, Circuit Judge, fourth Judge of the Court of Appeals, and Chief Justice of Kentucky" (Edwards, 1870, p. 15). Shortly after he established his successful career as a lawyer and judge, Ninian married Elvira Lane in 1803. They eventually moved to Russellville in Logan County, where they came into contact with Benjamin and Lucy Stephenson.

The Stephensons had moved to Logan County in 1806. The bond between Lucy and Elvira Lane Edwards became almost unbreakable during this period. Lucy honored this friendship by naming her second daughter Elvira Amanda Stephenson in 1809. Ben and Ninian, brought together by the friendship between their wives, also quickly established a lasting friendship. Ninian was a longtime member of the Society of Freemasons, and in January, a new lodge of free and accepted Masons was established in Logan County. Benjamin Stephenson was included as a member of the lodge. The Society of Freemasons was an organization of considerable significance in the early 1800s. The society included among its members most of the leaders of the day, including George Washington. Being accepted to a lodge of the Masons meant that a man had been accepted into the upper levels of society. No doubt Ben's friendship with Ninian Edwards was a major advantage in his acceptance. The year 1809 was marked as well by the birth of Ben and Lucy's third child.

It was also the year of another turning point in their life together.

CHAPTER THREE

Seven Flags over Illinois

In 1787, the Second Continental Congress created "An Ordinance for the Government of the Territory of the United States, North-West of the River Ohio." The act, probably one of the most important and influential ever passed in the United States, became known as the Northwest Ordinance. The ordinance ultimately led to the creation of five new states: Ohio, Indiana, Illinois, Michigan, and Wisconsin. The ordinance was necessitated by Great Britain ceding its claims in the vast interior of America at the end of the Revolutionary War. A huge area from the upper Ohio River all the way to the Mississippi now belonged to the United States.

Several of the original 13 states claimed large portions of this area for their own. Virginia, for example, claimed a vast area from its borders all the way to the Mississippi. In addition to Virginia's claims, Massachusetts, Connecticut, and New York all believed that they too had claims on large areas of the region. This created a problem since many of the original 13 states had no possible claims to any of the land. States that had no claims, and no chance of future territorial expansion, were in a potentially weak political position. They feared that those states making claims, like Virginia, were in a strong position to expand and become economically and politically dominant. States like Maryland, with no claims, refused to ratify the Articles of Confederation until the states that had claims renounced their rights. Eventually, all of the claims were renounced, clearing the way for the passage of the Articles of Confederation.

Before the claims were dropped, though, the situation did create some unusual historical twists. The laws of colonial Virginia prohibited the use of the Virginia militia outside the borders of the colony. However, during the Revolutionary War, Patrick Henry, the governor of Virginia, sent a militia unit under the command of George Rogers Clark all the way to Kaskaskia, Illinois, to conquer the Illinois Country. Legally, this was only possible because the Illinois Country was considered a part of Virginia.

When the states ceded their rights, the problem of what to do with the resources of the area became pressing. There was also the problem of how to govern the population. The Northwest Ordinance was created to solve these problems. Between 1787, when the ordinance was passed, and 1809, when Illinois became a territory, political control of the Illinois Country changed several times. On the third of February 1809, the 10th Congress of the United States passed the bill that created the new Territory of Illinois. The bill was signed into law by the new president, James Madison, and came into effect on March 1, 1809. The Territory of Illinois became the seventh different entity, or "flag," to have ruled the Illinois Country.

The earliest of these political entities had been the great Mississippian culture of Native Americans, which was centered at the massive site of Cahokia just 15 miles south of modern Edwardsville. The Mississippians ruled over the area for almost 300 years, from around 900 to 1200 C.E. After the decline of Cahokia, Native American cultures that came after them, including the Illini Confederation, took over the area. In the late 1600s, the French arrived from Canada and raised the flag of France over the Illinois Country. They settled at the Peoria Lakes in the north, and to the south they built Fort Chartres near Prairie du Rocher. In southwestern Illinois, they settled in towns like Kaskaskia, French Cahokia, St. Philippe, and other small settlements in the Mississippi floodplain. After the French and Indian War, the British seized control of the area. British rule lasted for little more than a decade before George Rogers Clark conquered the Illinois Country during the American Revolution. The Illinois Country then came under the flag of Virginia and was considered a county of Virginia. In 1787, the Northwest Ordinance made the entire area north of the Ohio and east of the Mississippi into the "Northwest Territory," which became the fifth entity to rule the area. In 1801, the Northwest Territory was divided into two: the Ohio Territory and the Indiana Territory. The Illinois Country then became part of Indiana and raised the flag of the Indiana Territory. In 1809, when the 10th Congress of the United States divided the Indiana Territory and created the Illinois Territory, the seventh flag flew over Illinois, though it would not be the last.

Like most things in the history of American politics, the 1809 bill creating the Illinois Territory was not passed by Congress without controversy. The Indiana Territory had been created in 1801 when Congress decided to split the Northwest Territory into the Ohio and Indiana Territories. William Henry Harrison became the governor of the new Indiana Territory. Harrison had earlier become a military hero during the Battle of Fallen Timbers. He was a junior officer in the army sent to defeat the Shawnee, Miami, and allied tribes that had decimated St. Clair's army in 1791. In 1794, the troops led by General "Mad Anthony" Wayne engaged and defeated the Natives in an area recently devastated by a tornado, hence the name "Battle of Fallen Timbers." Based on his military experience and political savvy, Harrison became a very successful politician.

In 1803, Harrison was reappointed governor of the Indiana Territory, with its capital established at Vincennes. He did a number of significant things during his term as governor, including making crucial treaties. He negotiated a large number of treaties with Native American tribes, which ceded Native land to the United

Seal of the Illinois Territory, 1809. "Official State Symbols," Office of the Illinois Secretary of State. https://www.ilsos.gov/publications/illinois_bluebook/statesymbols.pdf

States. At the end of the revolution, the British had ceded their claims to the entire territory. However, British claims, while "legal," were almost worthless in reality. The British had *never* "controlled" the area. Control had always rested with the Native Americans, who had, so far, successfully resisted attempts to remove them by force. The Continental Congress, which created the Northwest Ordinance, was well aware of the difference between claims and control. It was aware too that settlement in the area would be much harder, if not impossible, without some way of satisfying the claims of the Native Americans. Article III of the ordinance largely dealt with religion, morality, and knowledge, and it encouraged schools and "the means of education." And the article went on to state that "utmost good faith shall always be observed towards the Indians: their lands and property shall never be taken from them without their consent." Article III came to be interpreted as requiring the government to "extinguish" all Native claims to lands by treaty before any American settlement could begin. While illegal settlement, or squatting, was common, territorial leaders like Harrison honored the intent of the article by negotiating treaties with tribes. While treaties were "negotiated," the unspoken threat of force was present in every negotiation. Whatever the tenor of the negotiations, Harrison succeeded in obtaining large tracts of land through treaties with a number of tribes.

Despite Harrison's success, almost from the beginning of his tenure, there was dissatisfaction among the settlers of the territory who resided in Illinois Country. Probably their biggest complaint was that the capital of the territory was far away in Vincennes, Indiana, as was the Territorial Court. Anyone living in Illinois Country was separated from the seat of political power and the protection of the court by a significant distance. Legal business with the court required a long trip through a region still inhabited by hostile Natives. Furthermore, Article VI of the original ordinance said, "There shall be neither slavery nor involuntary servitude in the said territory." Most of the leading citizens of the Illinois Country, as well as a number of settlers in both Ohio and Indiana, were southerners who had brought their enslaved persons with them. Although Harrison tried, unsuccessfully, to get the prohibition against slavery removed, he was blamed for the prohibition. Harrison responded by passing a law that allowed indentured servitude. For many years the law allowed slaveowners to keep their enslaved persons by calling them "indentured servants." Furthermore, and not surprisingly, Harrison was accused of political favoritism. Such a charge was inevitable given the distance between Vincennes and the western part of the territory. At one point, the settlers in Illinois Country wrote a petition asking that the area be annexed to the new Territory of Louisiana (Howard, 1972, p. 71). Most of the settlers in Illinois Country were clustered around Kaskaskia, which had a substantial French population. To be annexed by Louisiana, with its French heritage, probably seemed logical to anyone living in Kaskaskia. The petition went nowhere, however, and rule from Vincennes remained unpopular.

As seems appropriate and almost inevitable to any modern Illinoisan, the Territory of Illinois owes its birth to a political deal. In 1808, Jesse Thomas, an influential Indiana politician, ran for the office of territorial representative from Indiana to the United States House of Representatives. Thomas lived in western Indiana and was familiar with many of the people living in Illinois Country. Thomas campaigned in Illinois Country with the promise that, if he were elected, he would make sure that Illinois became a separate territory. Thomas was elected with the overwhelming support of the residents of Illinois Country. Unlike any number of other politicians, Thomas kept his campaign promise. Largely through his efforts, a bill authorizing the Territory of Illinois was passed in February 1809 and took effect on March 1, 1809.

President James Madison moved quickly to appoint political leaders for the new territory. The Northwest Ordinance had stipulated that the president would appoint a governor, three judges, and a secretary. The governor would serve a term of three years, receive a salary of $2,000 a year, and receive a "freehold" of 1,000 acres of land. The secretary would be appointed for four years at a salary of $1,000 and receive a freehold of 500 acres. The three judges appointed to the Territorial Court were given a salary of $1,000, a freehold of 500 acres, and were appointed to an unspecified term conditional only on continued "good behavior." The governor and at least two of the three judges were charged with adopting and publishing laws of the existing states or territories until a legislature came into being. No legislature could be organized until "there shall be five thousand free male inhabitants of full age in the district." Thus, the governor and the three judges had substantial power to adopt whatever laws they liked as long as those laws were in effect in one of the existing states.

The governor also had substantial power to appoint officeholders. The governor was the commander-in-chief of the militia and appointed all of the officers below the rank of general. Generals could be recommended for appointment by the governor but had to be appointed by Congress. The governor also appointed most civil officers, including sheriffs and justices of the peace. Additionally, the governor could create new counties and appoint county judges and civil officers.

President Madison's first choice for governor was Judge John Boyle, an associate judge on the Kentucky Court of Appeals. Boyle declined the appointment, and Madison then appointed Ninian Edwards on April 24, 1809 (Edwards, 1770, p. 27). Among those

Portrait of Ninian Edwards. Robert Sobel and John Raimo, eds., *Biographical Directory of the Governors of the United States, 1789–1978*, vol. 1 (Westport, CT: Meckler Books, 1978). 4 vols.

writing letters of recommendation for Edwards was Henry Clay, who eventually became one of the most powerful political figures of the 19th century.

At the same time, President Madison appointed Nathaniel Pope as territorial secretary. Pope was the brother of a serving senator of Kentucky and a cousin of Ninian Edwards. In addition, three judges of the Territorial Court were appointed: Alexander Stuart, Obadiah Jones, and Jessie Thomas. Governor Edwards needed time to clear up his affairs in Kentucky and transport his cattle and enslaved persons to Kaskaskia. Nathaniel Pope acted as governor from April until Edwards finally arrived and took the oath of office on June 11, 1809 (James, 1901, p. 7). Throughout his first years in office, Edwards was busy appointing county clerks, justices of the peace, county judges, county surveyors, and numerous other officeholders. As the commander of the Illinois militia, he also appointed a large number of lieutenants and captains to numerous militia units.

On June 28, 1809, Governor Edwards "removed James Gilbreath from the office of Sheriff in Randolph County. The Governor commissioned Benjamin Stephenson sheriff of Randolph County during the pleasure of the Governor for the time being, in the place of James Gilbreath, removed" (James, 1901, p. 8). Benjamin Stephenson had arrived in Kaskaskia some time shortly before in late June 1809. On first glance, the removal of Gilbreath as sheriff and the appointment of Benjamin Stephenson looks like a classic case of political cronyism. However, there was more to the appointment than first appears.

Gilbreath had served as sheriff from 1804 to 1809, under the administration of Governor Harrison of Indiana, while Randolph County was part of the Indiana Territory. He had been reappointed by Nathaniel Pope while Pope was the acting governor. Pope, new to the territory, was unfamiliar with Gilbreath's past actions. Far removed from the seat of power in Vincennes during his term in office, Sheriff Gilbreath had become something of a law of his own. His principal duty was the assessment of property and the collection of property taxes. He was also charged with the sale of property for which the owner had failed to pay taxes. Because of the distance and difficult journey between Randolph County and the governor and Territorial Court in Vincennes, it was almost impossible for a resident of Randolph County to get relief from one of the sheriff's edicts. Gilbreath seems to have taken advantage of this opportunity to pursue a number of nefarious schemes. The principal scheme evidently involved levying and collecting property tax, pocketing the money, and later declaring the taxes to be delinquent. He then was able to sell the property to one of his friends or partners at a tax sale. Apparently, he also kept some of the property and sold it later. According to a letter written by Benjamin Stephenson in 1816, Gilbreath was still selling property, acquired illegally while he had been sheriff, two years after he was removed from office. The territorial judges and the governor addressed the problem on July 20, 1809, by passing an act titled "A Law respecting Arrearages Due the Former Sheriff." The law stated:

> Whereas it is represented to the Legislature that the late sheriff of the county of Randolph has neglected to collect all of the county levies . . . Be it therefore enacted: That James Gilbreath, late sheriff of the said county . . . shall at the next county court . . . deliver and produce on oath . . . a full, just and true account of all the sums which he has collected, or ought to have collected . . . noting therein the names of delinquents and the sums due; and he shall also deliver a true and perfect account of all monies by him paid for the use of the county, stating therein the amounts paid to whom and by what authority, and produce to the court his original vouchers and receipts. (Philbrick, 1950, p. 11)

When Ninian Edwards removed Sheriff Gilbreath, it made sense to appoint Benjamin Stephenson. Not only was Stephenson a good friend and ally, but he had experience as a deputy sheriff in Virginia.

There was no single definition of the duties of the sheriff of Randolph County in 1809. Many of the duties were inherited from the laws of the Indiana Territory. When Ninian Edwards and the three Territorial Court judges came into office, they began adopting laws from other states. Frequently, these laws were adopted with amendments and were again amended later. The duties of the Randolph and St. Clair county sheriffs were enumerated in a number of sections of the various laws and acts adopted by the governor and the three judges. For example, the act regulating the county courts required that the sheriff attend each session of the court and, in the absence of the two judges, was required to open a session of the court. The sheriff was then required to adjourn the court on a day-by-day basis. The law concerning grand juries "required the sheriff of each county . . . before each meeting . . . to summon twenty-four of the most discreet housekeepers," and those housekeepers, "or any sixteen of them, shall be a grand jury" (Philbrick, 1950, p. 26). The sheriffs were also empowered to arrest or collect bond, not less than $200 or more than $500, for anyone indicted by a grand jury. The sheriffs were also required to issue merchant fees for $15 per year. The number of duties was substantial, but the major duty of the sheriffs remained the levying of taxes and their collection.

Assessing taxes was not the sole responsibility of the sheriff. In the beginning the sheriff did an assessment of the property, and two "freeholders" in the county were appointed by the court to create an independent assessment. Land, houses, "mansions," town lots, and town "out-lots," windmills, and "water" were all assessed. When the two lists were brought into conformity, the tax was calculated by the court. Later, a county assessor position was created, and the sheriff then became responsible only for collecting the taxes. The 1809 property tax rate was set at no more than 30 cents per 100 dollars in assessed value. In addition to levying the taxes and collecting them, the sheriff was responsible for dealing with the issue of delinquent taxes. "The act for levying and collection of a tax on land" required that the sheriff give the county clerk a list of all landholders and their taxes by the 18th of September of each year. The sheriff was then authorized to collect the taxes. The auditor of public accounts was subsequently ordered to

> deliver a list of delinquent accounts to the sheriff who shall advertise the said land as listed for sale in some newspaper most convenient to Kaskaskia. Be it further enacted that the

> sheriff shall have the power and shall be his duty to demand of every inhabitant of this county the amount of the tax due him . . . before June yearly, and on failure of any person to [do so], the same shall proceed to sell the land or so much thereof as will pay the taxes . . . and costs. (Philbrick, 1950, p. 14)

The laws and duties of the sheriff were constantly evolving because the judges and the governors were adopting and amending laws, seemingly on a daily basis.

When Benjamin Stephenson was appointed sheriff, one of his first duties was the levying and collecting of taxes. By the act of the governor and the judges, he was supposed to provide a list of landowners and taxes by September 18. Ben had been appointed on June 28. He quickly discovered that the former sheriff, Gilbreath, had kept hardly any records. With no records, it was almost impossible to quickly determine who owned property and its past assessment. Since there were no records of assessments or taxes paid, it was also impossible to quickly determine whose taxes were delinquent. In early December of 1809, Ben must have taken his problem to the governor and the court. They relieved him from the requirement to finish his list of owners and taxes in September. In an act titled "An Act for the Relief of Benjamin Stephenson," the court changed the date for the completion of the list from September 18 to December 25, 1809. It might be called the "Merry Christmas Ben Act."

The magnitude of the problem Ben had inherited became clear when he advertised the sales of land being offered to satisfy delinquent taxes. The closest newspapers were in St. Louis. In June of 1810, Ben began placing ads. He placed two ads in the *Louisiana Gazette*. The first stated:

> Notice—On the first Monday, the 2d day of July next, it being the first day of the county Court, the following tracts of Lands will be exposed to public sale, at the door of the house where the said court is held in Kaskaskia, or so much thereof as will pay the taxes thereon, and continue during the sitting of each succeeding court, until sold, or the taxes thereon paid.

The list of property accompanying the notice is remarkable for its length. On the first page, 84 properties were listed. Nine of the properties totaled 2,178 acres of land. One additional property was 1,428 acres. The remaining 70 properties consisted of 400 acres each. A second ad, placed on June 7, stated that starting on July 7, 1810, there would be additional sales involving four properties totaling 18,588 acres.

By the middle of July 1810, life had finally begun to slow down and assume a more normal pace for Ben. He had settled into the job of sheriff, and much of the mess left behind by Gilbreath was well on its way to being resolved.

Life in Kaskaskia was fairly comfortable and never boring. The population was an eclectic mix. Kaskaskia was first settled in the late 17th century and the beginning of the 18th century. Father Gravier, a Jesuit priest, established a mission among the Native Kaskaskians in the late 1600s and became the founder of the village of Kaskaskia. The Jesuits followed the Kaskaskia tribe who had moved to the area shortly before 1700. "For some time it was only a missionary station and the inhabitants of the village consisted entirely of natives" (Eastman, 1883, 14). Kaskaskia was located on a peninsula between the Mississippi River and the Kaskaskia River. It was surrounded by water on three sides. The Kaskaskia River, which traverses much of Illinois from the northeast to the southwest, leaves the bluffs east of the American Bottoms nearly 10 miles north of Kaskaskia. The river then flows almost due south, parallel to the bluffs before emptying into the Mississippi south of the little town of Kaskaskia. The location was extremely favorable since the soils in the American Bottoms were conducive to agriculture. There was plentiful water and ready access to both fish and a variety of mammals and birds, including masses of migratory waterfowl.

The most important thing about the location of Kaskaskia was its proximity to the two rivers. In the 17th and 18th centuries, most transportation was by water. From Kaskaskia, the Mississippi provided a transportation route north to the French town of St. Louis, a center of commerce. The Mississippi also provided an easy route south to New Orleans, the center of the French occupation of the Mississippi Valley. In 1733, the French built Fort Kaskaskia on the bluffs overlooking the town of Kaskaskia. Earlier, in 1720, they had built Fort Chartres near Prairie du Rocher. The original wooden fort there was destroyed by Mississippi floods, and a second wooden fort was built in 1725. Between 1754 and 1760, a stone fort was completed. Fort Chartres became the military center of the French empire in North America south of Canada.

By the 1750s, Kaskaskia and the Mississippi floodplain, from Kaskaskia north to French Cahokia, was a French colonial district of considerable importance. The population of Kaskaskia had swelled considerably and probably numbered well over 2,000. A small settlement of the Kaskaskia, the remains of a once powerful tribe, had a village just north of the town. The French had always had good relations with the Natives. Unlike the British, the French were content to live in harmony with the Natives, marry their women, and carry on a lucrative trade in furs. Also unlike the British, the French were never interested in bringing in large numbers of immigrants and establishing large farms and estates. The French *voyageurs* were basically rivermen who transported goods, especially furs, along the inland rivers of North America by canoe. They were among the earliest French settlers. They were accompanied into the area by *coureurs de bois*, literally "runners in the woods." They were fur trappers and traders who also made their homes in the area and married Native American wives. Both the voyageurs and the coureurs de bois were happy to escape the political control of the French aristocrats in Canada and even more delighted to escape the moral strictures of "the black robes," the ubiquitous Jesuit priests. In the middle of America, they were free to pursue a much more unfettered lifestyle:

> The French colonists almost entirely escaped the Indian hostilities by which the English settlements were repressed and weakened . . . Frequent intermarriages of the French with the Indians strongly cemented their union. For nearly a hundred years, the French colonists enjoyed continual peace, while the English settlements on the Atlantic coast were in a state of almost constant danger from savage depredations. (*History of Madison County*, 1882, p. 30)

Some of the variation between French and English relationships with the Native Americans owed to differing levels of aggression in the French and English approaches to settlement:

> The English colonists excited the jealousy and fear of the Indians by their rapid occupation of the country. New settlements were constantly being projected and . . . settlement pushed further and further into the wilderness . . . When the Indians saw their . . . territories being broken up and the . . . hunting grounds invaded . . . distrust and jealousy led to warfare. (p. 30)

Unlike the English, the French saw no need to expand settlements. They tended, by choice, to cluster in towns. They found isolated farms in the forest socially unattractive, whereas social life within the towns was appealing. Furthermore, the French land system differed notably from the English system. The English favored individual ownership of land and found the accumulation of property a means to greater social status. The French thought otherwise. Towns like Kaskaskia were surrounded by "common fields." Heads of household in the town were assigned areas to farm in the common fields. The size of the area assigned to a person depended on family size and need. When all of the land in the common fields was assigned and more was needed, the borders of the common fields were expanded by clearing more forest. No French settler had to venture into the wilderness to find land to farm.

The French settlements, like Kaskaskia, were compact towns. Although there was plenty of land available to allow for large lots and broad streets, the French chose to cluster houses close together and create narrow streets. Togetherness and neighborly interaction was a staple of French colonial life. The French grew abundant food in the common fields; they kept cattle and hogs; and they joined the Natives in hunting in the forest.

By 1810, the Kaskaskia tribe, living near the town of the same name, probably numbered fewer than 200 people. The Kaskaskia had been a member of the Illinois Confederation, which was a loose alliance of tribes: the Kaskaskia, Peoria, Tamaroa, Cahokia,

Moingwena, and Michegamea. The Wea and Piankishaw were closely related tribes and may have been part of the Illinois Confederation in earlier times. When Jacques Marquette and Louis Joliet had descended the Mississippi River in 1673, there were somewhere between 10,000 and 15,000 Illini. Over the next 150 years, they were almost completely exterminated by a number of more powerful tribes. They were attacked from the north and east by the Iroquois, who were armed with British guns. From the northwest they were attacked by the Saux and Fox tribes, and they were attacked from the north by the Winnebago and the Kickapoo. They also suffered attacks from the east by the Shawnee and other tribes being pushed west by English and then American expansion. By the time Benjamin Stephenson arrived in Kaskaskia, the Illini were almost extinct. The remnants of the Kaskaskia and Peoria probably numbered fewer than 400 people.

The French and Indian War never reached the American Bottoms, but at the end of the war, the French ceded the area to the British. Fort Kaskaskia was renamed Fort Gage by the British. Eventually, Fort Chartres was abandoned to the British, and all French military presence was removed from Illinois. With the advent of British rule, many of the French residents moved to the French settlement of Cape Girardeau, just across the Mississippi from Kaskaskia, or to St. Louis. Undoubtedly, they wanted to escape the possibility of political rule by the British, their traditional European enemy. Furthermore, many of the French citizens of Kaskaskia were slaveholders, and they were convinced that the British would require them to free their enslaved persons. Thus, the population of Kaskaskia declined. It declined even further starting in 1778. On July 4, 1778, an "army" of 175 men led by George Rogers Clark captured Kaskaskia without firing a single shot (Howard, 1972, p. 52). Clark was able to reassure most of the French population that the Americans would honor their traditions. French belief in Clark's reassurances was helped by news that the French had just recently joined the American Revolution. Nevertheless, still more French speakers left Kaskaskia for Missouri after the American takeover. By the time the 1810 census was conducted, the population of Kaskaskia had declined to 662.

When the Stephenson family moved to Kaskaskia, the bulk of the population was still French. A number of the French, like Pierre Menard, had prospered after the American takeover and became rich and politically significant. Most of the French who remained after the British takeover were happy to be American citizens rather than British subjects and adjusted well to American rule. In addition to the French, there were a few English settlers who remained after the revolution. They included John Edgar, a veteran of the British navy, who had obtained a number of large land grants from the British king. He had become one of the largest landowners in the territory. The French, English, and Native populations of Kaskaskia were joined by a number of Americans. Some had come with George Rogers Clark and stayed in the area. A number of veterans of the revolution came to the area. Thomas Piggot, a compatriot of Van Swearingen in the 8th Pennsylvania, settled in the American Bottoms just north of Fort Chartres. Some of the Americans were Yankees from New England, but the Yankees were considerably outnumbered by Americans who came from southern states, especially Kentucky. Those from Kentucky included most of the new political elite: Ninian Edwards, Nathaniel Pope, the judges, and other public officials like Benjamin Stephenson. They were joined by other American settlers who came for a variety of reasons. The nine brothers of the Rector family came to the area around 1809. The Rectors were surveyors, and the oldest brother, William, became an important surveyor in the area and a leading citizen of the territory before moving to St. Louis.

Governor Edwards, Nathaniel Pope, Judge Jesse Thomas, Judge Stuart, Benjamin Stephenson, and several of the Rector brothers established a small settlement just south of Prairie du Rocher, not far from Kaskaskia. Edwards was supposed to receive a 1,000-acre plantation as part of his compensation as governor. He was not able to get a title to his land for some time because of the restrictions of the Northwest Ordinance. Nevertheless, he moved onto a large tract of land and named his farm and mansion "Elvirade" after his daughter Elvira.

The Stephensons must have enjoyed their life in Kaskaskia. They were surrounded by interesting people with interesting stories to tell. Additionally, the town of Kaskaskia had become the capital of the new Illinois Territory. As the center of political and judicial power, the town drew people from all over the territory and also from neighboring states and territories. They came for economic reasons as well as legal and political reasons. The town had only 662 residents in 1810, but it probably was bursting at the seams.

The 1810 census shows that Benjamin Stephenson was the head of a household of 27. Clearly, not all 27 were members of the family. The family consisted of Ben, Lucy, and three children: Julia, James, and Elvira. The 27 people included "1 white male under ten, 9 white males 16–26, 7 white males 26–45, 2 white females under ten, 3 white females age 16–26 and 5 other free persons, except Indians, not taxed," who were probably the indentured servants. Leaving aside the five indentured servants and the five members of the family, there were 17 people not identified. Who were they, and why were they staying with the Stephensons? There is probably no good answer. In the early 1800s when people traveled, they frequently stayed with friends or relatives, or they just became guests in the only available house. Whatever the case, the Stephenson household was clearly a bustling place. Thomas Swearingen, Lucy's brother, was also in Kaskaskia and is shown as a single man, in the 16–26 age bracket, and the head of a household.

There was a lively social life in Kaskaskia. The French had always been sociable, and many of the new American settlers were people who had grown up in well-to-do families used to social gatherings. Only four months after the Illinois Territory was created, in 1809, there was a large celebration of the Fourth of July in Kaskaskia. According to an article in the *Louisiana Gazette*, the celebration followed what had already become a standard format for the period. Almost all of the townspeople, along with Governor Edwards, assembled in the early afternoon and sat down to dinner. Following dinner, toasts were offered, accompanied by volleys fired by the militia. According to the paper, 17 separate toasts were offered. They honored the president, vice president, the Constitution, the heroes of the revolution, Congress, industry, the union, the militia, the punishment of traitors like Aaron Burr and Benedict Arnold, virtue, liberty, George Washington, Thomas

Jefferson, the arts and sciences, economy, and "the American fair—their smile to the good and brave, their contempt to the vicious and base." After dinner the governor retired, and additional toasts were proposed and accompanied by firing a six-pound canon. These toasts honored Governor Edwards, William Henry Harrison, and Albert Gallatin, secretary of the U.S. Treasury Department. The newspaper reported that "the celebration of the day was closed by an elegant ball in to evening at Major B. Stephenson's, where a brilliant circle of Ladies attended, whose smiles seemed to speak the language of their hearts."

While the Stephensons enjoyed their time in Kaskaskia, their life, like those of most early settlers in the territory, was not without problems. The weather was a common problem. Because Kaskaskia was located between two large rivers, flooding was a threat, particularly in the spring. Since most transportation was by water, floods would disrupt the arrival of food and other goods. Several times the local newspaper suspended publication because severe flooding had stopped the delivery of newsprint. In the summer, the mid-continent heat dried up the numerous sloughs, floodplain ponds, and swamps, and the stink of dead fish decaying in the oxygen-starved water could become overpowering. Furthermore, stagnant water was a breeding place for clouds of mosquitoes, which carried malaria. Insects like horseflies and black flies, which delivered painful bites, were found in profusion. There were also significant natural disasters to suffer apart from springtime flooding.

In June 1814, the *Missouri Gazette* featured an article, reprinted from the Kaskaskia paper, describing one such disaster:

> This place was visited on Friday night . . . by a violent tornado which blew down and tore to pieces every building which was situated in that part of the village through which it raged. It demolished houses, fences, barns and stables. Nothing could resist its force—the roofs of several houses were carried to such a distance from where they stood that they are not yet found and the parts of others were on the opposite bank of the Kaskaskia river; we are happy however to state that in the wreck of property there was no lives lost, and not more

> than 12 or 14 much wounded not one of whom are considered very dangerous. Many Cattle, Horses, &c. were killed and wounded by the flying timber with which the atmosphere was clouded from the neighboring ruin. The space in which it raged most violent was not very wide, and the iron hand of misfortune has stricken those who were least prepared to bear the blow.

The fear and destruction wrought by the 1814 tornado pales in comparison to the earlier disaster of the New Madrid earthquake. The earthquake was really a series of earthquakes

> that took place over a period of months, beginning on December 16, 1812, until March of 1812. During this time, there were over 2000–3000 tremors, three of which were estimated to have measured over 8.0 on the later-devised magnitude scales. At least 6 other shocks were estimated in the 7.0–7.5 range. (Farrar & Mateyka, 2011, p. 9)

Two accounts of the earthquake were written by residents of Kaskaskia. Mr. Morrison, an attorney in Kaskaskia, wrote to the Cincinnati *Western Spy* in January, and his account was published February 22, 1812:

> We have been very much alarmed by a repetition of earthquakes since the morning of the 16 of Dec. The first happened about half past 2 o'clock–it was extremely severe and was succeeded by another just at sunrise the same morning, but somewhat less terrible. The subsequent ones have been more gentle, and occurred three times in about every 24 hours, for more than 10 days. For about 20 days past, we have not experienced more than 3 or 4 shocks, and these but slightly felt.

A more subjective take on the event offers another account:

> The years of 1811 and 1812 were years of trouble and dismay in Old Kaskaskia. In the first of these years, the inhabitants

> were frightened beyond description by a terrible earthquake which was felt in different degrees of intensity by the whole Mississippi valley. At Kaskaskia, the earth several times moved like a river agitated by the winds; the steeple of the church bent like a reed; the old bell rang with tremulous strokes like some unseen demon pulling on the bell cord; the cattle wild with nameless fear, ran to and fro filling the air with howling; the soil cracked so deeply in the very streets that they could not sound the bottom of the crevice, and the water drawn from it exhaled a most disagreeable odor; stone and brick chimneys fell down; houses cracked as if it were doomsday. The people, believers and nonbelievers, flocked to the church and listened with Catholic zeal to the stout old Father Donatien Oliver as he implored mercy from Him whom the elements obey. (Brown, 1906, p. 140)

Disasters wrought by the forces of nature were a common and vexing problem, but fear of tornadoes, floods, and earthquakes were nothing compared with fear of Native attack.

Conflict between the American settlers and the Natives was not a new phenomenon. Leaving aside the brief period of amity between the Pilgrims and the Natives, there had been trouble between the two sides from almost the first moment European settlers set foot on the continent. As European settlement spread, the conflict grew. After the Revolutionary War, the Americans began to broach the barriers of the Allegheny and Blue Ridge Mountains and to cross the Ohio River into the Ohio and Illinois Country. The conflict became characterized by appalling cruelty on both sides. Ever since the end of the revolution, British agents in Canada had been supplying arms and leadership to Natives fighting against the American settlers. Now, as England and America lurched again toward war, the problem became considerably worse. The War of 1812 was largely a result of British interference in American maritime trade and the British practice of impressing American merchant seamen into the British navy. The British agents in Canada believed it was their duty to encourage the Natives to increase their attacks on the settlers on the frontier. Even before the establishment of the

Illinois Territory, Native attacks were being carried out on isolated farms on the frontier. As the American presence increased, the intensity of the attacks increased in step. Most American settlement in the Illinois Country was south of modern Edwardsville. Most of the Native settlement was confined to the area from modern Springfield north to the Great Lakes. The 100 miles or so between the two areas was almost uninhabited and was used largely by the Natives as a hunting ground. Small parties of Natives tended to slip south from their villages to the isolated farms and settlements in both Illinois and Missouri. While many of the raiders were content to steal horses and other goods, other raids turned deadly.

In early July 1810, a party of Natives raided Portage des Sioux on the Missouri side of the Mississippi and stole a number of horses, deer hides, a pack saddle, and a considerable quantity of deer jerky. The Natives crossed the river to Illinois and headed north toward Peoria. William Cole, Cornelius Gooch, and James Moredough, the owners of the stolen goods, were joined by Sarshal Brown, Abraham Patten, and Stephen Cole; they immediately pursued the Natives. Near dusk, they caught sight of the Natives on the prairie about five miles ahead:

> Night coming on, and their horses becoming very fatigued, the pursuers concluded to follow no further, and pitched their camp near a small branch. But about two o'clock in the morning, while sleeping around their watch-fire, they were fired upon by the Indians and four of the party, consisting of Gooch, Abraham Patten, W. T. Cole and Sarshal Brown [were] instantly killed. Stephen Cole was wounded in two places and also tomahawked, but he recovered from his wounds. (Edwards, 1870, p. 37)

Cole and James Moredough escaped. The day after the two men reached safety, a party of settlers started back and recovered the bodies of the other men. A day or two later, another settler came across two Potawatomi sleeping in the woods. They had a number of horses with them. They said they were just coming back from a buffalo hunt and were tired. The settler, knowing nothing of the killings, thought nothing of the encounter until later.

Learning that the raiding party had included Potawatomi, "a requisition was made by the Governor of Louisiana Territory, upon Governor Edwards, to deliver them up for punishment" (Edwards, 1870, p. 38). Edwards did nothing about the requisition for nearly a year. But a series of incidents in 1811 forced Edwards to act:

> on June 2, 1811, at a cabin about two miles northeast of the present village of Pocahontas, most members of the Cox family were absent picking strawberries when three Potawatomi warriors rushed their cabin. Disappointed in their hope of a raid on the Osage, they had turned toward the settlements looking for plunder. In the cabin they found Elijah Cox, twenty years old, and his younger sister, Rebecca. The intruders held the young man screaming on the floor, first slicing off his scalp and then cutting the heart from his living body. They threatened his sister with the same fate if she did not turn over the hidden family savings. Terrified, but still defiant, Rebecca brought out only a small part of the money hidden in the house. Taking with them the money, a couple of guns, five horses, one scalp and the captive girl, the Potawatomi set out for the Indian country . . . Major William Pruitt led a party of eight or ten militiamen in pursuit of the murderers . . . About fifty miles north of what is now Springfield, and not far from the Potawatomi village, Pruitt and his men caught up with the murderers . . . The militiamen were reluctant to press their attack too closely, for fear that the Indians would kill their prisoner, but the brave Rebecca took matters into her own hands. She broke away and ran toward her rescuers, suffering tomahawk wounds to the back and head. (Ferguson, 2012, pp. 30–31)

Pruitt and the militia returned home accompanied by Rebecca, who eventually fully recovered.

Only a few days later a second deadly incident occurred. On June 20, 1811, two men by the name of Price and Ellis were attacked.

They had built a small cabin near Hunters Spring in what is now known as Lower Alton. Price and Ellis were plowing a corn field when,

> according to most accounts, five Menominee warriors approached the two farmers. When the two men warily asked the Indians whether they came in peace, the leader of the Indians, who was a large and powerful man, put down his weapons and advanced toward the men with hand outstretched, calling "Bonjour, bonjour." Price relieved, took his hand, but the Indian held him fast, while the others tomahawked him, while in another version, shot him through the heart. Ellis also was wounded, but managed to unhitch his plow horse and escape. He succeeded in reaching the Wood River settlements, where he told his story before dying of his wounds a few weeks later. (Ferguson, 2012, p. 31)

In the same month, Michael Squires, who operated a ferry across the Mississippi near Alton, fired on a canoe full of Natives, killing a Potawatomi chief (Ferguson, 2012, p. 32).

The settlers reacted to the Cox and Price killings. In late July, a group of settlers from St. Clair County sent a petition to Governor Edwards, asking for government protection. Edwards forwarded the petition to U.S. secretary of war, William Eustis, who sent the request to Congress.

Generally, raids resulting in mortality were infrequent. Nevertheless, the newspapers in St. Louis seemed to report a new raid in every edition. Fear among the settlers continued to escalate. When Ninian Edwards had assumed the governorship of the Illinois Territory, protecting settlers on the frontier from raids became his problem. As troubles grew in 1810 and 1811, he took a number of actions. As the commander of the militia, he greatly increased the number of militia units and appointed new officers at all levels of militia organization. Benjamin Stephenson was appointed a major of the militia and named brigade inspector. William Rector was appointed to the rank of general of the militia. Although he had no military experience, Edwards retained command of the militia in its initial campaigns. In addition to augmenting the militia, he took a number of other steps.

He created a network of informants, or spies, to keep him informed of the plans of the Natives. His network included traders and even a number of Natives. One of the most important of the spies was Thomas Forsyth. Forsyth was the son of a Scots-Irish Presbyterian immigrant who had arrived in America in the 1750s and fought beside the British in the French and Indian War. Unlike most of the Scots-Irish during the revolution, he was a Loyalist and was interned during the war. His son Thomas became a successful fur trader working among the Natives. Thomas founded a fur-trading company with his half brother John Kinzie. Kinzie worked out of a trading post near Chicago, while Forsyth founded a trading post along the Illinois River at Peoria. Because of his father's pro-British sentiment and the fact that much business of the Kinzie and Forsyth Company was transacted in Canada, Forsyth was assumed to side with the British and the Natives. He was, however, decidedly pro-American and quietly held several American appointments. He was an invaluable aid to Governor Edwards because he was in a position to learn the plans of the British and the Natives. Forsyth wrote many letters to Edwards, detailing the situation among the Natives who lived or traded around Peoria. Useful though he was, Forsyth was only one member of a network of spies that Edwards employed.

Edwards also opened communications and negotiations with many of the Native leaders. He invited Native leaders to meetings in Kaskaskia and sent emissaries to Peoria to meet with them and work toward peace. Edwards sent two such expeditions to Peoria.

The first, in July 1811, was led by Captain Samuel Levering. Levering was accompanied by Captain Edward Herbert, Henry Swearingen, Nelson Rector, a French interpreter, a Potawatomi Native, and eight French boatmen. Between August 3, when they arrived at Peoria, and August 18 or 19, Levering met daily with the Native chiefs in the area. His charge from the governor was "to demand of them the authors of the murders which had been committed, and the property that had been stolen by the Indians in the Louisiana and Illinois Territories, during the preceding two summers" (Edwards, 1770, p. 38). During the two weeks of negotiations, Levering met with Gomo and Little Chief of the Potawatomi and with Miehe Pah-ka-en-na, a Kickapoo chief. Levering delivered a lengthy letter from Governor Edwards. In it Edwards recounted all of the deaths that had taken place and enumerated much of the property stolen during the preceding two years. He reminded the Natives that, though the Americans had not been strong in the period just after the revolution, they had grown much stronger. Despite his growing military strength, the governor said that he wanted peace. The way to peace was for the Natives to turn over all of the stolen property and surrender the warriors who had killed the settlers.

In response to Levering's speeches and Edwards's letter, Gomo said he was just a chief and had no real power. He did not know who the guilty warriors were, nor could he surrender any of the Natives even if he had known who they were. He said that, in the past, a Potawatomi named Turkey Foot had killed an American; when the territorial government demanded that the tribe surrender him, the Natives had killed him themselves. When Kickapoo who had killed settlers were surrendered to the Americans, they were "tied up with ropes around their necks." This was not what they had been promised, as they were supposed to be put to death with dignity. "Our custom is to tie up a dog in that way" (Edwards, 1870, p. 48). He went on to say that the French had always given gifts to the Natives and that the French built no forts or garrisons. By contrast, when the Americans gave presents to the Natives, the Americans built forts, garrisons, and blockhouses wherever they went. "We infer that they intend to make war upon us. Whenever the Americans give the Indians presents, they afterwards say that we must give them such a tract of land; and after a good many presents they then ask [for] a larger piece" (Edwards, 1870, p. 48). Gomo concluded by saying that the Potawatomi, Ottawa, and Chippewa wished to live in peace and quiet with all men. The young men of the tribes did not believe the Americans wanted peace, which is why there had been trouble and killing. The chiefs were unaware of the killings at the time, and the only desire of the older people was to live in peace. Finally, Gomo finished by asking a question:

"Do you think it possible for us to deliver the murderers here today?" (Edwards, 1870, p. 49).

Little Chief then responded to the demands of Levering and Edwards. Little Chief blamed the trouble on a shaman known as Tenskwatawa, or "the Prophet." The Prophet was a Shawnee, the younger brother of the great Shawnee chief named Tecumseh. The Prophet had been a most strange and violent person when he was young. He had created trouble within the tribe, was a drunkard, and was not well liked. After he reached adulthood, he claimed to have had a vision and could foretell the future. At one point he predicted a solar eclipse, and when the eclipse came to pass, the Shawnee forgot about his past problems and viewed him as a great religious leader. The Prophet had been predicting war, and Little Chief ascribed the current problems to the Prophet's influence on the minds of the young men.

Levering's negotiations with the Natives ended in late August without any of the warriors being surrendered, but a number of the Natives quietly supplied the names of most of the warriors involved in the raids. They also suggested where they might be found, although all of the places suggested were well outside the area into which the Americans might travel safely.

Encouraged by Levering's ability to open talks with the Natives around Peoria, Edwards send a second emissary to negotiate. In March 1812, Captain Edward Herbert was selected to lead the negotiations. He was told to "request" that all of the traders around Peoria withdraw until a settling of all Native disagreements was reached. The traders were promised that the territory would withhold any future cooperation unless they complied. Herbert's visit to Peoria ended with an agreement that the chiefs would journey to Cahokia to meet with Governor Edwards. The resulting council was held at Cahokia starting on April 16, 1812 (Edwards, 1770, p. 56).

The council was attended by a number of chiefs representing the Potawatomi, Kickapoo, Ottawa, and Chippewa. Governor Edwards opened the proceedings with a lengthy speech. He asked that, in the event of war between the Americans and the British, the Natives would remain neutral. He told the assembled chiefs that the British had made many promises to the Natives in the past and had always broken them. He said that, if war broke out, the British would once again make many promises and ultimately break them all. (In fact, at the end of the War of 1812, that is exactly what happened, and the Natives were left in an untenable position.) In closing, Edwards made a hollow declaration: "My children, we do not want your land. We have more land already than we can use, and I shall neither propose to buy it, nor does your Great Father, or myself, wish to take a foot of it from you" (Ferguson, 2012, p. 46).

The chiefs of all of the tribes briefly spoke but decided that Gomo would give their collective reply. Gomo, like Edwards, a tireless orator, gave a lengthy reply to Edwards's lengthy speech. Gomo said that he was not a powerful chief and could not surrender the murderers without being killed himself. He did not want to join the British, nor did he trust the Shawnee Prophet. He concluded by saying, "the Great Spirit had given the land to all the Indians, and that no chief could sell their land" (Ferguson, 2012, p. 46). The council concluded in seeming harmony, but in fact nothing had been resolved in the negotiations between Edwards and the chiefs.

Edwards took a further step. On June 22, 1811, he sent a letter to Secretary of War William Eustis (excerpted in the July 11 issue of the *Lancaster Intelligencer*), stating that "blockhouses are erecting on the frontier in front of the settlements." A chain of blockhouses, a type of defensive structure, erected about 20 miles apart spanned the width of the territory from the eastern border with Indiana all the way to the Illinois River in the west. Some 25 blockhouses were supplemented with more than 20 family forts, which were built by neighboring settlers in the area between the Mississippi and the Kaskaskia Rivers (Ferguson, 2012, p. 32). The anchor of the defensive line was Fort Russell, built during the summer of 1812 about a mile and a half north of today's Edwardsville. Although its location and its size are disputed, the fort was probably located just off of modern Springfield Road, northeast of Edwardsville and Cahokia Creek. It likely enclosed about half an acre. No troops were ever permanently stationed there, but the fort was used for mustering militia troops. Ranger companies, commanded by Colonel Russell, occasionally used the fort. Throughout the War of 1812, the fort served as a place of refuge for the citizens of Edwardsville in case of attack, although no attack ever came. It also served as a military depot for munitions and military stores (Ferguson, 2012, p. 33).

The year of 1812 was a momentous year for the Stephensons. Their fourth child and second son, Benjamin V., was born. Although he was always referred to as Benjamin V., he was almost certainly named after his father and Lucy's father, Van Swearingen. Van was such a common name among the Swearingens that it would have been hard for Lucy to avoid it. But 1812 was momentous for another reason. On June 1, 1812, President James Madison sent a message to Congress asking for a declaration of war with Great Britain. The declaration was passed by both houses of Congress, and Madison signed the declaration on June 18, 1812. For the most part, the war was fought in the Atlantic Ocean and along the eastern seaboard of the United States. On the frontier, the War of 1812 was essentially a continuation of the long struggle between the Natives and the settlers. Because the federal government was occupied with fighting the British in the East, the governors of the western states and territories were left to fend for themselves, protected only by their militia.

The opening salvo of the war in Illinois occurred in faraway Chicago. Almost the entire white population of Illinois at the time lived south of Edwardsville. Chicago had almost no resident white population other than a few traders and a small military detachment. The military was stationed at Fort Dearborn along the shore of Lake Michigan. According to a number of sources, Fort Dearborn had been an unhappy outpost for some time. The problem was traced to antagonism between John Kinzie and the military leaders of the fort. Kinzie was the half brother of Thomas Forsyth, and Kinzie ran the trading post at Chicago while Forsyth worked at Peoria. Forsyth seems to have gotten along with almost everyone while Kinzie seems to have gotten along with no one. Kinzie was involved in a running feud with the commanding officer of the fort. When that officer was replaced by Nathan Heald, the feud continued. The garrison of the fort and the few civilian traders and their wives were divided in their support of the trader or the commander, and there was tension among all those involved. The situation turned desperate when the War of 1812 was declared. In

July, Fort Mackinac was surrounded by the British and surrendered. American general William Hull, in command of Fort Detroit, the strongest fort in the entire area, inexplicably surrendered his practically impregnable position. After the surrender, Hull sent an order to Captain Heald at Fort Dearborn to surrender the fort at Chicago. What happened next has been debated for years.

The most credible account is supplied by Captain Heald, whose official written report recounts the disaster that followed General Hull's order:

> Sir,
>
> I embrace this opportunity to render you an account of the garrison of Chicago.
>
> On the ninth of August last, I received orders from general Hull to evacuate the post and proceed with my command to Detroit by land, leaving it at my discretion to dispose of the public property as I thought proper. The neighboring Indians got information as early as I did, and came in from all quarters in order to receive the goods in the factory store, which they understood were to be given them. On the 13th, Captain Wells, of Fort Wayne, arrived with about 30 Miamies, for the purpose of escorting us in, by the request of general Hull. On the 14th, I delivered the Indians all the goods in the factory store, and a considerable quantity of provisions which we could not take away with us. The surplus arms and ammunition I thought proper to destroy, fearing they would make bad use of it if put in their possession. I also destroyed all the liquor on hand soon after they began to collect. The collection was unusually large for this place; but they conducted themselves with the strictest propriety till after I left the fort. On the 15th, at 9 o'clock in the morning we commenced our march. The situation of the country rendered it necessary for us to take the beach with the lake on our left, and a high sand bank on our right, at about 100 yards distant.
>
> We had proceeded about a mile and a half, when it was discovered that the Indians were prepared to attack us

> from behind the bank. I immediately marched up with the company to the top of the bank, when the action commenced; after firing a round, we charged, and the Indians gave way in front and joined those on our flanks. (Brannan, 1823, pp. 84–85)

By marching up the bank, Heald had left unprotected all of the militia troops, the wagons full of supplies, and the women and children. The Natives quickly closed in behind Heald and proceeded to slaughter almost everyone who had been left on the beach. By this time, half of Heald's troops had been killed or wounded. When the slaughter on the beach was over, the Natives approached Heald and offered him the chance to surrender, which he did.

Heald was severely wounded, and he later found out that his wife had also been wounded but survived. Heald and his wife were later taken by boat to Michilimackinac, and from there to Detroit, before being exchanged and ending up in Pittsburgh. Heald's report includes a summary of the fate of his command:

> Our strength was fifty-four regulars and twelve militia, out of which, twenty-six regulars and all of the militia were killed in the action, with two women and twelve children. Ensign George Ronan and doctor Isaac V. Van Voorhees of my company, with captain Wells, of fort Wayne, are to my great sorrow, numbered among the dead. Lieutenant Lina T. Helm, with twenty-five non-commissioned officers and privates, and eleven women and children, were prisoners when we were separated. (Brannan, 1823, p. 85)

Most of the prisoners were divided among the various Native groups. Over the next several weeks, a number of prisoners were subjected to brutal torture and eventually killed. Some were kept in captivity and later released through the intervention of Thomas Forsyth. John Kinzie, who had been with the militia, the women, and the children on the beach, was spared when one of the chiefs put him under his protection. Kinzie's escape did nothing to help his reputation among the Americans.

The massacre was a shock that reverberated throughout the territory, and the loss of Forts Dearborn, Mackinac, and Detroit to the British and the Natives made it much more likely that the Natives would turn on the Illinois settlements.

Governor Edwards finally decided that, in modern parlance, "the best defense is a good offense." In a long letter to the U.S. secretary of war written on November 18, 1812, Edwards detailed all of the steps he had taken since the beginning of the year. He emphasized the fact that, for most of the year, he had been taking defensive measures. However, beginning in August, he had learned that following the Fort Dearborn disaster, the Natives were massing near Peoria for an attack on the Illinois settlements. He reported that he had made arrangements to gather a militia army to ambush the Natives when they attacked. The Natives seem to have learned of his plans and called off the attack. Edwards went on to say:

> When I found that the Indians had retired from our frontier I began to prepare for an expedition against them, being fully convinced that I could so regulate it as to surprise them in their villages at the head of Peoria Lake. (Edwards, 1870, p. 70)

He then explained that he had been prepared to attack with only the Illinois militia, but Colonel Russell arrived with part of two companies of rangers and news that General Hopkins was marching from Kentucky to join the attack. Edwards, knowing that his little army had to move quickly to achieve surprise, left all of his wagons behind. The militia carried only arms, ammunition, and food. In order to resupply his troops, Edwards dispatched two boats upriver with orders to meet him at Peoria. One of the boats was heavily armed and the other filled with supplies (Ferguson, 2012, p. 82). The supply boats were commanded by Captain Thomas Craig, from Shawneetown on the Ohio. He had been appointed a captain in the militia on January 22, 1810, and on February 13 of the same year, Governor Edwards had appointed him a justice of the peace for Randolph County.

Edwards departed from Fort Russell on October 18, leaving behind several detachments of militia to guard the settlements in his absence. His little army numbered about 400 men. They were all mounted and were prepared to move quickly. According to John Reynolds, a young private in a company commanded by Samuel Judy, "the army was organized into two small regiments commanded by Colonel Benjamin Stephenson, and Elias Rector" (Reynolds, 1855, p. 137). At the time, Stephenson was still a major, but Reynolds was writing long after Stephenson had eventually been promoted to colonel. Furthermore, which Rector brother commanded the other regiment is unclear. William Rector was a general of the militia and probably was in command. But another source says it was Nelson Rector. Reynolds goes on to report that "Judge Pope, Nelson Rector, and a Lieutenant McLaughlin of the army were the aids to Governor Edwards . . . The army was ordered to pack on their horses provisions for 20 or 25 days" (p. 137).

The army followed the route that later became known as the Edwards Trace. Traveling north and slightly east, they followed the ridge dividing the streams flowing east to the Kaskaskia River and the creeks and streams flowing west to the Illinois and Mississippi Rivers. When they reached the Sangamon River, near modern Springfield, they encountered two sizable Kickapoo villages. The Natives had deserted the villages when the troops approached. John Reynolds says that one of the villages was on Sugar Creek, "where we saw on the bark of the wigwams much painting, generally Indians scalping the whites" (Reynolds, 1855, p. 138). The two villages were put to flames, with all material left behind by the inhabitants destroyed or burned.

Edwards then announced that they were going to march to Peoria and "cross the Illinois there" (Edwards, 1870, p. 72). The little army, fearing that the Natives at Peoria would discover them, marched through the night and did not camp until midnight. They were within four or five miles of the villages at Peoria when they stopped. The main village was large and was situated at the north end, or the head, of Lake Peoria. The population of the village was composed of Kickapoo and Miami. That night, Reynolds recalled that "all was silent as a grave, as we expected a night attack . . . when troops are silent, sulky, and savage they will fight" (Reynolds, 1855, p. 138). During the night, one soldier inadvertently fired his rifle and created a momentary panic that Governor Edwards quickly quieted. According to Reynolds, the men "lay with their clothes on with their rifles in their arms" (p. 138). Edwards sent four men to scout the Native village and find a route for the march the next day. In the morning, Reynolds remembered being told that, in the attack on the Shawnee Prophet's town at Tippecanoe, every soldier in William Henry Harrison's army wearing a white coat had been killed. Not willing to tempt fate, he removed his white coat.

There was heavy fog that morning. Moving silently through it, the leading elements of the army surprised two mounted Natives. A number of the men wanted to capture the Natives, but, according to Reynolds, Captain Judy said he had not left "home to take prisoners. I saw the dust rise off the Indian's leather shirt" when Judy shot him (Reynolds, 1855, p. 138). The wounded Native was able to get off a shot before dying, and one of the Americans was badly wounded. A number of shots were fired at the other Native, who was not hit. The Native turned out to be a woman, who was captured and, recalled Reynolds, well treated.

The Kickapoo and Miami village was on the floodplain of the Illinois River. After hearing the reports of his scouts, Edwards had planned to attack the village from the top of a small hill overlooking it, but in the fog, his scouts missed the hill and led the army onto the floodplain less than a mile below the village. Alarmed by the earlier shots and seeing mounted troops entering the floodplain, the villagers began fleeing the village on foot or on horseback. Edwards says, "In front of this village, the bottom, which is three miles wide, is so flat, wet and marshy, as to be almost utterly impassable to men on horseback" (Edwards, 1870, p. 71). Seeing the Natives running away, Edwards ordered an immediate charge. "We rushed upon them with such impetuosity that they were forced to scatter and take refuge in the swamp" (p. 71). According to Reynolds, "we all rushed shouting long and loud," but when the Natives took to the swamp, the Americans and their horses were mired in the mud before they knew it. Reynolds's horse fell down in the mud: "I went rolling over his head into the swamp. Near me I saw Governor Edwards' horse floundering in a deep mud hole, both down and covered with mud" (Reynolds, 1855, p. 138). Many of the Natives hid in the swamp, which was overgrown with cattails and brush so thick that it was dangerous to look for them without the possibility of being ambushed. The rest of the Natives running through the swamp were followed on foot to the river. Most of the Natives crossed the river and escaped. Three Americans, in their zeal, also crossed the river, only to discover they were alone and surrounded. They quickly retreated. A number of Natives had been killed in the swamp, and at the river, but the fight was now over.

Edwards's report to the secretary of war continues:

> The pursuit and fight over, we returned to the village, which, with a great quantity of provisions and other valuable Indian property, we burnt and otherwise destroyed. We brought off with us about eighty head of horses and four prisoners, having killed, according to the Indians accounts, frequently given, between twenty-four and thirty Indians without the loss of a single man. (Edwards, 1870, p. 72)

Edwards goes on to state that since General Hopkins had never appeared and he had few men, he decided to retire to Fort Russell with all of the plunder. Reynolds, having survived his battle without his white coat, says,

> We travelled on till dark in torrents of rain and camped on a high bluff without water or firewood. We were all exhausted and many laid down in the mud without food, fire or water to drink. I never experienced such a bad night. (Reynolds, 1855, p. 141)

The little militia army arrived back at Fort Russell after only 13 days.

When the army chased the Natives into the swamp, a number had been killed by troops commanded by Stephenson. Several women may have been among those killed. Afterward, articles appeared in several of the St. Louis newspapers, criticizing Stephenson and his men for what was deemed indiscriminate killing of women. Several of the men with Stephenson said that they had indeed killed one woman but were not at all ashamed of it. Given the level of hatred between the two sides, it is not surprising that such acts occurred.

While some of the papers criticized the killing of women, most published articles praised the expedition and its results. The *Missouri Gazette and Public Advertiser*, on Saturday, November 7, 1812, reported that Edwards's

> force consisted of 352 privates, all of whom he had raised in Illinois Territory, except 30 rangers who had lately arrived from Vincennes. With this force he proceeded to the saline fork of the Sanguemon, the late residence of the Kickapoos where he burnt two villages: from thence the little army progressed to the head of Peoria lake 20 miles above the village, here they found the Kickapoos and a party of the Miamies embodied but were vigorously charged upon and broken, and induced to take shelter in an immense swamp which skirts the Illinois river . . . Between twenty and thirty indians were killed, and a number wounded, four prisoners were taken; six American scalps, and some horses that had been lately stolen from St. Clair county were retaken . . . At the principal Kickapoo village upwards of 1000 bushels of corn was destroyed, besides a prodigious quantity of Beans and dried Meat, Pumpkins, Tallow Furs and peltry. Their houses were strong and well built, some large enough to accommodate 50 persons were found well provided with indian effects; & were in a few hours reduced to heaps of ashes. Eighty head of horses with their furniture, about 200 brass kettles, a great quantity and variety of silver and Indian ornaments, guns, bags of gun powder, flints &c. were brought off . . . Never was an expedition crowned with more success. Never have these Indians received so dreadful a blow. Indeed it would be invidious to eulogize any officer or private of the hardy band of heroes.

Meanwhile, after Edwards returned to Fort Russell, the two supply boats commanded by Captain Thomas Craig finally made it to Peoria on November 5. Edwards had left a note stating that the army had returned home, but it is not clear that Craig ever got it. Edwards was not there, and Peoria was deserted. Instead of turning around and going home, Craig decided to stay for a short while. What happened next was almost ignored in Ninian Edwards's biography written by his son. The biography's account of what occurred is brief:

> Sometime in the fall of 1812, Capt. Thos. E. Craig was ordered by Gov. Edwards to go to Peoria, and take prisoners those persons who were there for the purpose of assisting the savages to murder our frontier settlers. Capt. Craig was successful in the expedition and returned to Camp Russell on the 16 of November 1812, bringing a number of the inhabitants of Peoria as prisoners, together with a considerable quantity of different kinds of property. The prisoners were taken to St. Louis and discharged. (Edwards, 1870, p. 65)

This statement is "political spin" of the first order. The truth was far different.

When Craig arrived to find Edwards gone, and the village of Peoria deserted, he and his men looted the homes of the French and "liberated" their pigs and chickens (Ferguson, 2012, p. 94). After a fine dinner of pork and chicken, they slept on their boats moored across the river from Peoria. Late that night, six French employees of the trading firm of Kinzie and Forsyth came up the river. Craig's men stopped them and learned they had been sent ahead by Forsyth to scout the area. Craig released four of them and kept two as hostages. The next day Forsyth himself arrived with another group of French. That night, shots were heard, and Craig thought he was being fired upon from across the river. He was convinced that the shots had been fired by the French, and he was furious. Most likely the shots were really the work of a few Natives who quickly disappeared (Ferguson, 2012, p. 95).

Craig ordered the arrest of Forsyth and more than 40 of the French. Among those arrested was Jacques Mette, a trader for Kinzie and Forsyth (Edwards, 1870, p. 66). Mette later became a resident of Edwardsville and a close associate of Benjamin Stephenson. Craig seems to have been out of control, cursing and shouting at the captives and allowing his men to treat them roughly. The village was burned, and a number of pigs and cattle were shot. Some accounts say that all of the French were arrested while other accounts say that a number of women and children were left homeless and without food in the devastated village (Ferguson, 2012, pp. 96–97). Craig then returned to Fort Russell with his captives. All of the sources agree that the captives were taken to St. Louis and immediately set free.

Craig's actions were a public relations disaster. The French were outraged and, after many years of trying, later got compensation for their losses. Furthermore, Craig had arrested Thomas Forsyth, who was one of Governor Edwards's most important sources of intelligence. Even before the Peoria expedition, Forsyth had been appointed an "Indian Agent" by the federal government and a justice of the peace by Edwards. Craig claimed that he was unaware of Forsyth's significance and defended his actions. Despite the condemnation of Craig's actions from many quarters, he went on to a long career in Illinois. He was eventually promoted to the rank of major and became a judge of the Court of Common Pleas and later a judge of the County Court of Gallatin County.

Governor Edwards's foray to Peoria had been a great success. His little army had destroyed a number of villages, killed a number of supposedly hostile Natives, and, more importantly, destroyed or carried off a huge amount of food and equipment, leaving the Natives desperately short on supplies. The success of the mission clearly demonstrated the outline of a winning strategy. The way to beat the Natives was to send out sizable, and well mounted, militia units capable of moving rapidly and under orders to drive the Natives out of their villages and destroy as many of their goods as possible.

Benjamin Stephenson was chosen to lead the first expedition to test the new strategy. In early spring 1813, Governor Edwards ordered a contingent of Illinois militia, under the command of Major Stephenson, to march on the Native villages in central and northern Illinois Territory. The 1813 expedition was calculated to prevent the Natives from rebuilding and reorganizing after their defeat by Edwards the preceding fall.

Stephenson took command of three companies of militia led by captains James Moore, Jacob Short, and William Boone. The three companies mustered at Fort Russell and marched north on May 8. Following much the same route of Edwards's previous march, the unit followed the ridge between the Mississippi River, Illinois River, and the Kaskaskia River drainages. Today the route would be near the I-55 corridor. Stephenson's after-action report, written on May 20, 1813, was directed to Ninian Edwards and states, "I kept my course along the ridge that seperates the water of Kaskaskia from those of Illinois and Sanguemon rivers until I arrived at a point opposite the celebrated old Kickapoo Village of the Prairie" (Carter, 1948, p. 333).

There were two bands of Kickapoo. Those called the "Kickapoo of the Prairie" had established a large town, the Grand Village of the Kickapoo, just east of modern Springfield. The name derived from the fact that the Kickapoo of the Prairie were nearly the only Native group that settled on the prairies of Illinois. Almost all of the other groups tended, like their prehistoric ancestors, to avoid the prairies and settle in the more wooded parts of the territory. White settlement also tended to follow the same pattern. The forested areas and wooded sites near waterways were settled while the prairies were avoided.

Arriving at a point across from the Grand Village, Stephenson crossed the Sangamon River. He had already been on the march for seven days and was a day and a half from Crow Prairie on the Illinois River. Upon reaching the Illinois River, he was about 45 miles from Peoria:

> On approaching the town every precaution was adopted to surprise the enemy had they been there but unfortunately we arrived too late—none were found but from the sign we discovered it was very evident that a party of them had left that place not more than three or four days previous to our arrival & in its vicinity was an indian camp containing fourteen lodges of considerable size that had been recently abandoned

> which together with the Town—we burnt—in the latter there were some very large houses . . . and a considerable number of smaller ones. (Carter, 1948, p. 334)

Since he found no Natives, he divided his detachment into the three companies to return to Fort Russell by different routes. By taking different routes home, he hoped to encounter raiding parties returning home from the settlements. Ben accompanied Captain Short's company, and about 20 miles below the "old Town," they discovered a new village:

> in which the lodges were connected for about twenty five yards—Which must have been very lately and hastely deserted—some of the lodges not being entirely covered & fresh bark and other materials lying ready for the erection of others—Much other indian sign was discovered but it appeared to have been made about three or four weeks before and no doubt can exist that a considerable number of the savages had occupied that quarter and were driven from it by the terrer which was created by the march of the detachment lately commanded by Captain William B. Whiteside—Nothing further occurred except the discovery of six indians by three of Capt Moores men on their return home. (p. 334)

Stephenson's long report concludes:

> In common with all the officers and men whom I had the honor to command I regret that we had no oppertunity of a fair conflict with the enemy—Nevertheless I am persuaded that our tour must have an important effect in relieving the frontier from those Sanguinary savages that have so seriously infested it—Their Villages & Camps burnt—the heart of their own country penetrated—They must see the danger of and be detered from making their hostile incursions by the practicability of our discovering their tracks falling in behind them & persuing them into the settlements on which they meditate an attack—of the conduct of all the officers I cannot

> speak too highly—that of the men was equally correct. In a very fatiguing march thro praires in many parts so wet & miry as to sink the horses to their knees at every step not a murmur or complaint was heared—harmony pervaded the whole corps—every order was promptly obeyed—All were anxious for an opportunity of distinguishing themselves & I believe would have been willing to have gone double the distance to have obtained it—The Battalion which I have the honor to command, as well as yourself are convinced that it is impossible to keep the savages from our frontier without ranging at a considerable distance out side of the settlements and they are ready and willing at all times to encounter all the dangers & toiles that attend it—They have no wish to be idle. (pp. 334–335)

While it appears that, as military campaigns go, Stephenson's march was not only uneventful, but it was also of little consequence. In fact, though, Stephenson's command of the campaign was far more successful than his command of spelling and punctuation. The key passage in Stephenson's report validates the grand strategy that evolved from the Edwards's campaign against Peoria:

> Their Villages & Camps burnt—the heart of their own country penetrated—They must see the danger of and be detered from making their hostile incursions by the practicability of our discovering their tracks falling in behind them & persuing them into the settlements on which they meditate an attack. (p. 334)

The important point was that the Natives had abandoned their villages without a fight, and the troops were able to burn the houses and destroy all of the food and other items left behind. The strategy was based on the belief that, left homeless and without food and supplies, the Natives would soon lose interest in raiding the white settlements. Stephenson's performance in the campaigns of 1812 and 1813 earned him a promotion to the rank of colonel.

While the two campaigns by Edwards and Stephenson greatly slowed the Native attacks on the settlements, raids did continue in both the Missouri and Illinois Territories. The two territorial governors decided on a joint campaign. The 300 or 400 Illinois militia troops were led by Colonel Benjamin Stephenson. Colonel McNair led the Missouri troops. The overall command was held by General Howard, who had only recently finished his term as the first governor of the Missouri Territory. Stephenson's troops moved north from Fort Russell about the first of August 1813. They marched to the Mississippi opposite Fort Mason, just 10 miles below modern Hannibal. At Fort Mason the Missouri troops crossed the river, and the combined army marched upriver almost to the area of modern Quincy. There they turned east toward the Illinois River, 40 miles south of Peoria. They reached Peoria and marched to the northern end of the Peoria Lakes. Finding no Natives north of the town, they returned to Peoria. They camped at Peoria for more than 20 days and built a new fort named after William Clark. (Fort Clark remained a military outpost throughout the rest of the war. It was finally burned by the Natives in 1818.) Throughout the entire expedition, the army of almost 800 met no opposition. When the fort was completed, Stephenson and his men returned to Fort Russell in late fall of 1813.

Stephenson's military career was over. Nevertheless, in 1818, Governor Edwards sent a nomination to Washington City, promoting Benjamin Stephenson to the rank of major general of the militia of the Illinois Territory. All promotions to the rank of general had to be approved by Congress. The acting secretary of war, George Graham, in a letter to Edwards, promised that it "will be duly attended to when the Senate is in session" (Edwards, 1870, p. 545). However, the nomination was never acted on by Congress. The Territory of Illinois became a state before Congress could act. Since Ninian Edwards was no longer governor, his nomination was no longer valid.

Though Benjamin Stephenson's military career was over, he moved on to a new and even more important phase of his life.

CHAPTER FOUR

Colonel Stephenson Goes to Washington

After a trip of almost a month, Benjamin Stephenson, the newest member of the United States House of Representatives, entered Washington City in mid-November of 1814. Stephenson was met with a scene of devastation. Less than two months before, on August 24, 1814, a contingent of British troops had entered Washington City, almost completely unopposed, and began burning public buildings and almost everything else of value to the government.

Even before the British invasion, Washington City was a raw, unfinished place. Much of the city still was swampy, filled with hordes of mosquitoes, and many of the streets were a muddy mess in the spring. In the summer the city was hot and muggy, and the streets turned into dusty, potholed, and rutted washboards. In the late 1700s and early 1800s, there were few houses or residential areas. Also lacking were public accommodations. There were several taverns where government employees and members of Congress could stay, but there were not enough of them to meet the need. Slightly better accommodations were found in the few hotels, where, generally, at least two congressmen slept in a single room. Wealthy senators and representatives stayed in Georgetown, three miles south of Washington. For most, Washington was not a particularly enjoyable place to visit, much less to live.

Foreign visitors who came to the young capital were universally appalled by the frontier quality of the city and its residents. Dignitaries from Europe viewed most of the residents as unlettered, dirty, poorly clothed, and badly behaved. Those views extended to the House of Representatives, whose members resembled the general population. This foreign view of the representatives was not helped by the fact that arguments escalating to physical confrontation were all too common in the House chamber.

The raw and undeveloped parts of the city were somewhat relieved by the few impressive government buildings that had been built. The Capitol Building was already large and extraordinarily detailed with sculptures, beautiful wooden trim, and impressive crimson silk curtains. The White House had come a long way from the unfinished mess that President John Adams and his wife, Abigail, had found so depressing when they moved in on November 1, 1801. In the years since the Adamses became its first residents, the White House had been completed, making it beautifully furnished and richly decorated. Leaving aside the facts that the roof leaked, and that many of the floors were rotted from the continual damp, the White House had become a showplace for the new American nation.

President James Madison had signed the declaration of war with Britain on June 18, 1812. Just two months later, on August 24, 1814, Madison and most of the government had fled before the British army entered the city unopposed. In the next two days, almost all of the major public buildings were destroyed as well as a number of other facilities. When the British entered the city in the early evening, the Navy Yard and the ships there were already furiously burning. This extensive installation along the Potomac River housed most of the naval stores of the United States. A number of ships, plus several more under construction, were moored at the wharfs. The entire area had been set afire by the Americans to prevent the British from capturing the stores, ships, and other material.

The British immediately turned their destructive attention to the Capitol Building. The Senate chamber to the north and the House chamber to the south were almost entirely gutted by fire. The Library of Congress, housed in the east wing of the Capitol Building, was totally gutted, and more than 3,000 books burned. The chambers of the Supreme Court were also in the building, and they, too, were totally destroyed. By nine o'clock at night on August 24, the entire Capitol Building was engulfed in flames (Pitch, 1998, p. 106).

The White House was next. It was looted and burned during the early hours of the morning of August 25. The only thing left standing was the thick sandstone walls that survived the fire.

In addition to the Capitol Building and the White House, a number of other structures were destroyed. The structure housing the State Department and the War Department was looted and burned on August 25, and several houses and businesses were also burned. The offices of America's first national newspaper, the *National Intelligencer*, were given special treatment. Its editor had been vociferously anti-British, and the British were well aware of his editorials. The structure housing the newspaper was torn down, and the presses, newsprint, and books within the building were removed, piled in the street, and burned. At the same time, a contingent of the army moved into the arsenal and began destroying the arms and ammunition. Something set off an explosion among the barrels of gunpowder, and a large number of British soldiers were killed, wounded, or horribly maimed (Pitch, 1998, p. 138).

The British destruction was eventually stopped by a massive rainstorm in the early afternoon. A tornado imbedded in the rain generated terrible winds, and a number of structures, previously spared by the British, were either destroyed or damaged. The storm put out most of the fires, but the damage had already been done. The British finally abandoned the city, but the destruction was not over. Mobs of American looters managed to damage almost everything that was left (Pitch, 1998, p. 150). When Stephenson arrived nearly two months later, almost nothing had been done to rebuild, and the city was still a mess.

Stephenson had decided to run for the office of territorial representative in the United States House of Representatives shortly after returning from his campaign against the Natives in the summer of 1813. During the following year, he had been busy campaigning and keeping up with his duties as sheriff. In the election, Stephenson won rather easily. The election was held on the second and third of September 1814. There is no record of the total vote within all of the counties of the territory, but the vote in Randolph County was overwhelming. In Randolph County, where Stephenson had served for almost five years as sheriff, he received 118 votes, and Joshua Oglisby received but two.

Shortly after the election, Shadrach Bond, the first territorial representative to Congress, resigned from the House of Representatives to accept the position of receiver of public monies in the newly authorized federal land office in Kaskaskia. Since Stephenson had already been elected for the next Congress, Governor Edwards appointed him to serve the remainder of Bond's term. Normally, there were only two sessions of Congress during each two-year term, and Bond had retired after the second session of the 13th Congress. In 1814, however, there was an emergency third term necessitated by the problems of the war and the burning of Washington. Therefore, Stephenson had left almost immediately for Washington City to finish out Bond's term.

Despite the fact that his children were very young and the trip east was arduous, Stephenson took his family with him. He and Lucy must have decided that leaving his family on the frontier, with the ever-present threat of Native attack, was not a good idea. Even in the absence of Native attacks, the frontier was not a safe place for a young wife and four young children. The better option was to take the entire family and hope to leave Lucy and the children at Bellevue, the home of Lucy's uncle, Joseph, near Shepherdstown.

That Lucy and the children would stay in Washington was likely never seriously considered. Not only had it burned, but Washington was also well known to have an unhealthy climate: it was hot and muggy in the summer, and it was cold and bleak in the winter. Lucy had stayed at Bellevue with her uncle previously, and since her cousin Thomas had left for Kentucky, Joseph's large home was nearly empty. Joseph was probably excited to have Lucy and the children around, and Bellevue was a perfect place for the family to stay. It was located on the banks of the Potomac, where Lucy's father had grown up. It was the site of the original ferry crossing of the Potomac, and it was just across the river from Maryland. Shepherdstown was only 70 miles from Washington. Stephenson could stay in Washington and occasionally visit with his family on weekends and when Congress was in recess. In November 1814, he left his family in the care of Joseph Swearingen and traveled on alone to Washington City.

On Monday, November 14, 1814, he produced his credentials and took his seat as a member of the 13th Congress of the United States. After the Capitol was burned, the House of Representatives had moved into emergency quarters in what was known as Blodgett's Hotel. Construction on the building was started in 1896 by Samuel Blodgett, but it was not completed until much later. It really had never functioned as a hotel or tavern. Instead it had served as the city's first theater, and church services were also held at the site. It was an impressive building occupying a full city block between Seventh and Eighth Streets and between E and F Streets northwest. The building had a basement, two main stories, and a large attic. In 1810, the hotel was purchased by the government and housed the United States Post Office and the Patent Office. The British had burned almost all federal offices, but the Patent Office and the Post Office were spared. A number of citizens had convinced the British that the building was a private hotel, rather than a government building, and that all of its furnishings were private property. The House of Representatives met at the hotel for more than a year. After a year, the House and Senate moved to a new brick building built especially for Congress. Later, the building became the Old Capitol Prison, which housed Stephenson's great-niece Belle Boyd, the Confederate spy, during one of her several arrests during the Civil War. The prison also housed Mary Surratt after the Lincoln assassination. The prison was finally torn down, and the site is presently occupied by the Supreme Court Building.

Several questions were debated by the House during Stephenson's first few months in Congress. The most immediate was the question of the future location of the national capital of the United States. Washington City had been chosen many years before as a compromise between Alexander Hamilton and Thomas Jefferson. Hamilton had proposed that the federal government assume the war debts of the original states, and Jefferson opposed this on the grounds that Virginia had already paid most of its debts. Jefferson agreed to drop his opposition to "assumption" if Hamilton would support the location of the capital in Virginia. Now, with the

Capitol Building burnt to the ground, there was considerable talk of moving the seat of government to one of the major cities like New York, Philadelphia, Baltimore, or Boston, at least on a temporary basis. The original vote on the issue was taken in October before Stephenson arrived, and by a vote of 72–71, a motion to move from Washington was passed. However, substitute bills were introduced, and, after debating the question for nearly another six months, the House finally voted 83–74 in favor of staying in Washington and providing $500,000 to rebuild.

The second issue taken up at the start of Ben's term in Congress was the issue of compensation for members of Congress. A bill passed by the House and the Senate set annual compensation for the speaker of the house at $3,000, and $1,500 per year was to be paid to every other congressman, including territorial representatives. Before that, senators and representatives had always been paid a per diem rate rather than a yearly rate. There was much anger among the public about what seemed to be an unwarranted raid on the public treasury, and the act was rescinded at the end of the 14th Congress. By that time Stephenson had already been paid on a yearly rate and was on his way home at the end of his term.

As a territorial representative, Ben could speak in the House and participate on committees. He could also present petitions to the full House or to its committees. He was not allowed to vote, however, so it is not clear where he stood on the questions of whether to move the government and how to pay its Congress. Nevertheless, the debates on these matters were probably a good introduction for Ben on how things were done in Congress. The ability to accomplish anything as a territorial representative depended, in large part, on the delegate's ability to convince voting delegates to support his ideas. Since he had no vote, he could not "logroll," that is, promise his vote on another representative's bill in exchange for supporting one of his own bills. Instead, he had only his powers of persuasion, and Stephenson proved to be surprisingly adept at gaining support for his ideas. Without a doubt, he was greatly aided in gathering support by the fact that Remy Clay was the speaker of the house. Clay had been a young lawyer working in Kentucky at the same time that Ninian Edwards had started practicing law.

The two became friends, and Clay was inclined to help Stephenson because he was aware that Benjamin Stephenson and Ninian Edwards were closely allied.

Stephenson's primary focus during the third session of the 13th Congress was the continuing problem of Native raids on the frontier. On November 25, 1814, only 11 days after taking his seat in Congress, Stephenson introduced a resolution from the Territorial Legislature to increase the number of rangers employed in the defense of the frontier. The Territorial Legislature had been created in 1812. The Northwest Ordinance had provided that a territory could advance to the second territorial level when the total number of enfranchised freeholders reached 5,000. A territory of the second level was granted a single territorial representative in Congress and was entitled to have its own legislative body that would take over the duty of creating the territory's laws. In addition to introducing the legislative resolution from the territory, Stephenson and Rufus Easton, the representative from the Missouri Territory, jointly developed a plan to try to solve the Native problem.

Easton and Stephenson had a long-standing, and wary, relationship with each other. Stephenson, as sheriff of Randolph County, had become acquainted with the name of Rufus Easton through the controversy over the former sheriff Gilbreath. Easton was one of the people thought to have purchased land that Gilbreath had obtained by nefarious means. Additionally, after the New Madrid earthquake, Easton had been accused of buying land at fire-sale prices from frightened settlers. Throughout southern Illinois, southern Missouri, and northeast Arkansas, there was considerable political opposition to, and anger toward, Easton. On the other hand, Easton was a popular and highly successful lawyer and politician in St. Louis. Whatever their political and personal differences may have been, and there is no evidence that they ever exchanged a harsh word, the two approached the problem of Native raids as a coordinated team.

On December 17, 1814, Easton and Stephenson sent a joint letter to President Madison, proposing a federal military operation to clear the two territories of the hostile tribes. The letter probably was written by Easton, a highly educated lawyer and accomplished

Portrait of Rufus Easton. Creator unknown, Missouri Historical Society, identifier 1950-010-0001. http://collections.mohistory.org/resource/196870

writer. Stephenson, as his after-action report to Ninian Edwards showed, was not particularly skilled at writing. The letter is long and detailed. It starts with an estimate of the number of warriors of each of the tribes in the two territories. In the Illinois Territory, they estimated 1,200 Sauk and Fox warriors, 200 Folsavoins (also known as Menominee), 1,200 Potawatomi, 400 Winnebago, 1,000 Ottawa, 400 Kickapoo, and 200 Chippewa. The total of potential hostile warriors in Illinois was 4,600. In the Missouri Territory, they listed 11 tribes numbering 5,100 warriors.

The list from Missouri included several tribes that had moved westward across the Mississippi for various reasons. For example, the list includes 200 Shawnee in the Cape Girardeau area. They were remnants of the once powerful tribe led by the Prophet and his brother, Tecumseh. The Prophet had been discredited after the Battle of Tippecanoe, and Tecumseh was killed in battle late in the War of 1812. With the fall of the two leaders, the Shawnee lost cohesion, and separate bands went their own ways. One of these bands was brought to the Missouri Territory and settled near Cape Girardeau to act as a buffer against the Osage. The Osage were the most numerous of the Missouri tribes and certainly the most feared. They were a large people, with many warriors standing well over six feet high. The Shawnee also had a reputation as fierce warriors, and the government felt that the Shawnee could help keep the Osage from making trouble.

One of the most well-known incidents between the Shawnee of Missouri and the Osage is described in a book by a French traveler, Victor Tixier. In the book, Tixier relates the story of three Shawnee who were the victims of a raid by the Osage. The Osage stole a number of horses and escaped. The three Shawnee trailed the party to its village. That evening the three Shawnee put on their war paint and rode into the Osage village. They announced that if the Osage did not give back their horses, then they three alone would attack the village of hundreds of Osage in the morning. The Osage were so impressed by the show of bravado that they decided the Shawnee were too brave to die, and they returned the horses (McDermott, 1940).

The main purpose of the Stephenson and Easton letter, published in the January 21, 1815, issue of the *Missouri Gazette and Public Advertiser*, was to request that President Madison authorize a military expedition of 3,000 mounted men to launch a campaign against the hostile tribes in the two territories by April 20 of 1815. Stephenson and Easton suggested that the government immediately begin procuring meat for the expedition. They also requested that lead and gunpowder be brought by water and stockpiled in St. Louis. They recounted troubles that the Natives had already caused and suggested that the British "have it in view not only to take possession of the late province of Louisiana, but also to carry the war into the frontiers of the western states." The British did, in fact, have plans to take Louisiana, and they landed at New Orleans in January 1815, only to be defeated by Andrew Jackson. The dire predictions of disaster in the letter included a warning of what would happen in the absence of troops: "in that moment will the whole savage force be let loose upon our settlements, and the muddy waters of the Missouri will be crimsoned with the bravest and best blood of our fellow citizens." They went on to state that blockhouses had not been an effective deterrent to attacks. They suggested that the vast distances between Ohio in the east and the western border of Missouri, and between Arkansas in the south and the settlements at Peoria in the north, made protecting the thinly populated area practically impossible.

The heart of the letter illuminates the view of the two territorial representatives toward nearly all Natives:

> To avert a calamity so fatal and destructive, a campaign against the enemy, early in the next spring, is absolutely necessary and indispensible. It is important in a general and a local point of view: it is important to the whole western county–it is important to the nation at large, to the government, and the economy of the government.
>
> Halfway measures among Indians answer no valuable purpose–their maxim being "punish first, threaten afterwards." Administer to savages savage law–an eye for and eye, a tooth for a tooth, a horse for a horse, and a life for a life, are their ideas of justice. Govern them by their fears–make it their interest to be friendly–give them what is promised, and all will go right, in time of peace. In war they thirst for blood. To secure them, they must be furnished and employed or entirely exterminated.

The stark alternatives drawn here, either employing them or else exterminating them, probably sum up Stephenson's and Easton's view of Natives. Events intervened, however, before Madison could have taken any measures in response to the letter.

Negotiations were already underway in Ghent to end the war. Jackson's victory at New Orleans in January of 1815 actually came after the Treaty of Ghent was signed. While the end of the war did not stop all of the Native raids, a major change took place. Governor Edwards, in the council at Cahokia, had warned the Natives that the British would promise anything to get Native support and that they would eventually break all of their promises. That is precisely what happened at the end of the War of 1812. The British withdrew all support from the Natives, leaving them "holding the bag." Without British support, supplies, guns, and ammunition, the hopes of the

Natives to continue the war were shattered. Large-scale Native attacks were no longer possible, and even small raids were curtailed.

Stephenson's primary goal in running for Congress was stopping the Native threat to the settlements. With the end of the war, he had to redirect his efforts. He turned to solving a number of problems that had vexed the residents of the Illinois Territory since its establishment. One of the problems was military pay.

The militia was a territorial force under the command of the territorial governor. As a result, the issue of how the troops should be paid was a political hot potato. It could be argued that paying for a territorial force rightly fell to the territorial governor. On the other hand, the territorial governor was an appointee of the president, and the territories formed an arm of the federal government; therefore, paying for their defense should be a federal responsibility. Legally, there was little doubt that the responsibility for payment rested with Washington City, but the situation was complicated by the fact that the United States had almost no money. The war had disrupted international trade, and imports from Europe were much reduced. Since nearly 80% of the income of the federal government came from duties on imported items, its major source of revenue had dried up. The issue was finally solved by a resolution from the Illinois Territorial Legislature, which was introduced in the U.S. House of Representatives by Stephenson. The resolution allowed militia veterans to receive a pay certificate from the army paymaster, which could then be tendered in any government land office to pay for land. That Stephenson convinced the secretary of war and the army paymaster to pay the Illinois militia in land, given the political and economic situation, was a testament to his ability to persuade. Perhaps the political influence of Ninian Edwards, a friend of President Madison, made the difference, but the evidence strongly supports the idea that Stephenson was the deciding factor.

Stephenson's success put the heat on Easton. The Missouri militia had not been paid either. The territorial governor of Missouri was William Clark, a native of Virginia, a famous explorer, and a close friend and favorite of both Thomas Jefferson and James Madison. The failure to pay the Missouri militia was laid squarely at the doorstep of Rufus Easton, the territorial representative from

Missouri. A scathing letter to the *Missouri Gazette and Public Advertiser* on July 27, 1816, assigns blame with a rhetorical question:

> Why have not those excellent corps, the rangers been paid? And the same question may be asked in relation to our militia . . . Is it because the troops of our territory were less meritorious than those who have been paid or is it because our delegate Mr. E. has less influence than any other delegate or member of congress?

A second problem vexing the Territory of Illinois concerned the Territorial Court. The Northwest Ordinance had established territorial courts consisting of three judges. In practice, the three judges in the Illinois Territory met at Kaskaskia. The judges in Kaskaskia tended to take a narrow view of their responsibilities. Since they rarely met anywhere except Kaskaskia, it was difficult for most people in the territory to use the court. In an effort to deal with the problem, the Territorial Legislature wrote a new law establishing a circuit court system attached to counties. Under this system, the judges would be required to hold court several times a year in the various counties in the territory. The three territorial judges, led by Judge Thomas, objected to the change, saying that the legislature had no legal right to change the name of the court and that the travel required of the judges was objectionable since their pay did not cover the cost of travel. Furthermore, they argued that the Territorial Legislature did not have the authority to write a law that changed the system established by a federal authority. The judges sent their objections to Governor Edwards, who sided with the legislature. In the end, the law drafted by the legislature, the objections written by the judges, and Governor Edwards's reply were all sent to Washington and introduced in the House by Benjamin Stephenson. The document, introduced by Stephenson in January 1816, was a petition from the legislature, "praying they may be empowered in the future to pass laws regulating the courts of said Territory."

In the end, the act passed by the 14th Congress amounted to a limited rewrite of the act passed by the Territorial Legislature. The act established a circuit court system. The act said that whenever a new county was created, that county would be attached to the circuit court from which the largest portion of the new county was taken. The judges allotted to that circuit would be required to hold court in each new county twice a year at a time and place designated by the legislature. Further, if any judge was unable to hold court as required, the judge in the nearest circuit would be required to hold court. The act had a sunset clause: the system would remain in force until the end of the next session of the Territorial Legislature, after which that body had full power to organize the courts as it pleased. The law was a complete vindication of the positions taken by the Territorial Legislature, Ninian Edwards, and Benjamin Stephenson. The defeat suffered by the three judges led to real friction between Jesse Thomas and both Edwards and Stephenson. The friction never fully ended.

On the same day that Stephenson introduced a resolution calling for an increase in the number of rangers on the frontier, he also introduced a second resolution. This resolution requested that "the Committee of Public Lands be instructed to inquire whether any and what alterations or amendments are necessary by law to be made in the act confirming certain claims to lands in the Illinois Territory." The resolution was necessitated by President Madison's insistence that "squatters" be removed from federal land by force, if necessary. This was particularly problematic in Illinois. The Northwest Ordinance forbade that land be surveyed until all prior claims had been extinguished, and no land could be sold until it had been surveyed. The sale of land in the Illinois Territory lagged far behind other territories. Unable to buy their land legally, some settlers simply squatted on the land and began making improvements. Madison's order to remove squatters would have been a disaster for small farmers in Illinois. Stephenson's resolution was calculated to remove some of the impediments to the sale of lands and thus provide help to the small farmer. His resolution resulted in a lengthy act amending the original one. The amendment was passed by the House on February 27, 1815; it contained nine sections, with each of the first four addressing a specific problem.

The first section addressed the problem of islands in the Mississippi River. A number of people had settled on the islands, and several issues resulted. The first was the question of whether the Illinois Territory or Missouri Territory held jurisdiction over the islands. The act drew a line down the middle of the river, and everything east of the line was Illinois Territory while everything west of it became Missouri Territory. Even though the river might change course, or the islands might be reshaped, the original line would remain the dividing line between Illinois and Missouri. Another issue was that the islands had not been surveyed, and the original law said that land could not be sold before it was surveyed. The amended law also mandated surveys on the islands.

The second section of the act dealt with the problem of settlers residing on land of less than 160 acres. Originally, federal land was sold in units no smaller than a square mile. A square mile of land was labeled a *section*, and each section contained 640 acres. Federal land generally sold at two dollars an acre, so a section required a payment of $1,280. The law favored the rich, since most settlers were lucky to have 10 dollars in their pocket. Over the years the law was amended to allow the sale of half-sections of 320 acres and eventually allowed the sale of quarter-sections of 160 acres. Still, the average settler was lucky to afford merely a quarter of a quarter-section, or 40 acres. Settlers who had squatted on land were entitled to purchase their land from the government under the original act. However, the act stipulated that purchases could only be made for 160 acres or more. The amendment made it possible for those squatting on less than 160 acres to obtain a legal title for their land by purchasing it from the government. The change was a huge victory for the small farmer.

The third section of the amendment dealt with squatters who occupied land designated for educational institutions. The land survey system introduced in the late 1700s had divided land into rectangular portions. The basic unit was called a township and contained 36 square miles of land. Each township was six miles long east to west and six miles broad south to north. Each township included 36 sections, each measuring a mile square. As explained above, each section contained 640 acres. The original Northwest

Ordinance and the Land Ordinance of 1785 set aside one entire township in each territory for the support of "Seminaries," a term meaning institutions of higher learning. Within all other townships, section 16 of those townships was set aside for the support of common schools. This provision rested on the 19th-century belief that an educated populace was the cornerstone of democracy. This belief gained full expression in the language of the Northwest Ordinance, which stated that "religion, morality, and knowledge being necessary to good government and the happiness of mankind, schools and the means of education shall forever be encouraged." An enormous amount of land was involved, much of which was not sold until after the Civil War. Some settlers who had arrived prior to the official surveys had settled in the township set aside for seminaries. Others had settled in one of many sections set aside for the support of schools. President Madison would have forcibly removed them. The amendment, however, allowed settlers in such a situation to stay on their land while an equal amount of land from another section was set aside for the schools or seminaries.

The fourth section of the bill gave relief to settlers who had failed to exercise their right to purchase the land on which they squatted in the time allotted by the original law. Those who had failed to act quickly enough had seen their land expropriated and sold to others. Once again those most affected were those least able to take advantage of the original law. The amendment pushed by Benjamin Stephenson allowed those who had lost their land to be given the opportunity of first choice on newly surveyed lands, provided that they pay the purchase price.

The first four sections of the act Stephenson had set in motion provided a series of benefits to small farmers who had squatted on lands and would have lost them under the provisions of the original act and the directives of President Madison. Sections five through eight of the act consisted of administrative details concerning the implementation of the first four sections.

The ninth section of the act pertained to an entirely different and interesting situation. It stated:

> And be it further enacted, That it shall be lawful for Ann Gillham to locate any unappropriated quarter section within the Illinois territory, and whenever the said Ann Gillham shall enter with the register of the land office at Kaskaskia, any unappropriated quarter section, it shall be the duty of the register to issue to the said Ann Gillham, a certificate, specifying therein the quarter section so located; and it shall be the duty of the commissioner of the general land office to issue a patent for the land so located, whenever the certificate aforesaid shall be presented to him for that purpose.

In plain English, the section said that Ann Gillham had the right to select any previously unselected 160-acre tract of land within the entire territory. It also required the officer at the land office in Kaskaskia to give her a certificate that she could send to the commissioner of the land office in Washington. The commissioner, upon receiving the certificate, had to provide a patent or deed to the land to Ann Gillham.

The provision of 160 acres of land, free of charge, is an interesting case. Ann Barnett had married James Gillham in South Carolina, and shortly after the Revolutionary War, the couple moved to Kentucky. In June 1790, James and his son Isaac were hoeing a corn field some distance from their house. While they were too far away to see what was happening, a party of Kickapoo entered the house and surprised Ann and her three other children. When James and Isaac returned to the house after work, they discovered that the three children, ranging in age from 3 to 12, and their mother, Ann, were gone. The house had been ransacked and everything remaining was covered in feathers. The Natives had slit the ticks of the mattresses, shaken out the feathers, and used the empty ticks as sacks to haul off whatever they could carry. Ann had been so frightened that she had no recollection of the first part of her ordeal. She finally recovered enough to understand that she and her children were prisoners, and they were being marched off in the direction of the Ohio River. Afraid of being pursued, the Natives forced the captives to move as quickly as possible and threatened them with violence whenever they showed signs of fatigue. The children were without shoes, and Ann was forced to rip her skirt into rags to bind her children's feet. The only food available was some venison jerky to be eaten on the march. The Natives and their captives did not stop to eat all day.

Finally, after what seemed to Ann and the children an eternity, they finally stopped to rest. The Natives sent out a hunting party, which returned with only a single raccoon. The mother's reaction is recorded in an account of the kidnapping:

> Mrs. Gillham, who was afraid that either the children would perish with hunger, or that the Indians would kill them to save them from starvation, afterwards said that the sight of this one poor coon gave her more satisfaction at that time than any amount of wealth could furnish. The coon was dressed by singing off the hair over a blazing fire, and after throwing away the contents of the intestines, it was chopped in pieces and with head, bones, skin, and entrails, boiled in a kettle, and made into a kind of soup. The Indians and their captives sat around the kettle, and with bone spoons and forked sticks, obtained a scanty relief from starvation. (*History of Madison County*, 1882, p. 72)

At the Ohio River, the Natives made three rafts of logs, tied together with bark, and crossed the river. Moving north and avoiding all of the American settlements, they eventually reached the Grand Village of the Kickapoo near Springfield. It was the village that was destroyed by Ninian Edwards and Benjamin Stephenson almost 25 years later. All the efforts made by James Gillham to find his family initially failed.

After five years of searching, Gillham finally found several French fur traders who guided him to the Kickapoo village. A ransom was negotiated, and with the help of a trader from Cahokia, the ransom was paid and the family returned home. "The youngest son, Clemons, could not speak a word of English, and it was some time before he could be persuaded to leave the Indian country" (*History of Madison County*, 1882, p. 72). James Gillham had sold his farm in Kentucky and almost all of his property in searching and ransoming his family. He had searched large parts of southern Illinois and had been impressed with the land. When his family was released, he squatted on land in Illinois since he had no money remaining. Stephenson convinced the committees to add section 9 to the bill to provide relief for the family of Ann Gillham. She and her family eventually settled on their quarter-section near Long Lake in Madison County, not far from Edwardsville.

In addition to championing the multisection amendment sorting out problems of territorial land law, Stephenson was involved in a number of other legislative acts that had significant impact on the development of the Illinois Territory.

He was a supporter of an act to provide $8,000 to build a road from Shawneetown on the Ohio River to Kaskaskia. Until the road was built, the only way to go from the Ohio to Kaskaskia was to follow the trail from Fort Massac to Kaskaskia. This trail retraced the route of George Rogers Clark from almost 40 years before. In an era before steamboats moved up the Mississippi to St. Louis, an overland route was about the only way to move north into Illinois Territory.

Stephenson was also involved in the passage of an act that authorized the president to lease the saline near the Wabash River for a period of seven years. The salines of southern Illinois had been a major resource for populations in Illinois County for at least 1,000 years. The Native American Mississippian cultures had boiled water from the salt springs in huge clay pans to evaporate it and collect the salt. When the Illinois Territory was developed, the governor took over the leasing of the salt springs, and the sale of salt became a major source of revenue for the territory. The act to lease the saline along the Wabash was a way to increase the production of a commodity in great demand. Salt was the primary means of preserving meat. Salt beef and salt pork were sold by the barrel, and everyone in the territory used salt as a preservative. What's more, the salines were a source of money and political power for the territorial governor, who served as superintendent of the U.S. Salines. An early one-year contract signed by Ninian Edwards required that the annual production from the saline be no less than 120,000 bushels of salt, with a minimum price of no less than 80 cents per bushel and no more than one dollar per bushel (Edwards, 1870, p. 30).

For southern legislators, the salines offered something of a foothold for proslavery sympathizers. The Northwest Ordinance forbade slavery or involuntary servitude in any of its territories. Despite its ban on slavery, the ordinance had passed without a single southern vote in opposition, for the sentiment in favor of selling public land and settling the Ohio River region had been so strong. In an effort to gain southern support for the ordinance, the clause prohibiting slavery did include language requiring that escaped southern enslaved persons, who were apprehended in the territory, be returned to their southern owners. An exception to the territorial proscription on slavery applied to the U.S. Salines, as it was legal to use enslaved persons in the production of salt. The reason for the exception owed to the labor intensity of salt production.

Water from a salt spring was conducted to cast-iron kettles through hollowed log pipes, and long lines of the kettles were boiled over log fires. "From 125 to 280 gallons of water produced a fifty-pound bushel of salt and the daily yield ran from eight to one hundred bushels," explains one source: "Hauled by oxen to Shawneetown and reloaded into keelboats, the salt found a ready market in Indiana, Tennessee, Kentucky and Missouri. Illinois men rode more than a hundred miles for a packsaddle load" (Howard, 172, p. 154). At the Shawneetown saline, 1,000 to 2,000 enslaved persons were engaged in salt production. Enormous amounts of wood were needed to stoke the fires that boiled the water, and enslaved persons were kept busy cutting wood, stoking the fires, scraping salt from the kettles, and loading the finished product onto wagons. Most of the enslaved were leased from their Kentucky or Tennessee owners.

This exception to the rules of the Northwest Territory gave the proslavery forces some hope that the territorial prohibition could be overturned, while the antislavery forces kept a close eye on the administration of the salines. Even after the territory became a state and the Illinois Constitution, with its prohibition of slavery, was passed, the salines continued to be an exception until 1825.

The slavery question was, only then, finally settled by a total prohibition on slavery in the state.

During Stephenson's stay in Washington, two other things occurred that had a profound influence on his life. The first one was renewing his acquaintance with Josiah Meigs. Josiah Meigs was both a friend to Stephenson and later his supervisor. Meigs and Stephenson had become acquainted while Meigs, based in Cincinnati, was working as the surveyor general of the United States. In this capacity, Meigs spent considerable time in the Illinois Territory overseeing the beginnings of the General Land Office surveys of Illinois. During this time, Stephenson was the sheriff of Randolph County, and among his duties, he was in charge of appraising land

Portrait of Josiah Meigs. Courtesy of Hargrett Rare Book and Manuscript Library, University of Georgia Libraries, New Georgia Encyclopedia

holdings and of selling lands seized for delinquent taxes. The property rights mess in Illinois meant that the two men had to work together. When Stephenson went to Washington City as the territorial representative to the U.S. House of Representatives, he devoted much attention to land issues. This required working with Meigs, who had moved to Washington as the commissioner of the General Land Office. Thus, the two had a long-standing acquaintance and a working relationship.

Meigs sometimes sent friendly letters to Stephenson. On August 26, 1816, Meigs wrote to Stephenson, whom he addressed as "My Dear Friend." Meigs expressed interest in an article in the *Missouri Gazette* mentioning a petition from 1813 or 1814 that called for his removal as surveyor general. According to Meigs, Rufus Easton of Missouri had asserted that no such petition ever existed. The letter asked Stephenson to ascertain the truth of the matter. Stephenson responded in October of 1816, saying that such a petition had, indeed, been circulated. He suggested that several people had been involved, including William Rupel, Rufus Easton, and James Gilbreath. Rupel and Easton may have been involved in buying some of the land that Gilbreath had acquired under questionable circumstances. In addition to this exchange of letters, other official letters from Meigs to Stephenson report news and make other comments suggesting that Meigs and Stephenson were friends as well as colleagues.

Born in Middletown, Connecticut, in 1757, Josiah Meigs was the 13th child of Return Meigs and Elizabeth Hamlin but only the fourth child to survive infancy (Meigs, 1887, p. 1). Josiah was born in a turbulent period of American history. He was eight years old when the Stamp Act was passed, and he was only 18 when Lexington and Concord sparked the revolution. Two of his older brothers served in the Revolutionary War. His oldest brother, Return Meigs, was a member of the 6th Connecticut Infantry and ultimately rose to the rank of colonel. Josiah did not serve in the war and, for a time, worked in his father's hat store. Even though he seems to have had no formal education as a youth, he left the store in 1778 and enrolled at Yale (Meigs, 1887, p. 10). The Yale of 1787 bore little resemblance to the Yale of today. In 1778, the college consisted of only two small buildings and a chapel (p. 13). Instruction was largely under the direction of tutors, and the curriculum was dominated by classical subjects like Latin, other ancient languages, mathematics, philosophy, and religion.

Following his graduation, Meigs seems to have made a living as a tutor or teacher. In 1781, he was appointed a tutor of mathematics, natural philosophy, and astronomy at Yale. In 1782, he met and married Clara Benjamin. Concurrently, he studied law and gained admission to the Connecticut bar in April 1783 (Meigs, 1887, p. 17). In 1784, he left Yale and established the *New Haven Gazette*, a weekly newspaper. The newspaper had a decidedly literary character. There were few news articles, but there were lots of poems, reprints of classical writings from the Greeks and Romans, mathematical puzzles, sonnets, elegies, extracts from personal letters, extracts from books, and scientific observations (p. 18). During the Constitutional Convention, the paper carried articles about the convention and, during the adoption process, took a strong stance in favor of adoption. The paper ceased publication in 1788, and there is no information on its demise.

Meigs continued to tutor at Yale until 1789, when he left Connecticut to practice law in Bermuda. While his early years in Bermuda were quiet, he gradually became involved in legal cases involving British confiscation of American ships and the impressment of American sailors by the British navy. The arrogance of the British and the British navy through the period came to a head during the Napoleonic Wars beginning in the early 1800s. British privateers captured American ships and brought them before the Admiralty Court for condemnation so that they could be sold. Meigs was the only American lawyer in Bermuda, and he was in great demand. Meigs's success in defending the rights of the American ship captains and owners made him an object of bitter hatred among the privateers. So hated was he that the privateers had him arrested for treason on account of his strong language in court when defending the rights of the American sailors. He narrowly escaped conviction for treason, which would have resulted in his transportation to

Australia as a convict. After his acquittal, he was convinced that war was inevitable, and he took his family and sailed to New York (Meigs, 1887, p. 29).

Six months after his return to the United States, he was offered a professorship at Yale. He gradually became increasingly interested in politics and became a committed Jeffersonian. Unfortunately for Meigs, New England was a hotbed of Federalist beliefs. Meigs was a real misfit at Yale because of his politics. He was a strong supporter of the French Revolution, which the Federalists viewed as guilty of bloody crimes and promoting anarchy. Like most Democratic Republicans, he viewed the Federalists as being in favor of an absolute government that would support the privileged classes (Meigs, 1887, pp. 36–37). He managed to stay at Yale only by publicly declaring that he no longer supported the French Revolution (a nod to 18th-century political correctness). After six years of conflict at Yale, he finally left. His wife later wrote that they had been "exiled from his native State to the backwoods of Georgia only twelve miles from the Cherokee Indians for no earthly reason but his stern democracy" (p. 42).

In November of 1800, Meigs was appointed the first professor at the University of Georgia. He arrived in Athens in 1801 and was appointed president of the university in June. As the sole professor, he taught all of the classes, assisted by a single tutor. Additionally, he was in charge of constructing the first building at the university. He wrote to his brother:

> I arrived at this place two days ago. Here is the seat of the University of Georgia over which I preside. We are making bricks for a large Collegiate Building . . . We have plenty of timber all around us and thus far everything looks very favorable to the completion of the building. Our great difficulty is the procuring of lime [for the mortar]. (Meigs, 1887, p. 45)

He served as president for 10 years, but in 1810 he was forced to resign his position. The Arlington Cemetery website attributes his resignation to religion:

> Meigs worked long and hard to establish the foundation of [the] University, but a group of Presbyterians became entrenched on the board of trustees. This group was supported by various elements throughout the state who desired that education in the University have a definitely religious basis. He had neither a religious preference, or pretensions. In the face of this increased opposition, criticism of the discipline at the school and in reaction to his political pronouncements, Meigs was forced to resign his position in 1810. He continued as a professor for one more year, but continued to criticize the trustees so they dismissed him.

His biography does not mention the religious element and indicates that, once again, Meigs's Jeffersonian Democratic Republican sentiments were a source of friction with the trustees and the bulk of the citizens of Georgia, who had distinctly Federalist leanings. Whatever the reason for his leaving, Meigs was once again without a job.

Meigs wrote to Thomas Jefferson to ask for help in finding a position. He suggested that he be appointed to the chair of experimental and natural philosophy at West Point, but that position had already been filled. Jefferson wrote to Madison and mentioned Meigs's name in connection with the College of William and Mary. However, in 1812, shortly after receiving Jefferson's reply, Meigs received a letter from Madison appointing him surveyor general of the United States. The outgoing surveyor had been appointed to the same West Point position for which Meigs had applied. Although Meigs was a mathematician and a competent astronomer, he knew nothing about surveying (Rohrbough, 1968, p. 72).

His lack of competence in surveying never became a problem, though, because the War of 1812 disrupted surveying to such a degree that he never had to produce a significant number of surveys. The commissioner of the General Land Office, Edward Tiffin, was aware of Meigs's lack of surveying experience. Tiffin was tired of living in Washington and yearned to return to the Midwest. In 1814, Tiffin proposed to Meigs that they trade jobs. Meigs, an easterner, was happy to go to Washington, and he was also happy to be out from under the technical details of surveying. President Madison accepted the trade and provided new appointments for the two men. During his following eight years as commissioner of the General Land Office, Meigs remained a committed Democratic Republican. His political views cemented his relationships with Benjamin Stephenson and Ninian Edwards.

The second thing that happened in Washington with a profound effect on the rest of Stephenson's life was the passage of an act, approved on April 29, 1816, titled "An Act to Establish a Land District in the Illinois Territory, North of Kaskaskia." The act provided that all the lands north of the base line in the territory, formerly belonging to the land district at Kaskaskia, would be administered by a new land office established "at Edwardsville, Madison County, under the direction of the register of the land office and receiver of public moneys to be appointed for that purpose, who shall reside at that place."

By the time the act was passed, Benjamin Stephenson and his family had already left for home. The trip back to Kaskaskia from Washington was probably a little easier and faster than the trip from Kaskaskia to Washington in the fall of 1813. On April 22, 1815, Stephenson wrote to Ninian Edwards from "Summerset," by which he meant Somerset, Pennsylvania. The letter states:

> I arrived here this evening with my family, the road is extremely bad, in four days more I expect to reach Pitchburgh, when I intend to take water to furgusons ferry. I flatter myself with seeing you in Kaskaskia about the 15 or 10 of May??? If it wont be troubling you two much I would be very glad if you would rent me a house in Kaskaskia, I shall also want a hatters shop. I have a young man along which I wish to go to business immediately. I have every thing with me necessary to set him up, except fir. I am anseious to be in your county previous to the treaty with the Indians—gete any house that you think will answer, we won't be particular for the present.
>
> N.B. I am convinced my Friends have not received half the letters I wrote, I remember the number I wrote and paid.
>
> Yours Sincerely, B Stephenson.

The Stephensons' journey took them from Shepherdstown north to the National Road in Pennsylvania. From the National Road, there was stagecoach service through Somerset all the way to Pittsburgh. The trip would have been slow since it was early spring, and the roads were muddy and "extremely bad." There were a number of well-established taverns along the National Road where there were stagecoach stops allowing travelers to rest for a period during the day and to stop for the night. The trip to Pittsburgh would have been uncomfortable but relieved by the frequent stops to change horses and rest.

Once they reached Pittsburgh, the trip was easier because they could then float down the Ohio with the current. On their preceding journey toward Washington, the trip would have taken far longer since they were going upstream against the current. They unloaded at Ferguson's ferry near present day Golconda, Illinois. From there they would have taken a wagon northeast, following much the same route that George Rogers Clark had followed from Fort Massac to Kaskaskia in 1778. Following the same trail, they would have passed through the Shawnee Hills region near the U.S. Salines before entering the prairies. From there it was probably only a two- or three-day journey before reaching Kaskaskia.

On June 19, 1816, Stephenson had a letter addressed "To the Citizens of Illinois Territory" published in the *Western Intelligencer*, the weekly Kaskaskia newspaper. In the long letter, Stephenson recounted all of the legislative actions that he had worked on during his term in office. The letter gives a sense of Stephenson's character as well as the philosophy that guided his actions. The opening of the letter states:

> The period for which I was invested with the trust, with which your confidence honored me has expired, and my duties being now terminated, I consider it proper to give you a brief recapitulation of my own conduct, and of the principal measures of congress, which have been adopted during my term of service, in relation to the territory, and to the citizens thereof.

> I am aware that there may be some who doubtless will think, that more might have been done. But the liberal minded who reflect upon the difficulties I had to encounter, will, I am persuaded, find even in the success which it has been my good fortune to experience, a sufficient proof of the zeal and fidelity with which I endeavoured to serve them.
>
> If I had been able to effect much more than I have done, I would readily admit that I have not succeeded to promoting your interests to the full extent of my wishes. Nor do I think I have been as useful as it would be in my power hereafter in the same station, having now become more familiarized with the proceedings of the congress, having enlarged my acquaintance and acquired the confidence of friends who are both able and willing to afford their useful co-operation: without which, it is a melancholy truth, that a delegate of a territory, whatever may be his talents, cannot be very successful in advancing its interests.
>
> The two sessions in which I have served as your delegate have been particularly unfavorable for the territorial business, which has been unavoidably postponed, to questions of great national concern applicable in the first place to the war in which we were lately engaged; and subsequently to a permanent state of peace: the discussions of which, almost exclusively occupied the attention of congress, and consumed nearly the whole of both sessions.

The letter goes on to describe all of the legislative acts that concerned the territory, including his attempts to procure a military campaign against the Natives, the issue of militia pay, the controversy over the judiciary, changes in the land laws, and the new road from Shawneetown to Kaskaskia. In discussing several issues, Stephenson's concerns and beliefs become obvious. In one section of the letter, he discusses a petition from the Territorial Legislature that asked Congress to curtail some of the powers of the territorial governor. Both Ninian Edwards and Benjamin Stephenson supported the petition, even though it would have taken away some of the powers of the governor. Stephenson writes:

During the late session, I received and presented to congress the petition of the legislature, praying that the powers of the governor of the territory might be curtailed, and those of the people enlarged: and I gave to that petition, all the support in my power, but the most that I could obtain, was commendations of its decorous, temperate, and dignified style: for which it was viewed in as favorable a light, as any petition of the kind, that probably ever was presented to the congress; all similar applications from other territories had uniformly been rejected, and on enjoying equal privileges to those of any other territory, and superior to some of them: there appeared to be an unconquerable disinclination in congress, to make such radical alteration in the ordinance, what had existed for nearly thirty years, and probably the repugnance that was manifested to those changes resulted in part from the obligation that otherwise has been imposed of extending them to every other territory. But for my part, I can see no rational objection to extending to the citizens of a territory those principles of civil liberty which are recognized by the constitutions of almost every state in the union.

Perhaps the most revealing portion of Stephenson's letter concerns President Madison's attempt to forcibly remove squatters from federal lands. The letter states:

With a solicitude equally inspired by personal friendship, and a sense of duty, I exerted every effort in my power to avert the evils with which the President's proclamation threatened the settlers upon public lands. Having been for a considerable time associated with that class of citizens, in the defense of the territory, and knowing that of the seven or eight hundred men who were rallied in its defense in 1812, and to whose exertions, with the blessings of God, its preservation at that period may be justly attributed, there were not more than fifty freeholders; I could testify to the merits of the settlers upon public lands in our territory with the certainty of an eye witness. On all occasions I urged the ingratitude of such

> rigorous severity as was contemplated against them, and before the passage of the law upon that subject, which you have all seen, I had, I think, the good fortune to make such an impression in their favor, that no instructions for their removal were issued to the governor of our territory, as were given to the governor of the territory of Missouri.

This passage makes clear that Stephenson's thoughts were consistently on the side of the small farmer or settler. Practically all of the bills he supported were developed for the benefit of the poor rather than the rich. He was supported in his positions by Ninian Edwards, who, despite his substantial wealth, consistently supported the rights of the common man. These actions do not bolster claims, in the coming years, from political enemies who sometimes portrayed both Stephenson and Edwards as champions of the rich and famous.

One last revealing glimpse into the character of Benjamin Stephenson can be found in the editor's introduction to his long letter to the newspaper. The introduction was written by the young owner and editor of the newspaper, Daniel Pope Cook, who was a distant relative of Nathaniel Pope, the territorial secretary. Daniel was a young man in a hurry. He rose from newspaper editor to occupy, in later years, the powerful position of chairman of the House Ways and Means Committee, which wielded great power in Washington. When Stephenson returned from Congress in 1816, Daniel Pope Cook had not yet begun his meteoric rise to power. Cook's introduction to Stephenson's letter speaks to its author's character:

> In laying before our readers the following extract of a letter from our Delegate in Congress upon subjects local and highly interesting to our Territory we should do injustice to our feelings if we were to withhold from him an expression of our approbation of his conduct during the late session of Congress. He has promised to use his best exertions to serve his constituents, but he made no display of what he was going to do—but what he has done shows his devotion to the people he represents. He made no parade of extravagant

> promises, but he has shown emphatically "his faith by his works" . . . We will not say that his success has been unexampled, but we may safely say that is been very great—indeed unexpected. It shows that his vigilance never slept and that he must have obtained a character in Washington that enabled him to serve his constituents. We may indeed say that he deserves well of his country.

The statement that Stephenson's success, while not unexampled, was very great, "indeed unexpected," is revealing. Other descriptions of Stephenson paint him as a shy, quiet, and retiring individual. He was as uncomfortable a public speaker as he was a writer.

Stephenson's personal style was a significant departure from the typical 19th-century politician. Most of the politicians of the era were flowery orators, given to bombastic speeches and extravagant promises. Many of them were larger-than-life characters. The historical record indicates that Stephenson did not fit this type, and Cook's description of his service clearly indicates that Stephenson's quiet personality led others to underestimate his ability. Cook writes that Stephenson "made no extravagant parade of promises." Apparently, a politician who promised nothing, but delivered much, was as unusual in 1816 as such a politician would be today. Finally, Cook says, Stephenson's success in Congress shows that "he must have obtained a character at Washington that enabled him to serve his constituents." That character, demonstrated in the capital, would serve him well for the rest of his life in positions of public importance.

CHAPTER FIVE

Coming to Edwardsville

When Benjamin Stephenson returned to Kaskaskia in the spring of 1816, he was unemployed. He had resigned his position as sheriff of Randolph County in order to serve as territorial representative. His term in Congress concluded, he had announced he was not running for reelection in a letter to the newspaper. In his letter to Ninian Edwards, written at a stop in Somerset, Pennsylvania, he had asked the governor to rent a house for him and his family. The request might be interpreted as indicating that he was planning on staying in Kaskaskia. However, it more likely indicated that he was not planning to stay in Kaskaskia for any length of time. His letter also mentioned that he had a hatter with him, and he had almost everything needed to start a hat business except fur. Obviously, Stephenson had no intention of becoming a hatter. He might have been interested in being a partner in the business, but his interest might also have been purely altruistic: since there was no hatter in Kaskaskia, and the hatter needed a place to start a business, Stephenson may have brought him along simply to improve life in Kaskaskia.

Renting a house in Kaskaskia was a short-term arrangement, as his plans for the future were already well developed. Despite his status as an unemployed public servant, he was not without prospects. He had been a farmer most of his life. He had worked on his father's farm before becoming a deputy sheriff, and he had been a successful farmer in Logan County, Kentucky, before leaving for the Illinois Territory. But he almost certainly had no intention of becoming a farmer again. He knew that impending changes in

Washington could offer significant new opportunities. His work in Washington had concerned land law, and he had developed a good personal relationship with Josiah Meigs, the commissioner of the General Land Office. Before he left Washington, he knew that a bill authorizing a new land office in Edwardsville was making its way through Congress. Already an expert on land laws and a friend of the commissioner of the General Land Office, he had to have known he was a strong candidate for one of the two positions in the Edwardsville office. Still, he was probably reluctant to pin all his hopes on the possibility.

Although he was a perfect candidate for one of the land office positions, the positions were political appointments made by the president. It was entirely possible that someone else would be appointed to pay off one of President Madison's political debts. Madison might also give the job to one of his friends. Stephenson was in no position to gamble his future on the whims of a president. He had a wife and four children to care for, and he had become used to a level of economic security and social position far more significant than a farmer's life could provide. Unsure of the position in the land office, he had to have a backup plan. Clearly he had been thinking about what he might do for some time, for he seems to have already set an alternative plan in motion. During the War of 1812, Stephenson had mustered militia troops at Fort Russell on numerous occasions, and all three of his campaigns against the Natives had started at the fort. Fort Russell was just northeast of Edwardsville.

Governor Edwards had created Madison County on September 14, 1810. His proclamation stated, "I do appoint the house of Thomas Kirkpatrick to be the seat of justice of said county" (James, 1901, p. 26). Kirkpatrick's house was on Cahokia Creek, halfway between what became the town of Edwardsville and Fort Russell. Edwardsville, situated on a long ridge between several creeks, was named in honor of Governor Edwards by Kirkpatrick. In 1814, Kirkpatrick laid out a series of town lots along the top of the ridge. Even though the town was the seat of Madison County, there were few settlers by 1815–1816, and Kirkpatrick's lots did not sell quickly. Stephenson was familiar with the area, knew it was the county seat, and understood its potential for growth. He was also familiar with most of the people who lived there. He knew Thomas Kirkpatrick and the Whiteside brothers, who lived just west of town. The various members of the Whiteside family had been leaders in the militia during the war and had served under Stephenson on a number of occasions.

Just south of Edwardsville, Samuel Judy, another militia officer, had settled in the area known as the Goshen settlement. Stephenson knew that if Edwardsville became the location of a new federal land office, the town would become a beehive of activity and grow rapidly. Even if he was not appointed to one of the land office positions, there would be ample opportunity to grow with the town. He planned to open a general store. Almost certainly the store was a fallback position in the event he did not get a position in the land office. Obviously, he had been planning for both eventualities for some time. When in Washington, he must have investigated the possibility of purchasing wholesale goods in nearby Baltimore, which was only 40 miles away and was a major port. Imported goods could be purchased cheaply in the port city, and Baltimore was also a center of flour milling and furniture production. Sometime before he left for the Illinois Territory, he had purchased goods in Baltimore.

In early June 1816, not long after he returned to Kaskaskia, he received a letter from Commissioner Meigs. The letter was dated May 11, 1816:

> Herewith you will receive a commission, appointing you Receiver of public monies for the land district in the Illinois Territory north of the district of Kaskaskia: a copy of the act of Congress establishing the district, Forms and instructions for your government. The Register at Cincinnati has been directed to purchase Books and Stationery for you, for the Land Office and to forward them to the Register at Shawneetown, you will pay for them out of the first receipts for public Lands . . . I have to request that you will immediately qualify yourself [as Receiver] by taking an Oath to support

> the Constitution of the U States, for fidelity in Office, with a Bond executed by yourself and one or more good Sureties in the sum of Ten Thousand dollars.

At the same time, Major John McKee, a Kentucky militia officer whom Stephenson knew, was appointed the register of the Edwardsville office. General William Rector was appointed surveyor general of the Missouri Territory, Illinois Territory, and the Arkansas Territory. Stephenson was well acquainted with Rector and his brothers. They had served together in the militia.

Suddenly Stephenson was blessed with "an embarrassment of riches" when his appointment as receiver of public monies was shortly followed by the arrival of wagons carrying all the goods he had purchased in Baltimore for his store. By the time the goods for the store arrived, he had already traveled to Edwardsville and had rented a building for the land office on the west side of Main Street. When the goods for his store arrived, he housed both the store and the land office in the same building. He placed ads in the Kaskaskia newspaper announcing his new store:

> I have just received and am opening in Edwardsville a General and Elegant Assortment of Merchandize recently imported from Philadelphia and Baltimore which I am determined to sell at the most reasonable prices, as those shall see, who may favor me with a call. Benjamin Stephenson, Edwardsville, Nov. 18, 1816.

The ad ran weekly for a year and was replaced by a similar one that ran until April 1818, before disappearing from the paper. It appears that Stephenson maintained the store until all of his "General and Elegant Merchandize" was sold; he then ended his career as a merchant to concentrate on his position as receiver.

Receiver of public monies was a prized position. The receiver was paid $250 per quarter, and he also received a 3% commission on all land sales in his district. The register of the land office was similarly compensated. Some of the receivers and registers sold so much land that their salary and commission made them some of the most highly paid federal employees. Congress finally moved to limit the salary plus commission to no more than $3,000 per year. With an annual income of $3,000 per year, Stephenson was one of the best paid people on the Illinois frontier.

The receiver and register worked in collaboration. The register recorded all sales, completed the paperwork, and arranged for the buyer to get a "patent" issued by the government in Washington. The patent transferred title to the land from the government to the settler. For all intents and purposes, a patent could be thought of as a deed. The register was responsible for keeping a record of all sales, including the location of the land, the total acreage, and the sale price. The receiver of public monies handled the payments for the land and administered various payment schedules, which had developed over the years. The federal lands were sold at auction. The purpose of selling the land by auction was to make certain that small landowners or prospective settlers had an equal chance to buy the land before the rich and powerful could negotiate a secret deal to procure the property. The receiver was responsible for scheduling the land auctions and advertising the auctions in local newspapers. The receiver of public monies was also responsible for collecting the money and maintaining a bookkeeping record of all land sales, the size of the tracts sold, and the cost per acre. The register and the receiver kept separate books recording all land sales. The double bookkeeping system allowed the government to track all land sales, and it provided a check on the register and receiver. Both were required to send monthly reports to the General Land Office in Washington. The register's report had to be countersigned by the receiver and vice versa.

The sale of public lands began shortly after the end of the Revolutionary War. The treaty signed by the British ceded their rights to all the lands between the Allegheny Mountains and the Mississippi River. When the war ended, the new nation was governed under the Articles of Confederation adopted in 1781. The key to the adoption of the Articles of Confederation was the agreement on several issues among the political leaders of the time. One of these was an agreement on "assumption" made between Alexander Hamilton and Thomas Jefferson. This agreement allowed the federal government to take over all the war debts of the former colonies in exchange for locating the capital of the United States in Washington City. The other key agreement was the cession of claims to the lands west of the Ohio River by the various colonies that had charters giving them control of large tracts of land. Maryland had refused to sign the Articles of Confederation until the various states gave up their claims. The cession of land by the British, plus the cession of the rights of the various colonies, meant that the new United States held title to a vast amount of land.

At the end of the revolution, the new country was nearly broke. Most of the colonial income, and that of the new nation, came from duties, or taxes, paid on imports. Since it had been British policy to discourage manufacturing in North America, almost every manufactured item of any importance, like china, high-quality clothing, woolen and linen fabrics, and most luxury items had to be imported. The duties on these items had been a significant source of income. About the only thing that was not imported was food. The war stopped most of the imports, and the revenue from duties almost completely dried up. While the importation of goods from Britain and France resumed after the revolution, it was slow to rebound. Within a few years, the situation became increasingly complicated as a result of international tensions. The start of the Napoleonic Wars in Europe in 1803 once again began to reduce import duties. With the start of the War of 1812, the situation became even more difficult. The war curtailed most imports and greatly reduced the export of commodities.

Most American exports were commodities and came from the southern and middle states. From the South, cotton was exported in significant quantities, while the Mid-Atlantic exported a lot of tobacco. Most of the northern states had few agricultural products available for export, and their exports were limited to small amounts of whale oil and furs. Thus, with both import duties and the export of American commodities disrupted for most of the first 40 years of its existence, the United States was faced with a significant fiscal crisis. Large debts had been incurred during the revolution, and there was no federal income available to repay them. The only resource available in large quantities was land.

For settlers, land was "as good as gold." Owning your own land made you independent. You could grow enough food to feed your family and have enough left over from selling the surplus to buy most necessities and, maybe, a few luxury items. With settlers clamoring for land, the vast land resources of the mid-continent United States looked like a ready source of money to the government. Additionally, if the lightly populated territories west of the Alleghenies were settled, they would serve as a buffer between the hostile Natives and the more settled parts of the states in the East. Unregulated sale of land would have created chaos, so the Continental Congress passed the Land Ordinance of 1785.

Titled "An Ordinance for Ascertaining the Mode of Disposing of Lands in the Western Territory," the Land Ordinance of 1785 was the first of two pieces of legislation that rank among the most significant ever passed by any U.S. Congress. The Land Ordinance and the Northwest Ordinance are legislative companion pieces: the Land Ordinance of 1785 set the rules for selling land to settlers, while the Northwest Ordinance, passed two years later, set the rules for governing the settlers in the newly sold lands. Both acts had profound effects on the way the young United States developed.

The Land Ordinance not only changed the way land was sold, but it also changed the way the expanding country looked. From an aerial view, some of the southern colonies in the United States would have looked like a crazy quilt conforming to no discernable pattern in the settlement of land, while almost all of the post-colonial parts of the United States formed a checkerboard of rectangular tracts of land of different sizes. Whereas roads often meander in old towns of Europe, in most areas of the United States, roads, other than those connecting one city to another, tend to be laid out in straight lines and right angles, usually running north to south or east to west.

The rectangular, checkerboard pattern of properties is the result of a new survey system introduced by the Land Ordinance of 1785, which required that the geographer of the United States direct all surveys of land and oversee the conduct of individual surveys and surveyors. The ordinance also mandated a survey pattern that was much like the method that had developed in New England during the preceding century.

The New England system was based on a unit called a township. A township was a parcel of land six miles wide from east to west and six miles long from north to south. It contained 36 square miles of land. In New England, townships were purchased by groups who then subdivided the area according to their own desires. The Land Ordinance of 1785 adopted the township plan and required that townships be numbered from south to north. The act provided that the surveyors would be paid two dollars a mile, which included the wages for all other workers and expenses.

The instructions in the act called for the establishment of a north-south line and an eastwest line perpendicular to the north-south line. Both lines were required to begin on the west bank of the Ohio River at the western end of the Pennsylvania-Maryland state line. The first eastwest line, called the base line, continued all the way through the Northwest Territory. According to the act,

> The geographer shall designate the townships, by number progressively, from south to north, always beginning each range with No. 1; and the ranges shall be distinguished by their progressive numbers to the westward. The first range, extending from the Ohio to the Lake Erie, being marked No. 1. The geographer shall personally attend to the running of the first east and west line, and shall take the latitude of the extremes of the first north and south line, and of the mouths of the principal rivers.

The act stipulated that all of the lines would be measured with a chain and be exactly described on a plat, or map. The term *chain* refers to a surveyor's chain used to measure distances. Inherited from the British survey system, a chain is made up of 132 six-inch links. Thus, one chain measures 66 feet in length. Eight chains make a mile, and 10 square chains make an acre. In addition to chaining and platting each line, the surveyors were required to note on the plats "all mines, salt springs, salt-licks, and mill-seats, and all water-courses, mountains, and other remarkable and permanent things . . . and the quality of the lands." In practice, as the system developed, the qualities of the lands were described by their vegetation. Lands were described as prairie or wooded, for example. In wooded areas the size and species of the trees were recorded along the survey lines.

The act continued with specifications for partitioning the land into units:

> The plats of the townships respectively, shall be marked by subdivisions into lots of one mile square, or 640 acres, in the same direction as the external lines, and numbered from 1 to 36, always beginning the succeeding range of lots with the number next to that which the preceding one concluded.

The subdivisions of one mile square were called sections, and each township had 36 sections, numbered from 1 to 36. Any tract of land could be identified by its township, range, and section numbers. For example, Edwardsville, where Stephenson located the land office, was in Section 4 of Township 4 N, Range 8 W.

After the first seven ranges were surveyed and platted, the surveyor was directed to send the plats to the U.S. Treasury Department to be recorded. The secretary of war was directed to take one-seventh of the total land in the seven ranges to be used for providing land warrants to veterans of the Revolutionary War. The secretary of war was to continue taking one-seventh of all subsequent ranges until all eligible veterans had received warrants. The act also required the secretary of war to identify "certain officers in the hospital department" for receipt of grants of land from the lands set aside for the use of the Continental Army.

The act also stipulated that sections numbered 8, 11, 26, and 29 of every township were reserved by the government for future sale. Additionally, section 16 of each township was to be reserved "for the maintenance of public schools." One-third of all gold, silver, lead, and copper mines were reserved for sale by Congress.

Arrangement of Townships and Ranges in the Rectangular Survey System

T6N R6W	**T6N R5W**	**T6N R4W**	**T6N R3W**	**T6N R2W**	**T6N R1W**
T5N R6W	**T5N R5W**	**T5N R4W**	**T5N R3W**	**T5N R2W**	**T5N R1W**
T4N R6W	**T4N R5W**	**T4N R4W**	**T4N R3W**	**T4N R2W**	**T4N R1W**
T3N R6W	**T3N R5W**	**T3N R4W**	**T3N R3W**	**T3N R2W**	**T3N R1W**
T2N R6W	**T2N R5W**	**T2N R4W**	**T2N R3W**	**T2N R2W**	**T2N R1W**
T1N R6W	**T1N R5W**	**T1N R4W**	**T1N R3W**	**T1N R2W**	**T1N R1W**

Arrangement of Sections

6	**5**	**4**	**3**	**2**	**1**
7	**8**	**9**	**10**	**11**	**12**
18	**17**	**16**	**15**	**14**	**13**
19	**20**	**21**	**22**	**23**	**24**
30	**29**	**28**	**27**	**26**	**25**
31	**32**	**33**	**34**	**35**	**36**

Divisions of a Section

<table>
<tr><td colspan="3">Half-Section
320 Acres</td></tr>
<tr><td>¼ of ¼
Section</td><td></td><td rowspan="2">Quarter-Section
160 Acres</td></tr>
<tr><td>40 Acres</td><td></td></tr>
</table>

Three townships adjacent to Lake Erie were reserved for the use of the officers, men, and others who were refugees from Canada and Nova Scotia. Finally, the act "ordained" that the towns of Gnadenhutten, Schoenbrunn, and Salem, on the Muskingum River, along with all of the buildings and improvements, "would be reserved for the sole use of the Christian Indians, who were formerly settled there, or the remains of that society, as may, in the judgment of the geographer, be sufficient for them to cultivate." This section of the act was calculated to right a wrong committed during the revolution. The three towns specified in the act had been populated by members of the Leni Lenape, or Delaware, tribe. In the early 1700s, tribe members had converted to Christianity, settled into towns, and adopted white customs. In 1781, a contingent of the Pennsylvania militia, ignoring the fact that the Natives were peaceful and friendly, attacked the three towns and slaughtered 28 men, 29 women, and 39 children.

Thomas Hutchins, the geographer of the United States, was tasked with the job of laying out the first east-west base line and surveying all of the first seven ranges. Hutchins was born in New Jersey but had joined the British army as an ensign before the

French and Indian War. He was a gifted cartographer, and at the end of the French and Indian War, he was sent west and stationed at Fort Chartres just north of Kaskaskia in Illinois Country. When the revolution came, he resigned his commission in the British army after having served with the British for more than 20 years. He was promptly arrested for treason. In 1780, he escaped to France and met with Benjamin Franklin and asked for a recommendation to a position in the government. In 1781 he was named geographer of the United States. Within days of the passage of the Land Ordinance, Hutchins was given a three-year extension to his appointment as geographer at the rate of $6.00 per day. Hutchins and a team of surveyors started out from Pittsburgh in late September 1785, with the intention of laying out the first east-west line. They immediately came under attack by Natives and abandoned their efforts. His initial charge was to survey the first seven ranges encompassing a tract of 1,764 square miles. Constant Native attacks slowed the surveys substantially, and when Hutchins died in late April 1789, only four of the seven ranges had been completely surveyed.

Land sales began in some of the states before the seven ranges were completely surveyed. State land offices continued to control the sale of land throughout the 1790s. State control ended in 1800 when the first two federal land offices opened at Marietta and Steubenville, Ohio. In the next 10 years, land offices opened in a number of other Ohio districts and in the Indiana Territory.

The original bill mandated that the first seven ranges would be sold either as entire townships or in smaller lots. Odd-numbered townships were to be sold as complete townships. Even-numbered townships were to be sold in smaller lots. The size of the smaller lots was not specified, but the townships were divided into square-mile sections of 640 acres, and most sales were expected to be of entire sections. The sale of entire townships seemed to favor the rich, but many in Congress argued that it was good for the small settler. Their argument was that the large investor who purchased an entire township could subdivide the land into parcels of any size and sell to small investors.

Over the first 20 years of federal land sales, a number of rules set in the Land Ordinance of 1785 did not work so well in practice.

One of the provisions was that all of the land would be sold at public auction. According to the ordinance, the auction price was set at a minimum of one dollar per acre, but the minimum price was quickly changed to two dollars per acre. The change was made by Congress, which saw the sale of public lands as a cash cow. At two dollars per acre, an entire section of 640 acres could be purchased for $1,280 dollars. An entire township consisted of 23,040 acres and, with a minimum bid of two dollars per acre, could be purchased for $46,080. Since real money was scarce even for the rich, a time-payment system was developed. The time-payment scheme proved to be disastrous, however, and Congress's cash cow failed to yield a significant amount of income.

With the price per acre set at two dollars, the minimum purchase was initially to be a half-section consisting of 320 acres. There was an 8% discount for land purchased with cash. With the discount, a half-section of 320 acres could be purchased with cash for $588 plus a $10 filing fee. However, most people opted to buy on credit. They also frequently opted to buy considerably more land than they could afford. Most reasoned that, if they had the $588 needed to buy a half-section, they could buy two entire sections on credit by paying 5% down and a second payment of 20% made 40 days later. During the first year, the initial 25% payment required to purchase two sections was only $640 dollars. So, for $52 more than the $588 needed to buy a half-section, one could get four times as much land. Of course, that meant the buyer was on the hook for three additional yearly payments of 25%. In order to qualify for credit, the buyer had to pay a $5 fee and agree to pay interest at the rate of 6% beginning at the date of purchase. If the annual payments were not made, the buyer was given a fifth year to make the final payment before the government was supposed to foreclose on the property.

The credit system had the effect of encouraging buyers to dream big and buy more than they could afford. Many believed that, after two years of farming, they could make enough money to meet the second 25% payment including interest of 6%. Unfortunately, most farms produced very little the first year because the land had to be cleared. Consequently, most people could not make the first payment. Because the interest charges kept compounding, their debt increased every year, and many farmers failed to pay the third and then the fourth payment. They also frequently failed to make a payment at the end of the fifth year, and their land was subject to foreclosure.

By 1804, only four years after the first Ohio offices opened, significant changes to the sale of land began to be made. The minimum purchase was lowered to a quarter-section rather than a half-section. A quarter-section of 160 acres could be purchased for $320 plus fees, but with a discount for cash payment. The 6% interest charge was removed and was only charged when a payment became overdue.

Even these changes, though, failed to solve the problems. Albert Gallatin, secretary of the treasury, wrote Congress as early as 1803 to say that the land system could not work without major modifications. He suggested that three major changes be made. First, he recommended selling land in smaller tracts. He reasoned that most small settlers could handle the purchase of a quarter-section of 160 acres or an even smaller 80-acre purchase of half of a quarter-section. Second, Gallatin thought the minimum price of two dollars per acre was too expensive and said the price should be lowered. Finally, he argued that the credit system was totally unworkable as it encouraged settlers to gamble on imagined future profits. Therefore, he advocated the total abolition of credit. Eventually, all three of his recommendations were adopted, but, unfortunately, the changes were long in coming.

Ignoring Gallatin's warning, Congress made additional changes but kept many of the worst features of the law. Between 1805 and 1820, the system set the minimum purchase at 160 acres. The credit system was altered by charging a 6% interest rate only on overdue payments, rather than beginning at the date of purchase. The law still required a payment of 5% down and an additional 20% due in 40 days. In years two, three, and four, 25% payments were required.

For receivers like Stephenson, the piecemeal changes created enormous problems. Some lands were purchased on credit, and some were purchased with cash. Some buyers purchased the minimum 160 acres, while some purchased half-sections, full sections, or more. The worst problem was the credit system. Credit was supposed to be charged after a buyer defaulted on a contract. After five years, the land was supposed to be repossessed and resold. However, Congress, under pressure from voters, decided that foreclosures would be delayed for a year. And after that year had expired, Congress discovered that the payments still had not been made, and an additional 6% interest charge was now due. Instead of cutting its losses and abandoning the system, Congress continued to grant one-year extensions. After a number of yearly extensions, many settlers found the interest on their purchase had accrued to the point that they owed considerably more than the original purchase price.

Secretary of the Treasury Gallatin had suggested radical changes in 1803, but it was not until 1820 that all three of his suggestions were adopted. The Land Act of 1820, signed by President James Monroe, abolished the credit system and required cash sales. The minimum purchase was reduced from a 160-acre quarter-section to a half-quarter of 80 acres. The final change reduced the minimum auction price to $1.25 per acre. A settler could buy 80 acres for $100. The time-payment credit system had been in effect for 20 years and had been a disaster. In the 20 years, more than $44 million worth of land had been purchased, but almost half of that amount was still owed to the government. Over the entire time the system had been in operation, only about $400,000 worth of land had been expropriated from defaulters. In 20 years, less than 1% of land sold for credit had actually been repossessed and been made available for resale.

John McKee and Benjamin Stephenson had been appointed to the offices of register and receiver of public monies in the Edwardsville District land office in 1816. For the first four years, they operated under the credit system. For Stephenson, a major part of the job was keeping up with the paperwork on defaulting purchasers and the resulting interest charges. The paperwork requirements escalated every year as the number of buyers and defaulters increased.

There were multiple problems for both McKee and Stephenson. There was a huge pent-up demand for the sale of land in the Illinois

Territory. Land sales had been delayed for almost 10 years because of the difficulty of sorting out all the prior claims on the land. The original law required that all preexisting claims on the land be extinguished before surveying could begin. Sales had to be delayed until surveying had been completed and all the plats had been sent to Washington for approval. In Illinois, the preexisting claims were considerably more complicated than those in Ohio and Indiana.

First of all, there were a large number of Native groups living in the territory, and their claims had to be ceded by treaty. Some parts of the territory had been cleared by treaties negotiated by William Henry Harrison in the early 1800s. Shortly after becoming governor of the territory, Ninian Edwards had signed treaties with the surviving tribes of the Illinois Confederation. However, the Illini were so reduced in numbers that they no longer controlled much land. Consequently, there were still large parts of the territory occupied by groups that had not yet been pressured into signing away their claims. In addition to the Native claims, there were also French and English claims. The French had been in the area for 150 years, and claims had been granted by the French king and government. The Illinois Country had become a British possession after the end of the French and Indian War. In the 19 years of English rule, the king had granted a number of claims to English citizens. After George Rogers Clark's conquest of Illinois Country in 1788, a number of American settlers had arrived. While many of them squatted on land, some purchased claims from the French and English who had received earlier grants. In addition to all of the legal claims, there were a number of bogus claims. Some individuals fraudulently stated that they had purchased claims from earlier French citizens, who, they claimed, were now dead or had moved to Missouri Territory. Some of the claimants produced "witnesses" who swore that they had seen the purchases even though no paperwork could be produced. It took nearly 10 years for all of the claims to be adjudicated, and until they were settled, large parts of the territory could not be surveyed, much less sold.

The delay in selling Illinois land was not just an economic or social problem. It was also a significant political problem. The

Northwest Ordinance required that a prospective voter be a *freeholder*. The definition of a freeholder was a white male who owned more than 50 acres of land. Settlers who could not buy land could not vote, and the lack of voting rights was a huge political issue. All of the attendant social, economic, and political problems had to be held in abeyance until the sale of land could begin. The opening of the Edwardsville District land office coincided with the settlement of many of the claims. Settlement of the claims meant that surveying could start in earnest. William Rector, appointed surveyor general of the Illinois, Missouri, and Arkansas Territories at the same time that Stephenson was appointed receiver, began surveying almost immediately.

It is difficult to describe the relationship between William Rector and Benjamin Stephenson. They were not best friends, but they were more than mere acquaintances. They knew each other well throughout Stephenson's time in Illinois. They were both high-ranking officers in the militia, and they worked together on many occasions. Rector had been the first general of the territorial militia and had promoted Stephenson from the rank of major to colonel. Perhaps the best way to think of their relationship is to classify it as a "wary friendship." In an October 1816 letter, Benjamin Stephenson responded to a letter from Josiah Meigs about the petition that may have been circulated in the Missouri and Illinois Territories. The petition called for Meigs's removal from the office of surveyor general of the United States. In Stephenson's reply, he wrote:

> There are persons enough who about that time heard of such a petition, among others, Governor Edwards recollects that inquiries were made of him concerning it–I believe however that the bad prospect of success; or the fear of General Rector (who though a very amiable, is a very determined, and sometimes rather a desperate man) caused the petition to be suppressed–that is, if it did exist.

The description of Rector as amiable, but very determined and sometimes desperate, coupled with the comment that there was "fear of General Rector," suggests that Rector was one who needed to be treated with equal parts respect and reservation.

William Rector was the sixth child of 14 children of Frederick and Elizabeth Conner Rector of Rectorville, Fauquier County, Virginia. He left Virginia in the early 1800s and became the first settler in Perry County, Indiana. William Henry Harrison was the governor of the Indiana Territory, which included Illinois Country. Harrison was in charge of federal contracts in the territory and hired William Rector to survey a buffalo trail from the Ohio River to Vincennes. His surveying skills were so evident that he was subsequently hired to do further contracts in the Indiana Territory and Illinois Country. He was named the deputy surveyor general of the Kaskaskia District in 1807. He received a number of contracts for surveys throughout the Indiana and Illinois Territories before 1812. He was one of nine brothers, of which at least five came to Illinois to help conduct the surveys:

> All nine brothers stood over six feet tall and weighed at least 200 pounds. All of them laughed at danger. John Reynolds, who knew them, described the brothers' passionate and impulsive natures, called them the most fearless and undaunted people I ever knew. (Ferguson, 2012, p. 80)

The War of 1812 brought most survey business to a halt. In 1813, Rector and Stephenson served together in Governors Edwards's campaign against the Natives at Peoria Lakes.

After the war, Josiah Meigs appointed Rector the surveyor general of the Illinois, Missouri, and Arkansas Territories. Rector directed surveys of thousands of acres of public lands and hired dozens of surveyors to do the work. Because of his position, he was one of the most influential men in the three territories. During 1817 and 1818, many of the surveys were done in the Edwardsville District, and Benjamin Stephenson was authorized to pay Rector for the completion of the surveys. The payments were made out of the receipts at the Edwardsville office. Four separate payments totaling $60,000 were authorized by William Crawford, the secretary of the treasury.

Surveying was one of the most significant professions in the United States during the 18th and 19th centuries:

> The surveying experience was a frontier enterprise that bound together young, educated men with political or military connections and ties to the federal government. Surveyors, central figures on American frontiers, did not become household names, although national figures from George Washington and Daniel Boone to Abraham Lincoln surveyed dozens of properties. American surveys of private claims and federal land began in 1785 and lasted until 1946 . . . [and] federal contracts sent scarce money into frontier towns and were significant plums for those who were party to the survey economy. Skilled surveyors were also administrators who hired crews to negotiate natural obstacles and survive unpredictable weather. Surveyors were also experienced men in backwoods lifeways, living months in the open woods, out on the prairies, and in traversing swamps and wetlands. (Morrow, 2007, p. 4)

In addition to the natural obstacles that the surveyors confronted, there was still considerable danger from the Natives.

The original surveys of the Northwest Territory had often been disrupted by the danger of Native attacks upon the small and isolated survey parties (Rohrbough, 1968, p. 10). Danger from the Natives was still a problem as late as 1814 in the Illinois Territory. The March 12th issue of the *Missouri Gazette* published an extract of a letter from Ninian Edwards to William Rector. Edwards wrote:

> I avail myself of the opportunity of a ranger I find going to St. Louis to inform you that I have this day received certain intelligence from the U. States Saline, that a party of hostile Indians have made their appearance in that neighborhood, and that your worthy brother and my much esteemed and respected friend, Major Nelson Rector on Tuesday last returning from surveying received two balls in his side and his

> horse three from those Indians. He however made good his escape to the Saline and Capt. White immediately started out with a party of men in pursuit of the savages. The next day C. J. Tramel with another party followed on. I have reason to believe that your brother, though probably badly wounded, is likely to recover.

The same issue of the *Missouri Gazette* reported that William Rector had received a letter from his brother reporting the incident. According to Nelson Rector,

> it is with much regret and mortification that I have to inform you that on my way to this place from my camp (where I have been recently surveying) at the hour of 11 o'clock Tuesday the last I was fired on by a party of Indians consisting of from 5 to 8 in number, who have badly wounded me. My left arm is broken by a ball which still remains in it. I am also shot through the left side of my breast; the ball entered below my collar bone, and was extracted from my back by Doctors Shannon and Gainey; I have a third wound on the right side of my head, just above my ear. Which is very slight, as it only cut the skin, and knocked off my hat, with the above wounds it is unnecessary to tell you I suffered more than I can express before I arrived at the first house; which was 12 or 14 miles distance from the spot where I received my wounds: My broken arm knocking against every branch that came in its way: not withstanding the severity of my wounds, I am very sanguine of recovering, as they are much better than I could have expected in so short a time. Although the tawny sons of the woods were so sure of my scalp, they have missed it; not withstanding they were concealed under the bank of a creek, and did not shoot more than eight or ten paces from me. My horse was shot through his shoulders but carried me where I received assistance. I am here yet alive, and should heaven permit me ever to recover again, I will retaliate on the savage rascals in a four fold manner (if but my one arm is preserved) I do not think of dying.

Surveying could be a lucrative profession. By 1816 most surveyors working on government lands were paid three dollars per mile surveyed. At least five of William Rector's brothers performed a number of these surveys, and three of his nephews were also employed. The nepotism that characterized Rector's survey administration was common knowledge. Gershom Flagg, a Vermont Yankee who had settled on a farm outside Edwardsville in 1817, wrote to his brother Artemas Flagg on September 12, 1818:

> I have not been able to get any employment in surveying. The Lands have been principally surveyed in the winter of 1816–7. There was then upwards of 80 companies employed upwards of 4 months. They surveyed the Military Bounty Lands and most of the other lands where the Indian title was extinguished. 3 1/2 millions of acres of Bounty Lands were survd . . . between the Mississippi and the Illinois Rivers. There is now considerable surveying to be done but the Surveyor General Rector has so many connections that are surveyors that is not possible for a stranger to get any contract of any importance. Government gives 3 dollars a mile for surveying all public lands. Some who are not surveyors (but favorites) make contracts for surveying and then hire it done. I was offered 25 dollars a month last winter to go with another surveyor but did not choose to go under a man who did not know as much as I did myself. (Buck, 1910, p. 160)

The complaints were well known, and in January of 1823, the United States House of Representatives requested that the secretary of the treasury provide information on all surveying contracts. The House specifically wanted to know if the surveys had actually been done by the contractors rather than subcontractors, whether the contracts had been faithfully executed, and what price was paid by mile. The treasurer's office responded with the information for five surveyors general covering the states and territories of Illinois, Missouri, Arkansas, Ohio, Indiana, Michigan, Mississippi, Louisiana, and Alabama. Rector had let contracts in Illinois, Missouri, and Arkansas. During the years of 1819–1822, his surveyors had surveyed 87,573 miles at three dollars per mile for a total expenditure of $262,718.11. While he had supervised almost twice the number of surveys as the other four surveyors general, he paid the lowest price per mile of all the supervisors. The general price in the other areas was four dollars per mile, and Edward Tiffin, the former commissioner of the General Land Office, paid five dollars per mile for one survey of the boundary line between Ohio and Michigan. The House investigation did not elicit any information on the question of whether the surveys were made by the contractors or by subcontractors. In the absence of any information indicating wrongdoing, the House investigation did not result in any action against Rector. In late January 1823, however, the Senate called for information on all contracts let by Rector since January 1, 1819. The investigation revealed that, of the 93 contracts given by Rector, 17 were contracts with people named Rector.

While the Senate investigation was going on, Joshua Barton published a letter in the *Missouri Republican* accusing William Rector of hiring members of his family and overpaying the surveyors in his district. Barton was the attorney general of Missouri, the brother of a U.S. senator, the protégé of Rufus Easton, and a friend of Edward Bates, who became Abraham Lincoln's attorney general. It would be hard to find a more influential enemy, but William Rector's brother Thomas believed that the article was an affront to his family, and he challenged Barton to a duel. Barton agreed to the duel on the condition that Thomas Rector admit that the charges were true. Rector was so intent on destroying Barton that he admitted the charges in order to ensure the duel would take place. On June 30, 1823, at six o'clock in the evening, Barton and Thomas Rector met on Bloody Island, an island in the Mississippi. Bloody Island was clearly visible from the top of the huge Native mound near the Mississippi, and a number of the Rectors were on top of the mound to witness the affair. Barton was killed with the first shot. When the other Rectors knew Barton had been killed, they raised a victorious cheer. The intensity of the hatred was so great that they had agreed among themselves that, if Thomas should fall, another member of the family would take his place. They were determined to kill Barton whatever the cost. Barton was buried by his friend Edward Bates at St. Charles, not far from the old stone tower.

The Senate investigation did not find Rector guilty of any offense. However, the furor over the duel and death of Joshua Barton convinced President James Monroe to reverse his decision to reappoint Rector as surveyor general of the districts of Missouri, Illinois, and Arkansas. Rector returned to St. Louis, but Edward Bates offered to prove that no fewer than 20 relatives and connections of Rector had received contracts, and Rector then sublet the contracts at enormous profit. Though Rector denied the charges, he retired from public life. Thomas Rector was indicted for murder by a grand jury in St. Clair County, Illinois, for the killing of Barton. Illinois governor Edward Coles issued a warrant for Thomas Rector's arrest, but the state of Missouri declined to act, and no further action was ever taken. Thomas was killed several years later in a brawl. The rest of the Rector family sank into obscurity, and William Rector died in poverty in Illinois.

Settling claims and paying surveyors were only a few of the problems that Stephenson faced. A major obstacle was the lack of real money on the frontier. Native agents, like the surveyors, were also supposed to be paid by the government, but the distances and the glacial pace of travel made payment very slow. Many of the receivers of public monies were ultimately forced to become the "paymasters of the frontier." That was particularly true for those like Stephenson who were stationed at the far reaches of the frontier, far from Washington. Stephenson received periodic instructions from Josiah Meigs authorizing payments to the surveyors out of the receipts from the land office. He also received instructions from the secretary of war, directing him to pay the Native agents. All of these instructions added substantial paperwork requirements to the job but made the position of receiver substantially more important than it had been.

The lack of money resulted in other kinds of problems. Aside from the printing of dollars during the revolution, there was no United States paper money in circulation. During the Revolutionary War, "Continental dollars" had become so devalued that their lack of worth inspired a phrase: "not worth a Continental." The only money readily accepted everywhere in the country was gold or silver coinage. Most of the metal coins circulated were European. Most common were British, French, or Spanish currency, although other national coins were also in circulation. The Spanish silver dollar was a common form of money and could be cut into "bits." Two bits coincided with a quarter, and so on.

Early in the 1800s, state and local banks began to crop up east of the Mississippi. These banks were allowed to print their own paper money but with the restriction that they held gold and silver reserves equal to the amount of paper money they printed. Customers were supposed to be able to take their paper money to the bank that issued the money and exchange it for gold or silver coins collectively known as specie. The system of unregulated "wildcat" banking was a magnet for fraud and abuse. Many of the banks issued worthless paper money, and receivers of public monies were expected to keep track of which of the hundreds of banks could be trusted. The commissioner of the General Land Office sent regular reports listing those banks whose paper could be accepted and which banks were issuing paper that was not acceptable. In certain cases, some denominations of bills were acceptable, while other denominations from the same bank were not. The General Land Office reports were printed in local newspapers.

A typical ad in the *Edwardsville Spectator* in 1819 listed the banks from which the receivers could accept money. The same ad said, "Bills of the branches of the Bank of the State of Tennessee of the Indiana branch banks, and of the branches of the State Bank of North-Carolina, other than those above mentioned, are not receivable." In November 1819, Stephenson placed an ad in the *Edwardsville Spectator* saying that he had received a list of banks "whose notes are receivable," and since the Bank of St. Genevieve was not on that list, he would not be able to accept notes from that bank since he "had no authority to do so." Since the mail service was so slow, it was common for Stephenson to accept paper money from an acceptable bank on the list only to find out that a directive removing that bank from the list had been sent a month earlier. Sometimes such letters were delivered in time to stop the transactions.

The lack of banks on the frontier created another problem for Stephenson. What was he to do with the money that was received in the land office? There was no bank nearby in which to keep it. In Stephenson's case, he had to take the money to St. Louis and deposit it in one of the banks there. The frontier was not a place where an individual wanted to be known as someone who frequently carried a lot of money. The frontier was populated with a few people who were bad and a lot of decent people who were desperate. Not only was taking the money to St. Louis dangerous, but it was also quite expensive and time consuming. There were no bridges across the river, and Stephenson had to ride to the river, engage a ferry, make his deposits in a bank, ride the ferry back across, and make it home safely. The fees for the ferry were 25 cents each way for a person and 75 cents each way for a horse and rider, so the expense was not inconsiderable.

The primary duty of the receiver, in addition to handling money, was the task of scheduling and overseeing land auctions. Once the surveys were completed, the president issued a proclamation indicating that land would be sold at the offices of a specific district. It then became the duty of the receiver to place ads describing the amount of land to be offered and details about the auction. The typical auction involved a significant amount of land. It was not unusual to schedule an auction in which 20 to 30 entire townships were sold. The receiver was required to advertise the sale in a number of local newspapers. A typical ad placed by Stephenson appeared in the July 24, 1819, edition of the *Edwardsville Spectator*:

> The sale of the 30 townships of land advertised by the President's proclamation, to be sold at Edwardsville on the first Monday of August next, will commence on Monday the 2nd of August, at 10 o'clock in the morning, and continue for three weeks. During each week there shall be sold ten townships.

The scheduling of auctions depended on the completion of surveys, so the auctions were held sporadically rather than regularly. Prior to 1820, the minimum cost for an acre had been $2. In 1820, the minimum bid per acre had been lowered to $1.25 per acre. Most lands sold for the minimum bid. If a parcel was not sold, it was rescheduled for a future auction. Business at the Edwardsville office was constant. In the six years between 1816, when the office opened, and 1822, when Stephenson died, the office sold 3,446 parcels of land totaling 426,701.68 acres. The total income of the office during the period was $832,699.94.

The land offices had to contend with other difficulties of frontier life that would not trouble a business in operation today. In the days before the introduction of gas lamps and electricity, lighting was mostly provided by candles. Beeswax candles were expensive and did not last long. Tallow candles lasted even fewer hours and produced a lot of smoke. Even a large number of candles failed to illuminate most rooms well enough to work by candlelight alone. At one point, a frustrated John McKee tried to complete journal entries for the monthly sales figures. Part of the page shows the unfinished entries. Scrawled diagonally across the bottom of the page is a note saying, "I can't work in the dark!!!" In the winter, when the days grew short, there were times when the workday was greatly abbreviated. In the summer, the office frequently got so hot that sweat dripped on the pages and the candles melted.

One of the more trying realities of frontier life was waiting for the mail service. An *Edwardsville Spectator* article printed in February 1822 gives a measure of the wait: "William P. McKee, Esq. is appointed Register of the Land Office in this place. He received his commission on Saturday last, by the southern mail, which had been two months and a half on its way from Washington." Before 1822, mail service was even slower and was beset with other problems. In April 1817, Stephenson received a letter from Josiah Meigs with an admonishment:

> Your account of monies received in the month of December last has arrived, considerably damaged: in future protect your accounts with better envelopes. And instead of making them in the form of a long roll attach the sheets together in book form.

In October of the same year, Stephenson received another letter from Meigs complaining again of packaging inadequate to the task:

> Effectually to secure the documents you transmit to this office in the future, I have to request that may be well wrapped in paper, tied and put into a cover of leather or skin. Unscraped skins with the fur outside will perhaps be the best protection from the weather.

All of the problems in the land office were manageable except one: an eventual successor to the post of register.

John McKee had been appointed register at the same time that Stephenson had been appointed receiver. The two were acquainted and after their appointments became close friends. When McKee and his son, William, came to Edwardsville, they had no place to stay, and they boarded at Stephenson's house. They stayed with the Stephensons until McKee could purchase a farm and move his wife, Polly, and the rest of his children to Edwardsville. Stephenson and McKee worked well together and seem to have had almost no friction. In October 1818, the *Illinois Intelligencer* in Kaskaskia carried news of misfortune:

> Died–At Edwardsville . . . Major John McKee, Register of the Land Office at that place. By the death of Major McKee society has been deprived of a valuable and useful member. He was a correct, moral and honest man.

Territorial Secretary Nathaniel Pope was appointed the new register in November 1818. Pope and Stephenson were longtime associates and were also friends. Pope's appointment would have meant continued harmony in the land office. Unfortunately for Stephenson, Pope was elected to the House of Representatives and resigned as register. President James Monroe then appointed Edward Coles to be register.

Coles was a Virginian. He was acquainted with Thomas Jefferson and was a friend of James Monroe. He had served as secretary to President Madison, and he was a close friend of both Madison

Portrait of Edward Coles. Office of the Illinois Secretary of State. https://www.cyberdriveillinois.com/departments/library/heritage_project/images/2014/12/EdwardColesPortrait-e1418186963528.jpg

and his wife, Dolley. He had been born into wealth on a plantation that included a substantial number of enslaved persons. By the time he reached adulthood, he had come to loathe the institution of slavery and made his feelings known to both Jefferson and Monroe. Due to his political connections, he was appointed to the register position at Edwardsville by Monroe. He left Virginia with a number of enslaved persons. On the way down the Ohio River, he freed all of them. He also purchased 160 acres of land for each family of manumitted persons, and he tried throughout the rest of his time in Illinois to provide assistance to his former enslaved people wherever possible. He was a vociferous advocate of abolition. Described as "young, dignified, and courteous," Coles nevertheless "lacked the charm and finesse to be a successful politician. His blunt speech alienated some associates, and he antagonized legislators when he became Governor, by announcing government programs without consulting with the legislature" (Howard, 1972, p. 134).

Even though Benjamin Stephenson, a slaveholder, had maintained friendly relationships with many of the antislavery forces in the Illinois Territory, he was unable to maintain a good relationship with Coles. Although there is no public evidence of overt hostility and not even any recorded public exchange of harsh words, it seems that the two did not work well together. The only evidence of their disharmony is contained in an exchange of letters between Josiah Meigs and Stephenson. In a letter to Stephenson, Meigs commented on the fact that Stephenson's monthly report had arrived but had not been countersigned by the register. Stephenson was reminded that his report could not be accepted without the signature. He was ordered to obtain the signature and resubmit the report. Stephenson replied that he had saddled his horse and ridden the three miles to Coles's house and produced his report for signature. Coles had refused to sign it. Eventually the report was accepted without Coles's signature, and it is clear that the relationship had substantially deteriorated. Coles resigned in early 1822, and William McKee, the son of John McKee, was appointed to the position of register, which restored a much-needed level of harmony to the office.

The land office position was not the only one that Stephenson filled during the period. By 1811, treaties, many of which had been negotiated by William Henry Harrison in his role as governor of the Indiana Territory, had ceded almost all of the land in Ohio and Indiana to the United States. Much of southern Illinois had also been acquired. Almost all of the public lands in 1816 Illinois were those acquired before the War of 1812 and were concentrated in the southern third of the state. There were also two narrow corridors of land a little farther north, which included the floodplains of the Wabash in the east and the Mississippi in the west. Much of northern Illinois remained under the control of the Potawatomi, Sauk, and Fox, while the vast prairies of central Illinois were controlled by the Kickapoo. In 1816, this did not present substantial problems for the sale of land in the office of the Edwardsville District.

Early settlers, like most of the Native Americans before them, avoided the prairies. The prairies were inhospitable, with hot summers and cold, windy winters. Furthermore, the fine-grained loess soils of the Illinois prairies drained poorly and became sodden in the spring. Once they dried out in the summer, the ground became hard and intractable. For settlers from the wooded areas of the eastern United States, the prairies were not considered particularly attractive. The attitude of many early settlers in the area is probably best expressed by the English writer Charles Dickens (1842), who, when traveling across the Looking Glass Prairie near Belleville, wrote, "It is not a scene to be forgotten, but it is scarcely one, I think (at all events, as I saw it), to remember with much pleasure, or to covet the looking-on again, in after-life" (p. 125).

The prairies were looked upon by the early settlers as having soil too poor to grow trees and, therefore, too poor to grow crops. This view was reinforced by Vice President James Monroe, who had been sent to Illinois Country to judge its natural resources. His opinion was that the absence of trees proved that the soils of the territory were almost useless. Worse still, the dense roots of the prairie plants grew as much as 10 feet deep and created a tangled mass in the earth nearly impenetrable to a wooden plow pulled by a team of horses. Because of the attitude toward the prairies, the early sales of land in the Edwardsville office concentrated on lands in southern Illinois and along the narrow corridors up the major rivers. Since so much land was available for sale, the fact that the prairies covering most of the territory were still under Native American control did not present much of a problem early on.

By late 1817 and early 1818, the situation had changed for two reasons. First, the Edwardsville office alone had sold more than 300,000 acres of land, and the need for additional land was rapidly increasing as new settlers entered the area. Second, some settlers like Gershom Flagg, who in 1817 purchased a quarter-section (160 acres) just north of Edwardsville, had begun plowing and planting the prairie. Flagg's lengthy and enthusiastic letters to his family provided glowing accounts of the area and the potential of prairie soils for agriculture. The experiences of Flagg and others like him demonstrated the amazing fertility of the soil. The demand for the prairie lands of central Illinois quickly increased. The prairies remained difficult to plow because of the dense root mass. But the problem was solved by using the enormous power of a team of at least six oxen to pull a single plow. Once the prairie had been initially "broken" by plowing, subsequent plowings could be done by a team of horses. Since few settlers owned six oxen, people like Ninian Edwards made a significant income by renting ox teams they would advertise in the newspaper. Turning over the soil by plowing would bury the thick cover of vegetation, which, as it decomposed, added even more nutrients to the grassland soil. No longer spurned by settlers, the demand for prairie tracts exploded.

In Washington, D.C., the potential for future sales of land and the rich prairie farmland in Illinois did not go unnoticed. In July 1817, Benjamin Stephenson was appointed sub-agent of Indian affairs in the Illinois Territory. Although the original appointment letter has not yet been found, Stephenson's acceptance letter was sent in July of 1817. His acceptance is a model of brevity, consisting of a single sentence: "Edwardsville Illinois Territory 19 July, 1817. Sir, I have the honor of receiving the appointment of Sub-agent of Indian affairs in the Illinois Territory, and accept of the same with pleasure." The appointment was the first step in the plan to acquire the Illinois prairies. At first glance, Stephenson's appointment was questionable.

As sub-agent of Indian affairs, he would have to interact with the Natives on a sympathetic or, at least, a dispassionate basis, and Stephenson could not be called dispassionate about Natives. He had considerable reason to dislike them. His brother James had narrowly escaped death on St. Clair's expedition in which one of Lucy's cousins had been killed. Lucy's half brother, Thomas Swearingen, had been killed by Natives. Lucy's father, Van, and her brother-in-law, Samuel Brady, had been leading figures in the fight against Natives on the Ohio River frontier. Additionally, many times as a child, Ben had been told the story of his maternal grandmother, Margaret Floyd Reed. The story told by Margaret Reed relayed the Native attack upon her family in 1719:

> In the blackness of night, a terrible war whoop was heard: she remembers her father putting her on a horse behind her brother and telling them to ride for their lives as he gave the horse a cut with a whip. He turned back to get his wife and other children, was too late; they were all massacred by the Indians. (Riley, 1999, p. 10)

Both of Margaret's parents and three of her siblings were killed.

Before going to Congress, Stephenson had participated in three expeditions against the Natives in the Illinois Territory. He was familiar with the savagery of attacks on the frontier in the period before the end of the War of 1812, and he knew a number of people, like Ann Gillham, who had been attacked. The letter written by Rufus Easton and Stephenson in 1815 to President Madison about the proposed expedition against the Natives on the frontier made a summary statement: "In war they thirst for blood. To secure them, they must be furnished and employed or entirely exterminated." Though Stephenson was no compassionate supporter of Native rights, he nevertheless opened an Indian agency housed in the land office building on north Main Street in Edwardsville.

From another angle, Stephenson's appointment made sense in the context of land acquisition from the Native Americans. If anyone in Illinois was in a position to understand the value of the land and why the federal government coveted it, that man was Stephenson. His office was already concerned with the situation, since a portion of western Illinois between the Illinois River in the east and the Mississippi in the west had been set aside as "Military Bounty Lands" for veterans of the War of 1812. These lands were to be given to the veterans when they presented a warrant certifying their service. Since this "military tract" was isolated from all of the other lands for sale in the territory, few were willing to use their warrants. If they had moved into the military bounty lands, they would have been surrounded by Natives and cut off from the few American settlements that existed.

A step toward acquiring these Native lands took place on November 1, 1817. The acting secretary of war, George Graham, sent a letter to Ninian Edwards, the governor of the Illinois Territory, and William Clark, the territorial governor of Missouri. The letter said:

> I have the honor to enclose you a commission for the purpose of treating with the Illinois, the Kickapoos, the Potawatimies, and other tribes of Indians within the Illinois Territory. The object of this negotiation is to obtain a cession from the tribes who may have a claim to it, of all that tract of land which lies between the most northern and eastern points of the boundary of lands, ceded by the Kaskaskias in August 1803, the Sangamo and the Illinois rivers, and which tract of land

> completely divides the present settled parts of the Illinois Territory, from that part which lies between the Illinois and Mississippi rivers, and which has been lately surveyed for the purpose of satisfying the military land bounties, a circumstance which makes the acquisition of this tract of country peculiarly desirable. If either of the tribes who have a claim to the land is desirous of exchanging their claim for lands on the west of the Mississippi, you are authorized to make the exchange, and your extensive local knowledge of the country will enable you to designate that part of it, where it would be most desirable to locate the lands to be given as an equivalent. To other tribes who may not wish to remove, you will allow such an annuity for a fixed period as you may deem an adequate compensation for the relinquishment of their respective claims. To enable you to give the usual presents on such occasions, you are authorized to draw on this department for six thousand dollars. The contractor will furnish on the requisition of either of you, the rations that may be necessary for the supply of the Indians while attending the treaty. Your compensation will be at the rate of eight dollars a day for the time actually engaged with the Indians; and that of the secretary you are authorized to appoint, will be at the rate of five dollars a day.

Governors Clark and Edwards acted quickly, since they concluded a preliminary treaty on September 25, 1818. The treaty was minimally significant because it dealt only with the Peoria tribe. The Peoria were a subtribe of the Illini.

While the total population of the Illinois Confederation tribes can never be known with certainty, there is general agreement that their population had been around 10,000–15,000 in the middle of the 17th century. At that time they were scattered across at least 60 major villages from Wisconsin in the north to Arkansas in the south. By 1800, only 150 years later, the Illini had been reduced to a total population of 250–600 and had become almost powerless in the face of stronger tribes and American encroachment. Unlike many tribes that were destroyed by British and American contact, the Illini were destroyed by other, more powerful Natives. Their history is a tangled web of shifting alliances and enmities. The only constant seems to be their positive genius for choosing the wrong side in almost every conflict.

They engaged in a series of disastrous wars with the Iroquois, incurred the wrath of the Winnebago, fought for the losing French against the English, and allied themselves with the losing English against the Americans. They antagonized the Osage, allied themselves with the Shawnee shortly before the Shawnee were defeated by "Mad" Anthony Wayne, and fought against the Shawnee when they relocated to Missouri. At other times they fought with the Chickasaw, the Quapaw, the Sauk and Fox, the Kickapoo, and also the Miami. The final chapter in their destruction came in 1769 when the Ottawa leader Pontiac visited St. Louis and crossed the river to visit Cahokia. He was killed by a young Peoria warrior. Pontiac, a friend of the French, had nearly destroyed the English during "Pontiac's Rebellion" in the early 1760s and was still viewed as a heroic leader by many of the Native Americans. Enraged by what they saw as the murder of a hero, the Ottawa allied themselves with the Ojibwa, Potawatomi, Sauk, Fox, Kickapoo, Mascouten, and Winnebago. By the time the episode ended, the Illini numbered less than 600, most of whom were women and children.

The treaty signed by the Peoria, and the other remaining Illini, ceded all rights to their lands to the United States. Since their lands had already been taken by other tribes, it was really a legal charade and may have been the only good deal the Illini ever got in their dealings with either the Americans or other tribes. In exchange for the lands they no longer controlled, they were guaranteed the protection of the American government against other tribes, and they also received 2,000 dollars' worth of merchandise, an annuity of 300 dollars a year for 12 years, and the title to 640 acres of land in the Missouri Territory.

Among those who signed the treaty as witnesses were Benjamin Stephenson, subagent for Indian affairs and receiver of public monies at the land office, and John McKee. A number of the leading citizens, including Abraham and Jacob Prickett, William McKee, James Watts, and Josiah Randle also signed the treaty as witnesses.

William Clark and Ninian Edwards had gained little of real value in the treaty with the Peoria, as becomes apparent in a letter from the newly appointed secretary of war, John C. Calhoun, to Auguste Chouteau in St. Louis:

> Mr. Stephenson the sub-agent at Edwardsville has been appointed to treat conjointly with you with the Kickapoos and any other tribe who may have a title to the land ceded by the treaty of the twenty fifth of September 1818. The commission which you already have is sufficient without a renewal as the treaty, if made, will be but a supplement to the one already formed. You will consider the instructions under which you have acted as your guide and will exercise every economy in the formation of the treaty which may be practicable, as the State of the Indian appropriation is scarcely sufficient to meet the current expence. Should it be necessary to collect the Indians interested and to make an issue of provisions you are authorized to make a contract for such as may be wanted on the best terms you can obtain. The contract you will transmit to this department and you will cause the provisions to be issued and certified in conformity to the enclosed regulations.

The appointments of Chouteau and Stephenson to negotiate with the Kickapoo made considerable sense as each brought to the negotiation particular abilities and strengths.

In addition to Stephenson's expertise in land sales, he was familiar with much of the area in question since he had served in the territorial militia during the War of 1812 and had marched through the western portions of the area during the attack on Peoria. Auguste Pierre Chouteau was the son of Jean Pierre Chouteau, who founded the St. Louis Missouri Fur Company, which dominated the fur trade in the American West. Jean Pierre was the brother of Rene Auguste Chouteau, who, along with Pierre Laclède, founded St. Louis. Auguste Pierre was active in his father's fur company and is credited with developing the rendezvous system, which became famous among the "mountain men." All of the Chouteaus were viewed in a favorable light by most of the Native Americans. For one, they were French, and the French had always been more closely allied with the Native Americans than had either the English or the Americans. For another, the Chouteaus had extensive experience with the Native Americans in the fur trade and were, for the most part, viewed as being honest.

Chouteau and Stephenson moved quickly by organizing a meeting and concluding a treaty with the Kickapoo in just over three months. The treaty negotiations were held in Edwardsville and created a considerable sensation. A German traveler, Ferdinand Ernst, who was looking for places to settle German immigrants, happened to arrive in Edwardsville during the negotiations and wrote about what he witnessed:

> On the 23rd of July I entered Edwardsville. The most remarkable curiosity which met me here was the camp of the Kickapoo Indians who were now sojourning here in order to conclude a treaty with the plenipotentiaries of the United States, whereby they renounced all their rights and claims to the lands on the Sangamon, Onaquispasippi, and the entire State of Illinois; cedeing the same to Congress, and to immediately vacate the State of Illinois. Their color is reddish brown; their hair is cut to a tuft upon the crown of the head and painted various colors. Very few are clothed, in summer a woolen covering, in winter a buffalo skin, is their only covering. They seem to be very fond of adornments, as of silver rings about the neck and arms. They likewise carry a shield before the breast. (Sutton, 1976, p. 206)

The Potawatomi proved to be far less cooperative and appear to have threatened the Kickapoo in order to prevent their acceptance of the treaty. A letter conveying the news of progress toward the treaty was sent to Washington in time for the secretary of war, John C. Calhoun, to respond by July 16, 1819:

> I have receiv'd your letter of the ult. It is gratifying that you have so far proceeded, in accomplishing the object of your

> commission as to obtain the consent of the Kickapoos to remove west of the Mississippi. It is to be hoped that the Potawatamies will not be so indiscreet as to attempt to execute their threats upon the Kickapoos on their removal across the Mississippi. Should they however oppose the movement in that way, it will be considered an act highly unfriendly to the United States, and will be noticed accordingly.

The treaty as originally negotiated consisted of 10 articles. The first ceded "to the United States for ever, all their rights, interest, and title, of, in, and to, the following tracts of land." Stripped of all the labored descriptions and legal language, the section ceded almost all of the vast prairies of central Illinois to the government. Article 5 of the treaty agreed to pay an annual annuity to the Kickapoo of $2,000 in silver for a period of 15 years. Article 6 provided an immediate payment of $3,000 worth of merchandise and a tract of land along the Pommes de Terre and Osage Rivers in Missouri. Other articles promised that the United States would protect the Kickapoo from settlers and other U.S. citizens. The treaty also provided two boats and an escort to move the Kickapoo to their new lands and swore to put the Kickapoo under the protection of the government, protecting them from foreign governments and other Native tribes. In the 10th and final article, the Kickapoo relinquished all rights to any other tracts of land on the eastern side of the Illinois and Mississippi Rivers.

The treaty was signed on July 30, 1819. Chouteau and Stephenson signed for the United States, and 23 Kickapoo warriors also signed. Witnesses to the signing included Pascal Cerre, secretary to the commissioners; Ninian Edwards; Benjamin Stephenson's son-in-law Palemon Winchester; James Watt; Jacob Prickett; William McKee; and a number of other local residents and officials. Among the first of the witnesses to sign was Jacques Mette, who served as the interpreter for the negotiations.

Mette was an interesting individual who appears in a number of roles at various times during the life of Benjamin Stephenson. He is first mentioned in August of 1811 when Captain Samuel Levering reported to Governor Ninian Edwards that Jacques Mette "of

Peoria" had informed Captain Levering of the names of the three Natives who had committed a murder on Shoal Creek. Mette was living in Peoria with his wife and was cooperating with the Americans. Mette was, at the time, an employee of the firm of Kinzie and Forsyth. He had spent several winters among the Kickapoo as a trader representing the firm, was well known to the tribe, and spoke their language. Despite this apparent cooperation, in the fall of 1812, "Capt. Thos. E. Craig attacked the friendly French traders, and returned to Fort Russell, bringing a number of the inhabitants of Peoria as prisoners. The prisoners were taken to St. Louis and discharged" (Edwards, 1870, p. 65). Among those prisoners was Jacques Mette.

Despite his eviction from Peoria in 1812, Mette was apparently "rehabilitated" by 1819, since he appears to have been living in the Edwardsville area and was employed by Stephenson as an interpreter in the Indian agency. His skill as an interpreter must have been recognized by Chouteau since Mette had been employed as the official interpreter for the negotiations. He seems to have supplemented his income as the agency interpreter by serving as a teamster. Among the probate papers for the Benjamin Stephenson estate is a bill from Mette for hauling various loads of meat, barrels, and other items during 1819–21 and a bill for $5 dated December 15, 1821, for hauling all of the household furniture to the new brick home that Stephenson had built.

The Kickapoo treaty was met with great enthusiasm in the Illinois Territory. The August 7, 1819, edition of the *Edwardsville Spectator* contained an article summarizing the key parts of the treaty and describing the boundaries of the tract of land ceded to the United States. The article observed, "This tract contains between thirteen and fourteen millions of acres."

The receipt of the completed treaty was acknowledged by the War Department in September 1819:

> Gentlemen your communication of the 20th Ultimo, was received by the Secretary of War, the day before he left the seat of government for South Carolina, and by his direction I have the honor to acknowledge its receipt, and to express

> to you his approbation of your proceedings and of the treaty which you have concluded with the Kickapoos.

The treaty was finally ratified by the United States Senate after several minor alterations were suggested and negotiated by Stephenson and Chouteau with the Kickapoo.

Stephenson's greatest contribution to the treaty of 1819 may have come outside the negotiation process itself. While he was equally as important as Chouteau in the negotiations, he was even more important in his role as informal "paymaster on the frontier." As discussed earlier, money was scarce on the frontier, even for the United States government. Although the secretary of war had authorized Governors Edwards and Lewis to spend as much as $6,000 in their negotiations, he had not specifically authorized any sum for Chouteau and Stephenson for the Kickapoo negotiations. The letter from the secretary of war to Chouteau, authorizing Stephenson and Chouteau to negotiate with the Kickapoo, gave explicit directions for distributing rations to the Natives. It states, "The commission which you already have is sufficient without a renewal as the treaty, if made, will be but a supplement to the one already formed." The letter also claimed that there was not much money available to fund any treaty. Nowhere in their instructions were they given any direction, neither on the question of how much money they could spend nor on where to get the money. The fact is that the War Department had a budget for Indian affairs that was woefully inadequate and had no mechanism for paying anyone on the frontier in a timely manner. When Stephenson and Chouteau concluded the treaty, they were obligated to provide an immediate payment of $3,000 worth of merchandise. However, there was no money to pay for the items. Stephenson took $6,000 in State Paper (equivalent to $3,000) in the form of specie from the U.S. deposits and paid for the merchandise.

The only problem with this transaction was that the deposits came from the sale of land at the Edwardsville land office, and the office's money was controlled by the secretary of the treasury. Stephenson, a veteran of Washington City and no novice to politics, was well aware that the various departments of the federal government defended their budgets jealously. He subsequently wrote to Treasury Secretary Crawford explaining the situation. He obviously was well aware that he had crawled far out on a thin limb. An auditor had arrived in Edwardsville to conduct an annual audit of the land office's books, and Stephenson explained what happened in his letter:

> On the arrival of Mr. Dukins at this place, to examine my books, and count the money in my possession, I had to present him with drafts on the Hon. Secretary of War for $6264.10 ½ in place of that much money, which I had received and agreeably to his suggestion I beg leave to trouble you with the following explanation relative to said drafts. his instructions from the Secy of the Treasury I held in my hand money subject to certain drafts for Indian expenses. In the mean time Colo. Chouteau and myself acting as commissioners to treat with the Kickapoo Indian, had necessarily to incur expenses to the above amount, and having no other funds furnished to pay those expenses I paid them out of the money in my hands, and retained the drafts, well knowing that at any time, they would be as good, if not better, than the money which was given for them—but intending, in order to avoid any confusion in my accounts, to exchange them as soon as necessary for money, which in cash has been done and can be effected as to the balance without the least inconvenience. You will perceive that nothing but the public interest was consulted in the transaction and I apprehend no possible objection can be made to the proceeding, nor have I any reason to suppose Mr. Dukins thought otherwise.

Today, a federal employee of the Treasury Department who spent money budgeted for the secretary of the treasury to aid a project of the secretary of defense would probably get fired. Additionally, a select committee would probably investigate the situation for several years before placing blame on someone in the minority party.

In 1819, though, things were different. Nowhere in any of the communications thus far located, between Stephenson and the secretary of war and the secretary of the treasury, is there any response from either secretary to Stephenson's mea culpa. The fact is that the secretary of war got his treaty and the secretary of the treasury got his money back. Both seem to have been entirely satisfied.

Three weeks after the Kickapoo treaty was signed in Edwardsville, the following announcement appeared in the August 28, 1819, edition of the *Edwardsville Spectator*:

> **WAS LEFT**
> **With** the subscriber by one of the Kickapoo Chiefs, a **SMALL BLACK**
> **HORSE**, about eight years old. The owner is requested to prove property and take him away.
>
> Ben. Stephenson

No one seems to have claimed the horse. Three years later, after Stephenson's death, all of his personal property was sold at auction. Two items failed to appear on the inventory and sale records and were sold several weeks later. A five-volume set of the laws of the United States was purchased by David Prickett for $11.00. The horse was purchased by Lucy Stephenson for 87-1/2 cents.

CHAPTER SIX

Statehood

When Ben and Lucy moved to Edwardsville in 1816, the little community probably had only eight or nine houses, mostly log cabins, and no more than 70 residents. Shortly after they moved, they built the first brick home in town. The house was located on Main Street near the original location of the land office in Pogue's store. The house quickly deteriorated and was torn down only a few years later. The only clue to its demise is a small footnote in a single reference. The reference says that the first brick house in the town was built for the Stephensons by Nathaniel Buckmaster. The person who made the bricks used street dust rather than sand to bind the bricks, and in a few years the house "crumbled again to dust" (Hair, 1866, p. 137).

Edwardsville was founded by Thomas Kirkpatrick, who came from South Carolina (Nore & Norrish, 1996, p. 10). Thomas had married Susannah Gillham, and he and his two brothers, James and Francis, accompanied a large group of the Gillhams to the area in 1805 (Hanser, 2008, p. 7). Since the Native claims had not yet been extinguished and no surveys had been completed, most of the group squatted on any piece of desirable land. However, Thomas Kirkpatrick purchased two militia warrants, or claims, from French citizens of the area. The claims entitled the warrant holder to claim any piece of property in the territory that was not already inhabited. The first claim, entitling the holder to claim 100 acres of land, was purchased from Pierre Lejoy, who held a militia claim from 1790. Kirkpatrick selected a location for his 100-acre claim on both sides of Cahokia Creek. Kirkpatrick acquired another

100-acre militia claim from a second Frenchman, Louis Le Brun. Kirkpatrick chose an area south of Cahokia Creek on the top of the ridge upon which the town of Edwardsville eventually developed. The northern edge of the ridge started at the banks of Cahokia Creek, which, at that point, flowed from east to west. Just west of the ridge, Cahokia Creek turned south and paralleled the ridge for a considerable distance before exiting the bluffs to cross the American Bottoms, emptying into the Mississippi. Most of the top of the ridge was prairie, while the creek bottoms were heavily timbered. Kirkpatrick built a two-room log cabin and a lumber mill on his claim near Cahokia Creek. By 1810, the mill was in full operation, and he was selling lumber across the Mississippi in St. Louis. An ad in the *Missouri Gazette* in 1810 reported that he was selling cherry lumber for $3.80 per 100 board feet. Walnut or ash sold for $3.25 per 100 feet, while oak sold for $3.00 per 100 feet. Kirkpatrick employed a number of people at the mill, and he built a log cabin on his second claim on top of the ridge to house the workers. Aside from the Gillhams, there were very few other people in the immediate vicinity.

The closest neighbors, several miles to the southwest, were two brothers, Samuel and William Bolin Whiteside, who had claims acquired from their father, James Whiteside, and another militia veteran, Abraham Rain. Six miles south was a 400-acre tract occupied by Samuel Judy, who had acquired four militia claims from four separate veterans. Kirkpatrick's nearest neighbor was James Haggins, who inhabited a 100-acre militia claim on top of the ridge halfway between Kirkpatrick's two claims. One additional claim is indicated on the original township map surveyed in 1815 and completed in 1816. It is a 100-acre claim located northwest of Edwardsville at the junction of Cahokia Creek and Indian Creek. The claim was three miles west, or downstream, from Kirkpatrick's claim on Cahokia Creek. This final claim belonged to Nicholas Jarrot, a wealthy French entrepreneur who lived in the old French village of Cahokia. In 1815, John Robinson, an early resident of Edwardsville and a Revolutionary War veteran, investigated the Jarrot claim and suggested that it was an excellent place to build a seven-foot-high dam to create a mill pond (*History of Madison*

Map of Missouri and Illinois, 1823. Lewis C. Beck, *A Gazetteer of the States of Illinois and Missouri* [. . .] (Albany, NY: Charles R. and George Webster, 1823). Benjamin Ostermeier is the editor and creator of this site: https://whiteside.siue.edu/assets/photos/Map_1823.jpg

County, 1882). There is no evidence that a mill pond and a mill were ever built there.

In 1810, Governor Edwards had created Madison County. The original county started at the northern border of St. Clair County and extended north all the way to the Canadian border. Edwards named Kirkpatrick's two-room log cabin as the seat of justice for the county (James, 1901). Kirkpatrick's cabin became the first county seat and the first courthouse, as well as the first hotel. Shortly thereafter, it also became the first tavern when Kirkpatrick obtained a merchant's license and a permit to keep a tavern. Kirkpatrick's property became considerably more valuable in 1812 when

Fort Russell was built just about a mile northeast of his mill. In 1814, while the war was still going on, Kirkpatrick developed a plat for a new town, which he named after Governor Edwards. In the original plat, Kirkpatrick laid out two streets, which ran northwest to southeast along the top of the ridge. Main Street was on the east while Holland Street, or Second Street, was on the west. Town lots were designated on each side of the two streets. Throughout most of the War of 1812, there was considerable traffic through the area since militia units and the various ranger units frequently mustered out of Fort Russell. However, the frequent traffic did not result in settlement. It was not until the end of the War of 1812 when the community that Kirkpatrick had envisioned began to grow. Even as late as 1815, there were almost no houses in the area. Edward Coles ventured into the Illinois Territory in 1815 looking for a place to relocate. He wrote:

> The county had recently been laid out, and its seat of justice was located on Thomas Kirkpatrick's farm. There was but one small log cabin on the site of the old town of Edwardsville, and that having no person in it when I passed, and seeing no marks to show the town had been laid out, I passed on the road over the site without knowing I had done so. (Norton, 1912, p. 56)

The period of stagnant growth ended with the conclusion of the War of 1812 and the establishment of the land office in 1816. By early 1816 there were two general stores in Edwardsville. The first was opened by Robert Pogue and was shortly followed by the opening of Stephenson's store. Originally, the land office was housed in a couple of rented rooms in Pogue's store, but when Stephenson's goods for his store arrived, he moved the land office and his store a block or two south to a new building. The building was on the west side of Main Street just across the street from the courthouse square.

The land office was a magnet for settlers. Every settler who wished to acquire land had to come to Edwardsville to attend an auction, and each auction could last for weeks. In addition, Edwardsville was the county seat, and judges and lawyers attended court at Kirkpatrick's cabin. By 1817, a new log courthouse had been erected on the courthouse square. In addition, the square had a log jail and the Wiggins Hotel. Since the courts and the land office both transacted legal business, many lawyers visited the city at regular intervals. Because there were few houses available in the early years, the Wiggins Hotel had substantial business. The hotel was marked by a distinctive sign depicting the first president of the United States and was always advertised in area papers as "The Wiggins Hotel at the Sign of George Washington." One of the early female residents of the city recalled that, in the early years, young ladies would frequently stroll around the courthouse square and the Wiggins Hotel in the early evening. The courthouse square was where all the young, well-dressed, and handsome lawyers stayed while they were in town.

In 1818, a special census was performed as a requirement for the territory to be admitted to the union as a state. The census has always been criticized for its lack of precision. In order to achieve statehood, there had to be 60,000 people in the territory. Almost certainly there were fewer than 60,000 people in the territory at the time. There is wide agreement that the census count was inflated to reach the required number. While there is no truth to the claim that the census counted every person, every horse, every cow, and every dog and cat, it does appear that the census was somewhat flawed. Even with the possibility of inflation, the little town of Edwardsville showed only 18 households comprising 166 people. The total included 74 white men, 71 white women and children, 17 indentured servants, and 4 free people of color (Buck, 1917).

Despite its small size, Edwardsville was already one of the most important towns in the territory. It was the largest settlement north of the little French town of Cahokia, which was about 25 miles south. North of Edwardsville, there was no other settlement anywhere before reaching Peoria. Settlers from a large surrounding area came to the town to buy goods in the two stores, take care of legal matters, and buy land in the land office. At the time it was an unusual town. It was populated by a number of professional people like Stephenson and Edwards, a number of doctors and lawyers, and gentlemen farmers. There was almost no middle class. The problem was so pervasive that Benjamin Stephenson placed an ad in the *Western Intelligencer* of Kaskaskia on March 11, 1818, titled "Notice to Mechanics and Farmers." The ad said:

> Mechanics of every description are much wanted at Edwardsville: more particularly the following Taylor, Shoemaker, Waggon Maker, Hatter, Saddler, Tanner and Curriers. Four to six ax men, and from six to eight farming laborers, will find immediate employment, and good wages.

In the next several years, the town and its population seem to have grown significantly. In 1819, Edmund Dana published a booklet titled *Geographical Sketches on the Western Country: Designed for Emigrants and Settlers*. About Edwardsville, Dana wrote:

> Edwardsville is the seat of justice for Madison County. It lies eight miles from Milton, and 20 miles north east from St. Louis; is a flourishing town, containing 60 or 70 houses, a court house, jail, public bank, printing office, which issues a weekly newspaper, and a United States land office, of which colonel Stevens [*sic*] is the Register [*sic*]. As this county embraces all the lands above, east of the Mississippi, and all the bounty lands in Illinois, soldiers' patents and grants of Illinois bounty lands are recorded here. In the vicinity of this town is a society of Methodists. There is an extensive tract of land around this spot, of an excellent quality, on which many plantations have been opened. But, unfortunately for settlers, the most valuable tracts have been monopolized by speculating men, who are non-residents. (p. 143)

A second description of the growth of Edwardsville, in the period between 1816 and 1820, can be found in the letters of Gershom Flagg. Writing to his brother Azariah in June 1819, Gershom Flagg said: "We have a News Paper published in Edwardsville which has very lately commenced by the title of *Edwardsville Spectator*. There is also a Bank and Lawyers enough to sink the place. The county is settling with extraordinary rapidity" (Buck, 1910, p. 165).

Another description can be found in the letters of Ferdinand Ernst, the promoter of a German colony at Vandalia, who traveled through southern Illinois in 1818–1819. He arrived in Edwardsville during the treaty negotiations involving Benjamin Stephenson, Auguste Chouteau, and the members of the Kickapoo tribe. He seems to have been more impressed with the Kickapoo than he was with Edwardsville. All he said of Edwardsville is that it

> is a pretty town about six or seven miles from the bluffs of the Mississippi and 25 miles from St. Louis. This fertile region is covered with fine farms, and where one has the opportunity of admiring the astonishing productiveness of the soil. (Sutton, 1976, p. 204)

In contrast, Ernst spent a long paragraph describing everything about the Kickapoo.

The census results for Edwardsville in 1820 show that the city had grown considerably after the 1818 census. The 1818 census showed 18 households and a population of 166. The 1820 census showed 53 households and a total of 437 people. The total population was 445, but there were 8 white males between 16 and 18 years who were counted twice. They were included in their household counts but also included in a separate column listing young men of militia age. Thus, the total population in Edwardsville in 1820 was 437. In the two years between 1818 and 1820, Edwardsville tripled in both households and population. White males outnumbered white females 232 to 154. On the other hand, there were 15 enslaved women and 12 enslaved men. There were 4 free male "colored persons" and only 1 free female "colored person."

The disparity between white males and females was common on the frontier. Many men went west to look for land and only later began to look for a spouse. If married, they later sent back east for their spouses. Interestingly, there was a significant sex disparity among children aged 10 and under. Eighty free white male children aged 10 and under were recorded and only 47 free white females of the same age.

The paucity of middle-class occupations that had prompted Stephenson's advertisement of just two years ago began to noticeably change. The ads bought by tradesmen in the *Edwardsville Spectator* included those of a tailor, a shoemaker, a baker, and an ad stating that Daniel Tolman had just opened a joinery on Main Street. There was even an ad from a Doctor Dulany, who

> informs the public that he cures the most obstinate cancers, wens, tetter worms, scald head, scurvy, king's evil, white swelling, rheumatism, fits, female and various other complaints, hitherto thought incurable by the medical art . . . the necessary medicines and written prescriptions will be furnished for each case from 10 to 50 dollars, according to the magnitude of the disease.

Another sign of the development of the town occurred in early 1819 when the first public library was formed. It was stocked with books donated by residents of the town. Benjamin Stephenson donated a number of books, as did his son-in-law, Palemon Winchester. It probably is a clue to the character of both men that Stephenson donated a five-volume set of *The History of Modern Europe* and a volume of John Adams's *A Defense of the Constitution of the United States*, while Winchester donated a book of poems and a copy of *The Adventures of Telemachus, the Son of Ulysses.*

In 1819, the first state General Assembly granted charters to Belleville, Carmi, and Edwardsville. Benjamin Stephenson, Joseph Bowers, Robert Latham, John Todd, Joseph Conway, Abraham Prickett, and Theophilus W. Smith were appointed trustees. The trustees developed a number of town ordinances, which were published in the *Edwardsville Spectator.* They included establishing a $5 fine for running a horse in town, a $10 fine for any person causing a riot or fighting in the town, and a $5 fine for anyone causing any dead or putrid animal to be thrown in the streets or any of the lots. Failure to remove said animal after the first fine would be followed by a surcharge of $1 for every additional day of failure to remove the carcass.

Interestingly, early Edwardsville was a model of Thomas Jefferson's vision of America as a land of "yeoman farmers." For Jefferson, the educated farmer tied to his own land was the cornerstone of freedom and democracy. Edwardsville in 1820 fit this model perfectly. Of the 158 people of employment age, 128 identified themselves as "engaged in agriculture." Only 10 were "engaged in commerce," and 20 were "engaged in manufacture." On the other hand, many of those who identified themselves and members of their families as "engaged in agriculture" were, in fact, engaged in other things. For example, Ninian Edwards reported that he was engaged in agriculture. While he had lived on a 1,000-acre estate in Kaskaskia and sold horses while he was governor of the territory, a more accurate answer would have been that he was "engaged in politics." Likewise, Benjamin Stephenson said that three people in his household were "engaged in agriculture" and none in either of the other two categories. But, once again, he was a "gentleman farmer" who also was a federal employee at the land office and the president of the Bank of Edwardsville (discussed in chapter 7).

Among the few non-farmers engaged in manufacture or commerce, only a few can be identified by profession. James Wright was listed as having two individuals in his household engaged in commerce. Newspaper ads reported that Wright was a tailor. Robert Pogue was listed as having three people engaged in commerce. Robert and his brother, George, were the owners of Pogue's store, the most prominent general store in Edwardsville at the time. William Hopkins indicated that three members of his household were engaged in manufacture, although, more appropriately, they probably should have been listed as engaged in commerce. Hopkins advertised in the *Edwardsville Spectator* that he kept a "House of Entertainment." While the term "House of Entertainment" might be construed in a number of ways, Hopkins, it seems likely, meant a theater! William Wiggins listed two people engaged in manufacture, but once again, it is probable that this should have been listed as commerce, since Wiggins was the proprietor of the Wiggins Hotel. Walter Seely listed six people engaged in manufacture, but so far no evidence exists to indicate what he actually did.

Edwardsville and the large area around it had been settled by an eclectic mix of people. There were a number of early residents of French descent who lived farther south in Prairie du Rocher or Cahokia. A few French-speaking residents, like Jacques Mette, settled in Edwardsville. A few of the older settlers were veterans of the Revolutionary War, and many of them, like William Whiteside, came from the southern colonies. Apart from the limited numbers of early residents like the French and the Revolutionary War veterans, there were at least four principal types of settlers.

The largest class consisted of southern farmers like the Kirkpatricks and the Gillhams, who had migrated to the area before the War of 1812 from South Carolina. They were joined by other southern immigrants, like the Whiteside family, who were Scots-Irish and had originated in North Carolina. The first of the Whitesides to settle in the area was William, who had been one of the "over mountain men" who destroyed the British unit led by Patrick Ferguson at the Battle of King's Mountain in the Revolutionary War. Others of similar persuasion had come from Tennessee or Maryland.

A second, smaller class of original settlers had come from New York and New England. A number of the New Englanders had migrated first to Ohio and later moved to the Illinois Territory. Like the southern immigrants, the New Englanders were mostly farmers. After the War of 1812, the number of New England immigrants grew considerably.

A third class of early residents was also from the South but differed from the Whitesides, Gillhams, and Kirkpatricks in having an aversion to farming. They were subsistence hunters and gatherers. They made a meager living hunting, trapping, and collecting products of the woodlands like ginseng, honey, and beeswax.

The final class of settlers included the rich and powerful, who were appointed to political positions in the Illinois Territory. Most of them were well-educated Kentuckians who had originated in other southern colonies or states like Maryland, Virginia, and Tennessee. In addition to government positions, they were professional people: doctors, lawyers, justices of the peace, and judges.

Initially, the substantial differences among the four classes of settlers had been masked by the shared dangers of the War of 1812. Almost all of the early settlers had served together in the militia, and their differences had been subordinated to the need to defend their families. When the War of 1812 ended and the land offices of Illinois opened, new settlers flooded into the territory. When freed from the shared dangers of the war, and the ever-present danger of Native attack, regional cultural differences began to emerge as a substantial problem. The various classes of settlers were different in a number of ways. The early southern settlers and the New Englanders were both farmers and shared a disdain for the southern hunters, trappers, and collectors who were generally uneducated, poor, and somewhat ragged. In modern terms, the subsistence hunters might be called "rednecks" or "hillbillies."

One of the postwar New England immigrants was Gershom Flagg, a native of Vermont. Flagg first traveled from Vermont to Ohio, intending to settle there. In Ohio he had his first encounters with the southern "hillbillies." In a letter sent to his brother Azariah in November 1816, he reported his impressions of them:

> There is no regulations for educating the youth by common schools. The inhabitants are from all parts north and east of Kentucky and are the most ignorant people I ever saw . . . In speaking of the ignorance of the people in this state you will take notice that I have traveled in that part of the state which is inhabited by people from Pennsylvania, Maryland, Virginia, and Kentucky. I am persuaded the people who came from Connecticut who are settled in the north part of the state are more enlightened. (Buck, 1910, p. 143)

It is not unexpected that Vermonter Flagg found the Connecticut settlers "more enlightened." Feeling as he did, Flagg, to no surprise, left Ohio after six months and went to Illinois. He floated down the Ohio on a flatboat, sent his belongings up the Mississippi by boat, and walked the 174 miles from the mouth of the Ohio to St. Louis. In St. Louis he took a short-term job helping to paint the first steamboat ever to reach St. Louis. In 1817, he came to the land office in Edwardsville, purchased 264 acres, and shortly thereafter purchased another 420 acres. Eventually, he sold much of the land at a profit and settled down on a quarter-section of 160 acres. He developed a farm with a thriving orchard on the prairie just northeast of Edwardsville. His farm was located near the site of Fort Russell. He became one of the first settlers to tackle the difficult job of plowing the prairies. Eventually, he used his experience to supplement his income by plowing neighboring farms for four dollars an acre.

In Edwardsville, Flagg came into contact with the other three classes of settlers. He once again found a number of subsistence hunters and gatherers who had arrived before him, and he found them no more respectable than those in Ohio. Writing to his brother in September 1818, he stated:

> The people of this territory are from all parts of the United States and do the least work I believe of any people in the world. Their principal business is hunting deer, horses, hogs, and cattle and raising corn. They have no pasture but turn every thing out to run at large and when they want to use a horse or oxen they will have to travel half a dozen miles to find them . . . These kind of People as soon as the settlements become thick clear out and go further into the new Country. (Buck, 1910, p. 162)

Flagg, the irascible New Englander, was not alone in his disdain for those who "clear out and go further into the new Country."

When Benjamin Stephenson died in 1822, he owed considerable money to a number of people, but he was owed money by an equally large number of other people. In the probate process, Lucy Stephenson was required to list all of the people who owed money to the estate and to suppose which of those debts could be collected. The list of accounts she believed not collectable had a number of pithy comments about people that Gershom Flagg would have seconded. Lucy's list included the following names and comments: "Green Rice–a rascal, insolvent, in Alabama; E.L.R. Wheelock–insolvent in Mexico (if alive); Amos Ruder–may be got some day when he pleases; Jason Suttun–insolvent and now lives in St. Louis; John Starry–insolvent this five years running; James Tuttin–insolvent since time out of mind."

While the early southern farmers, the New Englanders, and the southern aristocrats were united in their disdain for the "hillbillies," they nevertheless had significant differences with one another. The southern farmers saw people like Ninian Edwards, Nathaniel Pope, the judges, the lawyers, and the doctors, along with those like Stephenson who held high-paying jobs, as rich snobs who took advantage of their political power. The New England farmers like Gershom Flagg also distrusted the southern elite. In a letter to his brother Artemas in 1822, he wrote:

> Brother I am full in the belief that we are carelessly suffering our government to waste the public Monies in giving high salaries, creating new offices for the sake of providing for their friends, &c. The people of the United States ought not to sleep while their Representatives are voting to themselves 8 dollars pr. day and giving such salaries to their officers because of the hundreds of applicants for one office. (Buck, 1910, p. 172)

In Edwardsville the rich and powerful were also separated from the southern farmers and the New England immigrants by geography. Governor Edwards and Benjamin Stephenson had moved to what came to be called "upper Edwardsville" while the original part of town, known as "lower Edwardsville," was where the less affluent lived. Contrary to the normal understanding of directional descriptions, lower Edwardsville was in the older northern part of the town, and upper Edwardsville was in the newer southern part of the town. The terms "upper Edwardsville" and "lower Edwardsville" are better understood as terms denoting social class rather than spatial relation. The residents of lower town used the term *buncombe* to describe upper Edwardsville and the people who lived there (*History of Madison County*, 1882, p. 132). Among other things, the term referred to political speech offering empty platitudes designed to win votes; it was obviously a derisive term. The divide between the two parts of town came to a head in early 1820.

Benjamin Stephenson and Theophilus Smith, with the blessings of Edwards and other residents of upper Edwardsville, made what appeared to be a generous offer to donate the money needed to build a new courthouse. The only stipulation was that the new courthouse be built on a new square located in upper Edwardsville.

Of course, locating the new courthouse near their own properties would increase the value of their holdings, so the offer was not wholly altruistic. That Edwardsville needed a new courthouse was not in dispute. The existing courthouse was seen as a disgrace by everyone in both lower and upper town. The original courthouse had been built of logs and was accompanied by a log jail also located on the town square. The courthouse and jail were totally inadequate. The floors were either dirt or plank, and both were small and unimpressive. The offer to donate the money for a new courthouse should have been welcomed, but the residents of lower Edwardsville viewed it as a power grab by the residents of buncombe. The residents of lower Edwardsville tried to make a counteroffer designed to keep the courthouse at its original location. Because the two sides could not reach agreement, the log courthouse and log jail continued in use for more than five years. Finally, with donated money in 1826, a brick courthouse was built near Main Street on the town square. It, like its predecessor, was wholly inadequate. Reverend Thomas Lippincott, a longtime resident of the area, said:

> I remember when Lorenzo Dow came to Edwardsville to preach, some years afterwards. When he was shown the court house as a place for the meeting he refused to hold service there—saying that it was not fit for a hog pen. It had not yet a floor, except a narrow staging for the court and bar. (Norton, 1912, p. 138)

Aggravating the regional and class divides were other social differences, one of which was language. The French spoke French, the New Englanders spoke a variant of English, the southerners spoke southern, and the subsistence farmers were sometimes thought incapable of any kind of coherent speech. Their diets were different too. The subsistence hunters ate deer, squirrels, raccoons, fish, ducks, geese, and anything else that swam, walked, or flew. They did a little gardening but subsisted on what plants they could collect. The New Englanders farmed wheat and raised cattle. They ate beef and white bread, plus whatever their gardens could produce.

The southerners also gardened, but they raised pigs and grew corn. They ate mostly pork and corn bread. While all of the groups at times ate whatever was available, their food preferences conformed to long-standing cultural patterns.

The differences among the groups were many—region of origin, education, occupation, wealth, and ethnicity—but the biggest one, and the greatest cause of friction, rested on the question of slavery. For the most part, division followed traditional lines that pitted settlers from the South against those from the North; however, there were striking anomalies. Theophilus Smith was a New Yorker who came to Illinois in 1817. He was a lawyer and judge and was a good friend of Benjamin Stephenson. Smith was an unrepentant supporter of slavery. In contrast, Edward Coles, a Virginian, was perhaps the most outspoken abolitionist in Illinois. The early French settlers were strong advocates for the retention of slavery, while some of the small farmers from the South had mixed feelings about the issue. Many of the subsistence hunters were southerners and were happy to support slavery. For them, enslaved persons were a class even lower on the social ladder than they were. Slavery gave them someone to look down on.

Whatever views the various groups held, the prevailing legal position was clear. The Northwest Ordinance had banned "involuntary servitude." Slavery was, de jure, illegal in the Illinois Territory. However, the law is a living thing: subject to growth, change, and repeal. From the beginning, the prohibition on involuntary servitude was constantly under attack. As already explained, slavery was allowed, by exception, among workers at the United States Salines. In addition, Governor Harrison had made a number of changes to the law to appease southern settlers in the Indiana Territory. When the Illinois Territory came into being, Governor Edwards and the three judges adopted a number of the Indiana laws, including all of the laws governing servitude. An Indiana territorial act of 1807, titled "An Act concerning the Introduction of Negroes and Mulattoes into This Territory," allowed southern immigrants to bring enslaved persons above the age of 15 into the territory if the enslaved person "owed servitude" to the owner. The owner and the enslaved person were both required to sign an indenture contract within 30 days of arriving in the territory. Any enslaved person refusing to sign an indenture had to be removed within 65 days. No enslaved person would be likely to refuse since he or she would have been sent back south, where the treatment of enslaved people tended to be worse than even the harshest treatment rendered in Indiana. The indentures were supposed to expire at age 35 for males and 32 for females. Children of the indentured brought into the territory were to be freed at ages 30 for males and 28 for females. This change to the original Northwest Ordinance was an additional attempt to appease the southern slaveowners who had already won a clause inserted in the Northwest Ordinance authorizing the capture of runaway enslaved persons in any territory in the Old Northwest.

When Governor Edwards and the three judges adopted the Indiana laws, they paved the way for the importation of enslaved persons into the Illinois Territory. The introduction of indentured servitude was a legal fiction that made slavery legal, even though it was called something else. The 1818 census listed 17 indentured servants in Edwardsville and 4 free people of color. For the entire territory, there were 317 free persons of color and 751 servants or enslaved persons. By the 1820 census, the number of indentured servants in Edwardsville had risen to 27, and there were 5 free persons of color in the town. South of Edwardsville, the number of indentured servants was considerably larger. The 1820 census listed 469 free people of color and 668 enslaved persons. But the 1820 census also listed another 375 people who were classified as Black without reference to their status as free or indentured. The total Black population in 1820 was 1,512 persons (Norton, 1934).

Governor Ninian Edwards and Benjamin Stephenson were among the largest slaveholders in the early Illinois Territory. Throughout the period of his territorial governorship, Edwards remained at Kaskaskia, where he lived on his farm, Elvirade. In addition to his political activities, he seems to have been a successful farmer and horse breeder. Horse racing was a favorite pastime among the early settlers, and Edwards advertised the stud services of his racing stallion "Pontiac." Throughout his childhood in Maryland and his formative years in Kentucky, he had been surrounded by slavery. He seems to have been untroubled by the existence of slavery and owned a number of enslaved people. He frequently advertised enslaved people for sale in the Kaskaskia and St. Louis papers. On June 27, 1812, an advertisement appeared in the *Louisiana Gazette* offering the sale of

> a family of negroes in the possession of Moses Austin consisting of a man, his wife and two children. One negro woman who is a excellent cook now in the possession of Capt Barton near Kaskaskia. A mulatto woman in my own possession who is a first rate cook and house servant. Four very likely young negro men and several boys. All of them are honest and valuable servants. I have also a gig for sale, and I will take a pleasant riding horse in part pay for it.

In November 1812, he advertised in the *Missouri Gazette* the sale of "several likely young negro men and women: and I wish to exchange for other horses a stud horse known by the name of Whistle Jacket." In October 1815, he placed another ad in the Kaskaskia newspaper called the *Illinois Herald*. In this ad, he proposed the sale of 22 enslaved persons of both sexes and suggested that, if they were not sold "shortly," he wanted to hire them out in Missouri. In the same ad, he advertised the sale of a stud horse, a large bull, and several young bulls.

Coupling the sale of enslaved persons with the sale of a gig, a stud horse, and several bulls is a remarkable reminder of the unthinking callousness of a southern slaveowner in the early 19th century. Clearly, enslaved persons, horses, gigs, and bulls were all simply property.

Benjamin and Lucy Stephenson never approached the level of ownership that characterized Ninian Edwards, but they did own a number of "indentured servants," or enslaved persons. When they came to Kaskaskia in 1809, Ben registered three indentured servants: Hark, Tobe, and Winny. Tobe, "a mulatto man about twenty three years and nine months of age," was indentured for a period of four years and three months. During the campaigns of the War of 1812, Stephenson was accompanied by a servant. Almost certainly, that servant who served in the territorial militia was Tobe. Hark, age 15 years and 6 months, was indentured until age 34. Winny was the daughter of Ester, one of Van Swearingen's enslaved persons. In Van Swearingen's will, he had bequeathed to his wife, Eleanor,

> one negro girl by the name of Ester, and her daughter Win, during her natural life, and at her decease the said Negro Ester to be set free—but the said Negro Win, with all the offspring of the said Negro Ester (if any more) to equally be divided between her the said Eleanor Swearingen's three children afore named.

When Lucy Swearingen Stephenson reached her 18th birthday, Van's will specified that she could receive "the sum of fifty pounds lawful money, or a small Negro girl of that value." Lucy chose Win.

In June 1810, Ben registered two additional indentured servants. Deborah, called Deb, was described as "about three years of age, brought from the State of Kentucky." Deb was indentured until she would reach the age of 32. Hannah was described as

> a negro woman of a black colour about twenty five years of age lately brought from the State of Kentucky and the said Hannah agreed and bound herself by an Indenture . . . for the term of thirty years now next.

When the Stephensons moved to Edwardsville, all the servants had to be registered again. On January 15, 1817, Hark, Win, and Deb, who had been registered at Kaskaskia, were still with the Stephensons. Hannah was not included, as she probably had completed her term of indenture. Tobe was also not registered since his four years and three months of servitude had been completed. Four additional children were registered as indentured servants. Moriah was six years old at the time, Caroline was four years old, and Louisa was two years old. Barksley was only 42 days old when he was registered. It is not clear what happened to all of the indentured servants. In the 1820 census, two "free blacks" were living with the Stephensons, but it is not certain who they were. It would be reasonable to conclude that Tobe was one of the two. The other might have been Hannah, who had been 25 years old when she was registered in 1810. Since indentured females were supposed to be freed at age 32, Hannah should have been freed in 1817, which would explain why she was not registered in Madison County.

In July 1821, two additional servants are mentioned in the records: "Jess a negro man belonging to Benjamin Stephenson wished his child registered to wit: Washing Will born the 5th of October 1820 done the 1st day of July 1821." In 1827, Jess Price agreed to be sold by Lucy Stephenson to James Mason for $300. He was freed before the 1830 census.

Caroline, one of the four children registered in Madison County in 1817, was sold to William Brown in 1820 and resold to William Linn and William Hasket of Vandalia. She was released from her indenture in 1839. At the time of her release she was described as "26 to 29 years old, 5'2" tall with a scar over her left eye and a scar on her left wrist and back of her left hand."

In the 1830 census, Lucy was still living in the same residence, but Palemon Winchester, her son-in-law, was listed as the head of the household. At the time there were 15 people living in the house, including three "Free Colored Persons." One of the free persons was a male under 10 years old, another was a male between 10 and 23, and the remaining person was a female between 10 and 23. Most likely, the young male was Washing Will, who had been born in 1821. The other young male was most likely Barksley, who had been indentured in 1817 at the age of 42 days. The free female was probably either Moriah, who would have been 19 at the time, or Louisa, who would have been 17 at the time.

The records mention Washing Will again in 1831, when Lucy sent a letter to Patronella (Patty) Canal, dated June 15. In the two-page letter, Lucy mentions that Mary, Mary's father, and Wash had gone to Ohio. It is not possible to identify "Mary and her father." Girls named Moriah were sometimes called "Mary," but any attempt to identify Mary or her father is speculation. This letter makes the last mention of Washing Will in any record thus far discovered. However, by the 1840 census, Lucy was living in Carlinville, Illinois, and "one free colored person between 10 and 23 years of age" remained in the household. Barksley would have been just over 23 at the time, while Washing Will would have been 19. Most likely, Washing Will was still with the family.

The special census of 1818 had been conducted in conjunction with the movement to achieve statehood for the Illinois Territory. The whirlwind push toward statehood was initiated by Daniel Pope Cook on November 20, 1817. Cook, only 22 at the time, was the editor of the Kaskaskia newspaper. He published a short paragraph suggesting a campaign for statehood: "While we are laboring under so many of the grievances of a territorial or semi-monarchical government, might our claims to a state government be justly urged?" He exhorted all readers to begin discussions about statehood and to get behind the movement.

The next edition of the *Illinois Intelligencer* included a lengthy discussion of Cook's ideas on the issue. The editorial was written by Cook, but he signed it "A Republican." The desire for statehood spread like a prairie fire driven by strong winds. Governor Edwards and the Territorial Legislature quickly backed the idea. Public support was also immediate, and a number of letters to the editor voiced strong support. Since statehood required a territorial population of 60,000, Governor Edwards suggested that a new census be taken in time for the legislature to act on the statehood issue at its next session. Cook was not prepared to wait. He had been elected to the position of the clerk of the territorial house of representatives, and Cook, "a young man in a hurry," urged the legislature to act before a census was complete. Pushed by Cook, the legislature drafted a proposal to Congress proposing that the territory be admitted to the Union as a state. Four days later, on December 6, 1817, the drafted memorial was adopted by the legislature and sent to the governor (Buck, 1917, pp. 210–220). The statehood request was sent to Washington on December 10, 1817. Nathaniel Pope, the territorial representative to the U.S. House of Representatives, presented the request to the House on the January 23, 1818, only 64 days after Cook had proposed the idea.

As it was initially proposed, the act had several significant provisions. One provision proposed that the northern boundary of the new state be set 10 miles north of the southern shore of Lake

Michigan (Denny & Nordhauser, 2011, p. 3). Nathaniel Pope, who was serving as the territorial representative in Washington, convinced the voting delegates to insert several amendments to the original statehood bill. One amendment moved the northern border of the state 51 miles farther north, thereby gaining a significant coastline on Lake Michigan:

> The other major change sought by Pope was to reduce the five percent of the proceeds from the government lands set aside for roads to only two percent. The remaining three percent was to be set aside for education. A portion of this three percent (one sixth) was set aside for the support of a college or university. (Denny & Nordhauser, 2011, p. 4)

The statehood bill was passed by the House on April 6, 1818. The act was then sent to the Senate and eventually to the president. The president signed the act on April 18, 1818 (Buck, 1917, pp. 225–231). Amazingly, only 152 days had passed since Cook had first published the idea. The statehood act specified that there would be an immediate constitutional convention. All free white males who had resided in the territory for six months could vote for delegates to the convention. Elections were held on the first Monday of July 1818. Smaller counties could elect two delegates while Madison, St. Clair, and Gallatin Counties could elect three delegates. The convention was scheduled to begin on the first Monday of August 1818.

In the election of delegates to the convention, there was considerable discussion of the kind of delegates who should be elected. Some argued that the delegates ought to be well educated and professional. The counterargument was that the rich and powerful would vote their own self-interest and the common people would be ignored. The big issue was slavery and indentured servitude:

> The two sides of the slavery issue stumped for the candidates sympathetic to their own issues. In the end, most voters simply supported people who were well-known in the county and had personal qualities which the voters admired. Thus, three doctors who had a wide circle of acquaintances and

> patients were elected. Five people who had been commissioners of the census and had visited many homes during the census were also elected. (Cornelius, 1972, p. 7)

Madison County had a strong turnout of voters: out of 1,012 eligible voters living in the county, 517 votes were recorded. Since voters had to travel to Edwardsville to vote, the 50% turnout was quite remarkable.

Among the three delegates elected to represent Madison County at the convention was Benjamin Stephenson:

> The delegates from Madison County were Benjamin Stephenson, Abraham Prickett, and Joseph Borough. All three fit the profile of the typical delegate. Stephenson was well known throughout the territory and had served in a number of offices. He had served in the congress and held the rank of colonel in the militia. As the receiver of public money in the busiest land office in the territory, he had been involved in business dealings with a very large percentage of land owners in the territory. Joseph Borough was also well known in the county. He was one of the five census commissioners elected as delegates. As a census commissioner he had knocked on the doors of many of the voters in the county. Additionally, he was well regarded for his service as a mounted ranger in the War of 1812. He had started as a private and attained the rank of lieutenant by the end of the war. Abraham Prickett was one of the earliest American settlers in Madison County. His father and mother, along with Abraham, and his brother, Isaac, came to the area from Kentucky in 1805. He was well known as a long time resident of the county and was familiar to most voters as one of the first storekeepers in Edwardsville. Additionally, he and his brother, Isaac, both served as postmaster in Edwardsville. As both storekeeper and postmaster, Prickett knew a large percentage of the potential voters and, since he owned one of the only stores in Edwardsville, most of the voters probably owed him money. (Denny & Nordhauser, 2011, p. 4)

When the delegates convened on August 3, 1818, Benjamin Stephenson was appointed to the credentials committee. When the final draft of the constitution was completed, it had only eight articles. Five of them were not at all controversial and had been copied with minor alterations from the United States Constitution and those of the states of Ohio, Kentucky, and Indiana. There were only three contentious issues, and two of them threatened to derail the entire process.

The least contentious of the three was the issue of compensation for state officers. The original drafted article dealing with compensation set the governor's salary and that of each supreme court justice at $1,250 per year. The provision for the judges' salaries was amended and lowered to $1,000 per year. This created considerable argument since the governor and the judges had always had a contentious relationship. Eventually a compromise was reached by the delegates, who settled the matter with an equalizing cut. The compromise reduced the governor's salary to the same level as the judges'. They would all now receive $1,000 per year.

A more contentious issue was the location of the new state capital. The issue was complicated by rampant real estate speculation from a number of the delegates. An area called Pope's Bluff, north of Kaskaskia, was suggested as a site for the capital. Just two days later, Nathanial Popc, John Messenger, and Benjamin Stephenson created a partnership, and the firm of Pope, Messenger & Stephenson entered claims on 1,600 acres of land at Pope's Bluff. Numerous other delegates owned land, or entered claims on lands, that had been suggested as a site for the capital. Some suggested a site on land they already owned. The speculation reached such a furor that the entire convention threatened to come apart. Finally, a resolution was proposed that "required the new state legislature, at its first session, to petition congress for the right to acquire four sections of land on the Kaskaskia River which were east of the third principal meridian." The genius of the resolution was that all of the land along the Kaskaskia east of the third principal meridian had yet to be surveyed and, therefore, could not be purchased by speculators. The resolution was adopted, to the chagrin of speculators like Stephenson.

The third and most contentious issue the constitutional convention had to settle was that of slavery. There were deep divisions between the slaveholders and those who adamantly opposed slavery. That the convention was able to reach agreement was possible only because slavery's defenders realized they faced total defeat unless they compromised. They accepted that there were two hurdles they could not jump. One, the original Northwest Ordinance had prohibited involuntary servitude. The most they could hope for was some continuation of the status quo, which allowed indentured servitude by registering enslaved persons as servants. Two, the proslavery faction faced the absolute certainty that the United States Congress would never accept a new state constitution allowing slavery. Those who held indentures with servants had to accept some form of compromise or else risk losing control over the indentured servants they thought of as "property."

The draft of Illinois's slavery article was taken from Ohio's constitution and prohibited involuntary servitude, but it allowed voluntary servitude. An amendment to the original proposal added the word *hereafter* to the key sentence. The new sentence read, "Neither slavery nor involuntary servitude shall hereafter be introduced into this state" (Cornelius, 1972, p. 15). The change meant that indentures already in effect in the territory could be retained; thus slaveowners could keep their enslaved persons for the years remaining in their indenturing contract. Another portion of the article on slavery retained all of the special provisions pertaining to enslaved persons and indentured servants employed in salt production at the United States Salines. Lastly, the article stated that the children of indentured servants were to become free at the age of 21 for males and 18 for females. Cornelius (1972) writes, "Illinois could conceivably be assured of some unfree labor until at least 1839" (p. 16).

After the many compromises over slavery, executive compensation, and the location of the capital, the draft of the constitution was finally passed and sent to Washington. Illinois became the 18th state.

Slavery was not just contentious in Illinois; it also created considerable controversy in Missouri. The relationship between Missouri and Illinois, and between Edwardsville and St. Louis in particular, suffered greatly because of it. Conflict was touched off on the Fourth of July in 1819. Like the celebration in 1809 in Kaskaskia, the 1819 celebration featured a large number of toasts. Most involved uncontroversial subjects like remembrances of George Washington, Revolutionary War heroes, and the Declaration of Independence, similar to those offered in 1809. Unlike the earlier celebration, however, several toasts were more pointed. In a toast to General Andrew Jackson, the hero of New Orleans, Abraham Prickett suggested "that every attempt to extend the reign of tyranny in the United States be met with approbation." The "reign of tyranny" was an unveiled reference to slavery. Daniel Pope Cook tried to introduce some levity to the proceedings with another toast to the "town of Edwardsville—More wives and fewer bachelors: and may they all be as celebrated for the discharge of their private duties, as they now are for their patriotism." At least three toasts to follow returned to slavery and the hope for its abolition. Edward Coles toasted the "rights of man—They appertain equally to him, whether his complexion be white, red, or black." The most controversial moment came when Daniel Smith proposed a toast that later managed to offend a number of influential citizens of Missouri. His poetic toast made mention of Missouri: "A comet appear'd last night in the sky / To give us a toast for the fourth of July. May she sail up Missouri and smite slavery and end it / And scorch with her tail those that wish to extend it!"

Several weeks later, the antislavery toasts were reported in the *St. Louis Enquirer*, accompanied by an article excoriating some of the citizens of Edwardsville and the *Edwardsville Spectator*. The *Enquirer* reported:

> Some strangers collected in this town [Edwardsville] have set up a newspaper and gone to work publically and regularly on the Missouri slave question . . . A few of the old settlers, without reflecting on the *consequences*, have also joined them. To say nothing of the impertinence of this interference in our domestic concern, it has an obvious tendency to destroy the harmony which has always subsisted between

> Missouri and Illinois, and to raise up the spirit of retaliation in the former.

The article went on to suggest that the people of Illinois were hypocritical since the state was full of enslaved persons disguised as indentured servants. Finally, the article suggested that much of the problem was related to the fact that many of those responsible shared blame for the failure of the St. Louis Bank and were now living in Illinois, where they would likely help bring about the failure of the Bank of Edwardsville. Obviously, Daniel Smith's toast had struck a nerve in Missouri.

On August 28, 1819, Hooper Warren, the editor of the *Edwardsville Spectator*, reported a stirring in the Missouri Territory:

> A meeting of the citizens of Howard and Cooper counties in the territory of Missouri, is proposed in the Boon's Lick paper for the purpose of raising a fund of nine thousand dollars, and the appointment of three missionaries, whose duty it shall be to proceed to the state of Illinois, and by the distribution of tracts, and by other means of moral instruction, to endeavor to civilize the people of this state.

It turned out that Daniel Smith's toast was only the opening salvo of his antislavery activity. Shortly after the Fourth of July, he appears to have traveled to Boone's Lick near Arrow Rock in central Missouri. Smith's activities at Boone's Lick were reported in the September 8 edition of the *St. Louis Enquirer*. According to the *Enquirer*, Smith attended

> a camp-meeting where there was a considerable number of people collected together both white and black. Smith was discovered to be very busy among the blacks, even so far as to encourage them to mutinize; some of the citizens remonstrated with him upon the impropriety of such conduct; in reply, Smith used insulting language, and declared that if the negroes in the territory would revolt and embody themselves, he would place himself at their head and lead them

> to battle if necessary; on his uttering these expressions, he was immediately chastised [beaten!].

The *Enquirer* concluded the article with an insult aimed at Hooper Warren:

> The Boone's Lick people need not attach any blame to the nominal editor in *Barrataria*—alias Edwardsville [Barrataria is an island near the mouth of the Mississippi, which was the lair of Jean Lafitte the pirate], who is a good-natured, pokeeasy creature—perfectly harmless in himself—who is the dupe of a parcel of fellows who are ashamed to acknowledge their own pitiful productions.

The citizens of Edwardsville targeted by slaveowners in Missouri in 1819 were left alone once the proslavery contingent in Missouri turned its anger to "Kansas, bloody Kansas." Illinois escaped the kind of savagery that characterized the late 1850s in Missouri and Kansas.

The compromise on slavery that concluded the Illinois Constitutional Convention of 1818 did not, however, end the internal struggle over slavery in Illinois. The following year the first state legislature once again took up the question and, on March 30, 1819, passed the so-called Black Laws. The act included 25 sections and was written in convoluted legalese. The first section of the act prohibited any Black or mulatto person from settling in the state without producing a certificate of freedom. Additional sections required that all Black and mulatto people with a certificate register their family by providing all names and ages, and the act prohibited bringing any Black or mulatto person into the state for the purpose of emancipation. If any Black or mulatto person was emancipated, the former owner was required to post a bond of $1,000 to ensure that the freed person would not become indigent. The law also prohibited the hiring of any Black or mulatto person who failed to produce a certificate of freedom. Anyone who hired a person without a certificate was subject to a fine of $1.50 per day. The act allowed the sale of indentures, and it also set punishments for indentured servants who violated any of the provisions of the act.

For example, "On the order of any Justice of the Peace any servant being lazy or disorderly, or refusing to work, may be whipped and have two days added to the period of indenture for every day of refusal." Any servant who was convicted of any act for which a free person could be fined was subject to 20 lashes for each $8 of fine. In other words, if a free person did something punishable with a $10 fine, a servant doing the same thing would receive 23 lashes. Any enslaved person or servant found 10 miles from the master's home without a pass could be apprehended by any citizen and taken before a justice of the peace, who could order up to 35 lashes. Any enslaved person or servant who "trespassed" on property without the owner's permission could be detained and punished with 10 lashes by the owner. In this case, there was not even the requirement that the enslaved person or servant be brought before a justice of the peace. Riots, "routs," unlawful assemblies, trespass, and seditious speeches by any enslaved person or servant could be punished at the discretion of a justice of the peace. Anyone, especially owners, could be fined 20 dollars for allowing an enslaved person or servant of color to assemble in groups of three or more in any house, shed, or yard for revelry at night. Any sheriff or judge who knew of such an assembly could jail those assembled and could have them punished by up to 39 lashes.

These Black Laws, or Black Codes, enacted in 1819, did include a few provisions meant to place some restrictions on owners. One section specified that owners had to provide sufficient clothing, food, and shelter. Of course, the word *sufficient* left room for argument. Any owner who failed to heed the provision could be brought to court. There is no evidence, though, that any owner was ever brought to court for violating it. Another provision made it illegal for a master and enslaved person to enter into additional contracts during the time of the initial indenture. Presumably, this would deter the owner from coercing the enslaved person or servant into further binding obligation or another period of indenture. Servants were classified as citizens while enslaved persons were not classified as citizens. This meant that a servant could complain to the circuit court if punished too severely. An enslaved person could be subjected to unlimited punishment without any form of legal recourse. Once again, there is no evidence that any servant ever went to court to complain about punishment. Servants, as citizens, were free to acquire property, and owners were required to care for any sick or lame servants at the end of their contract period. The law also provided that at the end of the indenture period, every servant had the right to have his or her freedom recorded.

The 1819 act had several other provisions. One of them forbade any Black or Native person from purchasing a servant who was not his own color. There were white indentured servants, so the idea of a white person being purchased by a Black or Native person was evidently anathema to the state legislators. An additional provision prohibited any enslaved person or servant from working for anyone other than the owner without the owner's consent. An indentured servant was prohibited from selling any corn or other commodity without the owner's consent. Anyone who hired a servant or received any commodity from a servant or enslaved person without the owner's consent could be fined up to four times the value of the work or commodity.

The 1819 Black Codes implicitly allowed slavery. Those working at the salines and those owned by the French were classified as enslaved, not servants. Those classified as indentured servants were subject to restrictions that were almost as severe as the laws governing Black enslavement in the southern states. The fact that such laws were enacted in Illinois is hard to fathom. In the South, there was constant fear that the large population of enslaved persons could revolt and overpower the smaller population of slaveowners. In the South, Black Laws were mostly a reaction to the fear of a revolt. In Illinois, the idea of such a revolt was preposterous. Servants and enslaved persons were a minuscule part of the total population, and any agitation for revolt would have been easily suppressed. The fact that Black Laws were passed in Illinois indicated that slaveowners were still convinced they could eventually legalize all forms of slavery in the state.

Four years after the Black Laws were passed, and a year after the death of Benjamin Stephenson, the Illinois legislature recommended a referendum on the question of convening a second constitutional convention. The purpose of the convention would be to alter the state constitution and allow full-blown slavery in the state. The referendum called for a vote on holding a convention and recommended that a vote be taken in 1824. There were a number of well-known and respected people in favor of the convention and slavery, including Jesse Thomas, a supreme court judge; Elias Kent Kane, who had drafted much of the first constitution; and Shadrach Bond, the first governor of the State of Illinois.

When the referendum passed, Edward Coles was the governor. Coles was a longtime foe of slavery, and he immediately began a campaign to defeat the convention referendum. As part of his campaign, he purchased the weekly Vandalia newspaper, the *Intelligencer*, which had been proslavery, and immediately changed its editorial direction. The proslavery group was so upset with Governor Coles that William May, supported by Theophilus Smith and others, went so far as to file a lawsuit against Governor Coles in 1824. Coles had manumitted all of his enslaved persons when he came to Illinois. May's suit demanded that Coles be fined $200 for every manumitted person he had brought into the state. The suit was brought under the 1819 Black Laws, which required a person to post a $1,000 bond for every freed person brought into the state. The purpose of the bond was to ensure that newly freed persons would not become wards of the state. Coles lost the initial suit and was ordered to pay $2,000. He appealed the decision, and finally, in 1827, the state supreme court set aside the judgment.

Coles was the undisputed head of the anti-convention faction, but he received considerable help from a number of influential allies in his fight. One of the most important of these was Hooper Warren, editor of the *Edwardsville Spectator*, the weekly newspaper that Warren had founded in 1819. Warren had lived in Edwardsville for six years after arriving in March of 1819. In the brief period between his arrival in Edwardsville and the death of Benjamin Stephenson, he became one of Stephenson's closest friends and most important defenders. In temperament, they were similar. Both were reticent, speaking rarely but earnestly, and exuded calm (Norton, 1912, p. 102). But on the matter of slavery, they were contrasts. Stephenson was a slaveholder, and Warren was one of the most important opponents of slavery in the new state of Illinois.

Warren was born in 1790 in Walpole, New Hampshire. When he was very young, his family moved to Vermont. As was common in the late 18th and early 19th centuries, he learned a trade as an apprentice. He apprenticed at the *Rutland Herald*, where he became a printer (*History of Madison County*, 1882, p. 202). In 1814 his apprenticeship ended, and he moved to Delaware. He then moved to Kentucky in 1817. Shortly thereafter, in 1818, he moved to St. Louis and began work at the *Missouri Gazette*. In the spring of 1819, Warren circulated a broadside in a number of newspapers, including the *Western Intelligencer* of Kaskaskia, seeking investors in a venture to publish a prospective weekly newspaper in Edwardsville. He suggested that the paper be sold at three dollars a

Hooper Warren Print Shop, Edwardsville, Madison County, Illinois, 1819. Historic American Buildings Survey, creator George Churchill, photograph, documented after 1933. Library of Congress. https://www.loc.gov/item/il0163/

year in advance, or four dollars per year if not paid within a year of subscription. The prospectus proved to be convincing to a number of investors, and the first edition of the *Edwardsville Spectator* appeared on May 29, 1819.

Featured prominently in it was an editorial by Warren setting forth his political sentiments and his future editorial policy. Much of the introduction to the editorial was a restatement of the information earlier provided in the prospectus. He repeated the statement that he was "by birth and education a republican" and that he would never fail to promote the cause of republicanism and liberty. Furthermore, he asserted, he had only recently arrived in the state and could, therefore, not have become biased in favor of any of the political groups that divided the state. He said he had not been able to find any significant differences in basic principles among these parties. In his view, the controversies arose from the personal merits of the various political opponents. He then vowed "a strict neutrality" with respect to political parties. The controversial portion of the editorial was still to come, however.

In the prospectus, Warren had congratulated the citizens of Illinois for the state's advantages. The advantages he cited were the state's geographical position, the productive soil, "and her constitution recently formed," which "secures to her citizens the enjoyment of civil and religious liberty, [and] has by the happy exclusion of slavery, ensured to the state an efficient population." His comments on slavery in the prospectus were minimal, yet they nevertheless had provoked an immediate reaction. He reported that, shortly after the circulation of the prospectus, he was "informed by several gentlemen, for whom he has the highest respect that this reference to the prohibition of slavery had given umbrage to many of the citizens," who "refused to subscribe for the *Spectator*; and the propriety of withdrawing the offensive allusion was respectfully suggested."

Warren went on to explain that the question of slavery was settled by the constitution, and what a newspaper said about it was not particularly significant. But it is clear that Warren was not about to knuckle under to the suggestion that he should abandon his opposition to slavery. His initial statement about slavery was minimal and relatively mild. When challenged by "several gentlemen" who had taken umbrage to his statement, he expressed his position in no uncertain terms:

> But with respect to the question now in agitation throughout the union, relative to prohibiting the further extension of this bane of man, this abomination of heaven, the editor now declares that, whenever a public discussion shall be required, of the comparative justice and advantage of LIBERTY and SLAVERY, of FREEDOM and DESPOTISM so he will not hesitate which cause to espouse.

Throughout his tenure as editor of the *Spectator*, Warren continued to be an outspoken and influential opponent of slavery.

His most significant contribution to the slavery debate came shortly after the death of Benjamin Stephenson. When the 1823 referendum proposing a new constitutional convention, which would allow slavery in the state, was passed, Warren took a leading role in the opposition. Over the next 18 months, there was a lively debate between the supporters of a convention and its opponents. Among the opponents were a number of leading individuals, including George Churchill, Daniel Pope Cook, and Judge Samuel Lockwood, the executor of Stephenson's estate. The *Spectator* was a leading voice for the opponents. Warren wrote a number of articles about the idea and published a series of articles by Governor Coles.

Warren became a target of the proslavery side for the *Spectator*'s anticonvention stance. Theophilus Smith believed there was no outlet for arguments in favor of the convention; therefore, he purchased a competing newspaper. The *Illinois Republican* published proslavery letters and editorials, and it published rejoinders to letters and editorials appearing in the *Spectator*. Smith was so incensed by Warren's anti-convention stance that, in July 1823, he appeared in the *Spectator* office armed with a whip and his small naval midshipman's sword, or dirk. When he threatened Warren, he discovered that Warren was armed with a pistol; the encounter gives credence to the adage that one should never bring a knife to a gunfight. The confrontation ended peacefully.

Even though Warren and Coles were on the same side, Warren found Coles to be too radical for his tastes. In return, Coles was exasperated with what he thought was Warren's lack of bold action. Coles finally purchased the Vandalia paper in order to publish his opinions. Despite their differences, Coles and Warren remained allies. The issue was finally decided in the general election of August 1824, when 4,972 voters supported the call for a convention while 6,640 voters opposed it (Cornelius, 1972, p. 23). The defeat of the call for a new constitutional convention finally settled the slavery question in Illinois. Coles and Warren were the leading figures in the fight. Even though the defeat of the referendum signaled the end of the fight to legalize enslavement in the state, the restrictive Black Codes were largely retained until the end of the Civil War.

By the time the Constitutional Convention of 1818 ended, Stephenson had already moved on to other things that consumed most of his efforts during what remained of his life.

CHAPTER SEVEN

Banker

Starting in 1816, when Ben and Lucy arrived in Edwardsville, and continuing until Ben's death in 1822, the Stephensons stayed busy and were deeply involved in most everything that went on in town. Lucy kept busy with a number of social and community activities in addition to family responsibilities. Julia, the older daughter, was married in 1820 at the age of 17. Lucy was certainly involved in preparing for the wedding. With few finished goods available on the frontier, the wedding dress became a joint project for Lucy and Julia.

Julia married Palemon Winchester, a member of the influential Winchester family of Tennessee. Palemon was a lawyer and the nephew of James Winchester, a captain in the Revolutionary War. James had been captured twice and exchanged both times. He moved to Tennessee after the revolution and entered politics. He became the first speaker of the Tennessee legislature. In the War of 1812, James was given a commission as a brigadier general in the United States Army. He was appointed to the position of commander of the Kentucky Militia in the River Raisin campaign. The campaign was intended to wrest control of Canada from the British. The River Raisin battle was a disaster, and Winchester was captured by the British for a third time. He and a number of his unwounded troops were marched off to Canada and later exchanged. The troops too badly wounded to be taken with the British were left in the care of the Native allies of the British. The Natives promptly slaughtered all of the wounded. "Remember the Raisin" became a rallying cry for those fighting in the war.

Lucy was also busy raising her three other children and managing the household. Nevertheless, she found time to devote to the newly established Presbyterian church in Edwardsville. She founded a Sunday school dedicated to the religious education of indentured servants, and she became a founding member of the Edwardsville Singing Society. Beginning in 1819, she increasingly became involved in the planning and construction of the new brick house that she and Ben were building. When the house was completed and the family moved in on December 15, 1820, she was kept busy with furnishing and decorating the house. Since there were not yet any schools, she was also the primary source of education for the younger children.

Meanwhile, Ben was busy doing a number of things in addition to his primary duty as the receiver of public monies in the Edwardsville District land office. He was appointed a trustee of the town when it was chartered. He was also appointed supervisor of the public roads leading to St. Louis, Belleville, Carlisle, and Ripley. His duties as supervisor of public roads involved the maintenance of a stretch of the roads beginning at the courthouse and extending for one and a half miles toward each of the towns. He was also involved in a number of other civic initiatives. As already mentioned, he helped establish the first public library in Illinois. He and Theophilus Smith offered to finance the construction of a new courthouse, which incited conflict between upper town and lower town. Stephenson and Smith also placed an ad in the *Edwardsville Spectator* several years later on July 13, 1822, titled "Education," which announced the opening of a subscription school:

> A seminary of learning has been opened in the brick building of Wm. May, in the town of Edwardsville, nearly opposite the Hopkins' Hotel under the superintendence of Rev. James Jesse Townsend; wherein will be taught the Latin and Greek Languages, Arithmetic, English Grammar, and Reading and Writing. The qualifications and character of the gentleman, who will conduct the institution, stands deservedly high . . . and it is presumed that those persons, who may entrust their children to his charge, will be satisfied with his literary and

> moral instruction. As the number of scholars will be limited application for admission should be made at an early period, to the instructor, or to either of the subscribers, from whom the terms may be learned.

Like Lucy's, a great deal of Ben's time and effort beginning in 1819 was taken up with planning and building their new home.

Also in 1819, the citizens of Edwardsville celebrated the 43rd anniversary of the signing of the Declaration of Independence. Benjamin Stephenson, just four days away from his 50th birthday, served as the president of the celebration committee and presided at the celebration. The participants met at the front of the Edwardsville Hotel and paraded to the site of the newly built joinery owned by Daniel Tolman. The celebration included a reading of the Declaration of Independence by General R. Hopkins, a surviving soldier of the revolution. The reading was followed by a patriotic speech. Dinner was prepared and served by M. C. Wiggins, the owner of the Wiggins Hotel. After dinner, "toasts were drunk, accompanied by appropriate songs." As discussed in chapter 6, the toasts angered the proslavery forces of Missouri. It is ironic that Stephenson, a slaveholder, was the chair of a celebration that caused such consternation among Missouri's slavery proponents.

Stephenson added a new and time-consuming duty beginning in January 1818 when he became involved in the creation of the Bank of Edwardsville. Stephenson's Bank of Edwardsville (unrelated to the contemporary bank of the same name) was a major undertaking and an important institution for Illinois. The bank was important because it would supply one of the most pervasive wants on the frontier: money, west of the Alleghenies. Most of the early settlers in the Northwest Territory, including the Illinois Territory, were subsistence farmers who had little money when they arrived. Individuals' lack of money was not the only problem, however. The larger problem was that there was hardly any money to be had anywhere. The federal government printed little legal tender of its own. The Continental Congress had printed paper money during the Revolutionary War, but in the absence of revenues from import duties or taxes, the government had no reserves to back the paper, which soon lost its value. As mentioned in chapter 5, the devaluation of the paper money printed during the revolution led to the phrase "not worth a Continental" to describe anything that was worthless.

In 1791, as part of Alexander Hamilton's push to federalize all of the colonial debts accrued in the Revolutionary War, a national bank, known as the First Bank of the United States, was chartered. As part of the same fiscal policy, the United States Mint was created the following year. Among the major purposes of the bank was to establish a monetary standard, which would bring some stability to currency. A second purpose of the bank was to ease the credit market and make loans more available. The First Bank of the United States Bank was in Philadelphia, but there were branches in the eight largest cities in the country. The bank's charter called for the issuance of 10 million dollars of stock, of which 2 million was held by the government. The remaining 8 million was supposed to be owned by private stockholders. The bank was chartered for 20 years. Although it was called a bank of the United States, the bank was not fundamentally a government bank. Most of the stock was held by private citizens. The bank existed largely to make loans, and it printed a limited amount of paper money.

When the charter expired after 20 years, the bank was sold to private interests on the argument that most of its stock was already owned by private investors. The U.S. Constitution granted only the government the power to tax and print money, so with its majority shares being held in private hands, the bank should be constitutionally ineligible to print money. With the expiration of the bank's charter, a number of problems began to appear:

> The war wrought great changes in the monetary system as well. It brought heavy pressure for federal government borrowing. New England, where the banks were more conservative, was opposed to the war and loaned only negligible amounts to the government, and the federal government came to rely on the mushrooming banks in the other states. These banks were primarily note-issuing institutions generally run on loose principles. Little specie was paid in as

> capital, and it was quite common for the stockholders to pay for their bank stock with their own promissory notes, using the stock itself as the only collateral. (Rothbard, 2007, pp. 4–5)

Since New England banks were conservative and demanded specie-backed notes, there was a rapid concentration of specie in New England banks and a corresponding decline in the availability of specie everywhere else. Prior to 1814, banks were supposed to maintain reserves of gold and silver sufficient to cover the amount of paper money they printed. By 1814, the lack of specie outside New England and the expansion of banks issuing currency in other regions led the government to suspend the requirement that currency had to be backed by specie. Since the state banks were largely unregulated, a number took advantage of the situation to print more money than they could back. Consequently, the banknotes issued by a number of banks outside New England became devalued.

The situation got so out of control that the government chartered the Second Bank of the United States in 1816. The bank was created with considerably more capital than the first bank and had 25 branches. Initially, the Second Bank of the United States was as poorly run as the state banks and nearly closed down after a year. New management finally stabilized the bank by 1822. The bank had a short life, however, because President Andrew Jackson opposed it. He refused to renew its charter in 1832 and withdrew most of the government's deposits from the bank. Afterward, it could no longer operate.

While the creation of the First Bank of the United States Bank and the U.S. Mint had eased the monetary situation in the East, it did little to improve the situation on the frontier. The second federal bank was supposed to solve the problems, but it was so poorly managed that it made them worse instead. In the Illinois Territory, the shortage of money was acute. Not only was it scarce, but the supply was also constantly shrinking. What little real money, in the form of banknotes and gold and silver coins, did make its way into the Illinois Territory was quickly transferred to other regions. Manufactured goods all had to be imported from the East or New

Orleans. Textiles, metal goods, and spices—almost anything other than food and liquor—had to be brought into the territory from somewhere else. Because of the need to import almost everything, money flowed out of the territory as fast as it flowed in. Even worse, what little money remained ended up being deposited in banks outside the territory because there were no territorial banks in the Illinois Territory.

This fact became intolerable when federal land offices opened in the territory. Large sums of money began to come into the territory, but just as quickly the money was taken out of the territory and deposited elsewhere. The federal land office for the Edwardsville District became one of the busiest land offices in the United States. But Stephenson, as receiver of public monies in the land office, was required to take the receipts to St. Louis to deposit the money in a bank approved by the federal government.

State banks had become common after 1816. By the 1830s, more than 1,600 banks had been created east of the Mississippi. On the one hand, the creation of these banks solved a number of problems. Money became more plentiful. Individuals could secure loans. Money, generated within a state, territory, or community, could be kept there rather than being sent east. On the other hand, in the absence of any form of regulation, other problems were legion. Fraud and counterfeiting were epidemic. Throughout the period, newspapers were full of accounts of nefarious schemes.

The *Western Intelligencer* in Kaskaskia ran numerous articles and ads detailing these problems. In 1817, an ad titled "A Swindler" was placed by Baptiste Montrieut. The ad warned the territory's citizens:

> A man by the name of Joseph Baker, came to my home not long since and gave me a bank note of $10, on the Patterson Bank, and the same person passed a note of $5 on the bank of New Brunswick, and a note to some other person, which notes have been shown to several persons in this place; who all pronounce them to be base counterfeits. I have thought proper to make his infamous conduct thus public to caution the people against such unprincipled wretches!

A second article in the *Western Intelligencer* detailed the appearance of counterfeit five-dollar bills "purported to be on the Bank of Marietta" on which "the cashier's name is a good imitation" but "the President's name is very indifferently written." The paper also ran an article from New York, stating that "the high constable of this city returned from Canada. He obtained there, and brought with him thirty-five plates on the following banks, and of the subjoined denominations." Another article from Kaskaskia cited problems in Ohio:

> We are informed that two trunks of bills lately struck off for the Mansfield Bank, were shipped from this place last week, for Ohio, where they are to be called up, and will probably be soon thrown into circulation. It perhaps is not generally known, that this association is nothing but a gang of swindlers who, under the specious name of "the President and directors of the Bank of Mansfield," are imposing on the community an immense amount of paper which they have neither the disposition nor ability to redeem.

Counterfeits came in all shapes and sizes. A common form of swindle was reported in a number of papers. The December 17, 1814, edition of the *Missouri Gazette* and the *Illinois Advertiser* cautioned readers: "The public are cautioned against a counterfeit of five dollar notes transformed into fifties. These counterfeits are of post notes of the Bank of Kentucky, with the usual insignia of Plough, Buck, & Co." This form of larceny was still being perpetrated five years later. The May 26, 1819, issue of the *Enquirer* reported:

> The one dollar notes of the Bank of Georgetown, Ky. altered to one hundred dollars; there are none but post notes of that denomination issued by said bank. Also, ones altered to twenties, fives to fifties, and tens to one hundreds, of the Bank of Georgia: these are very well executed.

In addition to the cases of outright fraud and counterfeiting, many banks succumbed to the temptation to print more money than they could secure. One author says of the situation, "the chief function of a western bank seems to have been to manufacture paper money and issue it on easy terms to the ambitious but impecunious inhabitants" (Dowrie, 1913, p. 366).

In December of 1816, the Territory of Illinois chartered its first bank. The case for creating the bank was made public by Daniel Pope Cook, editor of the *Western Intelligencer.* In a front-page article, on January 1, 1817, Cook pointed to the scarcity of "precious metals" and the difficulty of accepting paper money from banks in other states due to "the remoteness of our situation." Additionally, "the many frauds and deceptions that have been perpetrated in the country, by the circulations of spurious paper, purporting to be on bank at a distance, has very justly awakened the suspicion of those to whom such paper was offered and consequently cramped its circulation." Cook argued that money from a local bank would be much more familiar to people within the territory and thus more difficult to counterfeit. The Territorial Legislature and the governor obviously agreed.

The Bank of Illinois at Shawneetown was incorporated with $300,000 of stock at $100 a share. A total of $100,000 of stock was reserved for purchase by the territorial government at a future time. Purchasers of stock were required to pay 10 dollars a share in gold or silver coin with the remainder to be paid in paper money and on demand of the directors. The Shawneetown bank was allowed to open when it had received $10,000. The chartering of the bank solved one major problem for the territory. The bank was authorized to print its own paper money. The banknotes provided a medium of exchange at a time when gold and silver coins were in such short supply that there was no other effective medium of exchange. The Bank of Illinois at Shawneetown enjoyed great initial success. The stockholders, their friends, and their political allies obtained loans from the bank. They used the loans to fund large, speculative purchases of land. The gamble on speculation paid off for both bank and speculators. Since times were good, both made money. The initial reluctance of people to accept the paper money was eased when the Territorial Legislature passed another law: creditors could not demand payment unless they had notified the sheriff in writing that they would accept paper money from approved banks. Thus, creditors could not demand payment in gold and silver and were forced to accept the notes printed by the bank. The law was an open invitation to the bank to print more money than it had in capital.

The Bank of Illinois at Shawneetown was chartered during a period of economic expansion, and it was the only bank in the territory. It enjoyed such success that a little more than a year later, on January 9, 1818, three new banks were chartered. The Bank of Kaskaskia was unable to sell enough stock and never opened. The Bank of Cairo was chartered under a peculiar set of provisions. The holders of the charter owned 1,800 acres at the junction of the Ohio and Mississippi Rivers. The bank was chartered with the provision that the 1,800 acres would be subdivided into city lots that would be sold at $150 each. The first $100 of the $150 cost of each lot would be applied to bank stock. The bank was to begin business when 500 lots had been sold. The Bank of Cairo never opened. The Bank of Edwardsville was the third of the banks to be chartered. The provisions of its charter were similar to those of the Shawneetown bank. The Bank of Edwardsville was incorporated with $300,000 of stock at $100 per share. The terms for the purchase of the stock were even more liberal than those at Shawneetown. Stock in the Bank of Edwardsville could be purchased for five dollars down in gold and silver coin with the remainder to be paid in paper money upon the call of the directors of the bank. The bank could open for business when it had sold $50,000 in stock subscriptions and received $10,000 in specie payments.

Sale of stock commenced almost immediately. Advertisements appeared in both the Kaskaskia and Edwardsville newspapers, announcing that the sale of stock would commence on the second Monday of March 1818. Commissioners for the sale of stock included John Edgar at Kaskaskia, William Kinney at Belleville, Nicholas Jarrot at Cahokia, and Benjamin Stephenson, John McKee, James Mason, Abraham Prickett, and Joseph Conway at Edwardsville.

Initially, stock sales went well, and within several months, $30,000 in stock had been sold, with $22,625 of this stock purchased by Kentuckians. Principal among the buyers was General

John Payne. Payne's brother-in-law was Richard Johnson, who later became vice president of the United States. Richard Johnson and his brother, James, were deeply involved in the chartering of the Bank of St. Louis at the same time. An additional $5,475 in capital came from St. Louis stockholders, while the remaining $5,475 came from Illinois investors. Most of the Illinois investors were Edwardsville residents.

In the fall of 1818, stockholders in the bank met at Edwardsville to elect directors and officers. Directors included Colonel Benjamin Stephenson, Ninian Edwards, William Kinney, Abraham Prickett, Joseph Conway, Dr. Joseph Bowers, Robert Pogue, Theophilus Smith, and Robert Latham. It was an impressive set. Stephenson was of course receiver of public monies in the land office, and Governor Edwards was soon to be elected the first U.S. senator for the State of Illinois. Kinney would become a state senator, and Prickett would be a state representative. Conway was the clerk of the superior court. The remaining directors were respected professionals and businessmen in Edwardsville. At the first meeting, the new directors of the bank elected Benjamin Stephenson as president and Benjamin Seward as cashier.

Shortly after the bank opened, Stephenson, in his role as receiver, got a letter from William Crawford, secretary of the treasury. The letter, dated December 21, 1818, said, "From the favorable representations that have been made to me respecting the Bank of Edwardsville I have proposed to make it a depository of public money upon the usual conditions." The "favorable representations" were given to Crawford by Ninian Edwards, a fact that seems to have occasioned no concern on Crawford's part. The letter was of great significance since one of the principal reasons for chartering Illinois banks was to keep land office money in the state. Furthermore, the influx of substantial sums of land office money would put the bank in a favorable position. This position was enhanced by the fact that the secretary of the treasury had instituted a system that compensated the banks that became depositories of land office money. Rather than paying the banks for accepting the deposits, the Treasury Department deposited $40,000 in each of the banks. This was intended to be a permanent deposit for the bank's use and would remain in the possession of the bank as long as it was a depository of public money. Secretary Crawford's letter to Stephenson concludes with a cautionary note: "If any circumstance affecting the character of the Bank in which you may make your deposits should at any time come to your knowledge, you will communicate them to me." While the cautionary note appears to be a boilerplate addition to the letter, it would cause considerable problems a number of years later. Interestingly, Crawford never seems to have considered the issue of the obvious conflict of interest whereby receiver Stephenson was depositing federal land office money in a bank run by President Stephenson.

The bank began producing paper money in early 1819. Many denominations were printed: banknotes worth 25 cents and 50 cents, as well as bills in the amounts of 1, 2, 3, 4, 5, 10, and 20 dollars. The amount of paper money issued was never supposed to exceed the reserves in gold and silver coin held by the bank.

By the beginning of 1819, the directors and officers of the Bank of Edwardsville must have been celebrating their good fortune. A great deal of stock had been sold. The bank had been approved as a depository for the land office. A number of real estate developments were beginning in Edwardsville backed by loans secured from the bank. Additionally, new businesses and new settlers were flocking to town. Visions of fortune must have danced in front of all the investors.

Unfortunately for the investors, a number of factors came together that eventually destroyed the bank. The most significant of these was the recession that began in 1819 and extended into the early years of the following decade. Another important factor was the enmity of the *St. Louis Enquirer*, a newspaper that attacked the bank incessantly. A third significant factor was that the bank was under constant attack by other banks, including the Bank of Illinois at Shawneetown and, most notably, the Bank of Missouri.

The recession of 1819 was one of the early financial crises in American history. The crisis was precipitated by a number of causes. After its initial failures, the Second Bank of the United States had reinstituted the requirement that paper money be backed by specie. The federal bank, since it had limited amounts of gold and silver, began producing far less paper money than previously, so a credit crunch ensued. State banks were also required to limit their production of paper money according to the amount of silver and gold they possessed. This further curtailed the amount of money available, and credit became even more limited. During the boom period from 1800 through 1818, farmers had borrowed to buy land and borrowed to fund long-term improvements. The borrowing was fueled by easy credit from local banks that were printing money unsecured by specie. Land speculation had become rampant on the frontier. Even as late as June 1819, the boom continued. On June 12, 1819, Gershom Flagg wrote to his brother Azariah, "Land which was bought two or three years ago for two dollars an acre is now selling at 10 and 12. We have a fine country of land and a plenty of it" (Buck, 1910, p. 165).

Aside from the credit problems, the financial crisis was fueled by European recovery after the Napoleonic Wars. As Europe began an economic resurgence and saw increasing agricultural productivity, the need for imported American commodities lessened. This was particularly troublesome in the southern United States, where the cotton market crashed in January of 1819. Britain switched from American cotton to the importation of large quantities of Indian cotton. During the boom period, cotton prices had soared, so the loss of the British market was a financial disaster for southern farmers. All of these factors created problems affecting almost everyone.

Land speculators were hit hard. Those who had invested in new banks had purchased stock for little down payment, expecting to pay future installments on their purchases with their profits from the banks. When the banks ran into difficulties, they called on their investors to pay their installments. Most could not pay, and the banks fell into deeper distress. Merchants also suffered from the decline of prices and from declining demand:

> So low were prices and so scarce was the monetary medium in frontier areas that there was a considerable return to barter conditions among farmers and local inhabitants. Various

> areas returned to barter or the use of such goods as grain and whiskey as media of exchange. (Rothbard, 1962, p. 22)

There were widespread foreclosures, bank failures, unemployment, and declining agricultural production and manufacturing. The economy of the entire United States was affected, and the people of Illinois and Edwardsville were not immune.

In Edwardsville, the effect was felt at all levels. Farmers were pushed to the edge of bankruptcy. Gershom Flagg, one of the most successful farmers in the area, described the problems in several letters to his relatives. In a June 12, 1819, letter to his brother Artemas, Flagg described the recent boom in the population:

> The country is settling with extraordinary rapidity. Thirteen months ago there was not a family north of here and there is now perhaps two hundred some a hundred and twenty miles north of this. They settle on United States land. And as soon as it is offered for sale they will probably have to leave it or pay a high price for it. (Buck, 1910, p. 165)

A year and some months later, in October of 1820, he wrote his brother again, with grimmer news to relate:

> Money is becoming very scarce. Wheat now sells at 50 cts pr bushel and corn at 25. Beef and pork are also very low and the price of land has fell nearly one half within 18 months. The people are as is usual complaining of hard Times! Hard Times!! (p. 166)

On December 10 of the same year, Flagg wrote a letter to another brother, Azariah. He continued to quantify the economic woes for farmers:

> For this country this is called Hard Times. You may gather some Ideas of the circulation of cash here and of the great change of times from the annexed prices . . .

	1819	1820
Beef pr. lb	from 4 to 6 cents	from 2½ to 3½ cents
Pork "	" 5 " 6 "	" 2 " 3
Flour pr. Barrel	" $8. $12.	" $3.25 to $5.
Corn pr bushel	from 33 to 50 cents	12½ to 20 cents
Wheat do	" $100 [*i. e. $1.00*]	37½ to 50 cent[s]

Prices current in the vicinities of St. Louis and Edwardsville, from the letter of Gershom Flagg to Azariah Flagg, December 10, 1820. Solon J. Buck, "Pioneer Letters of Gershom Flagg," *Transactions of the Illinois State Historical Society* 15 (1910), 167. https://archive.org/details/transactionsofil1910illi/page/166/mode/2up

> Cows which sold last year for 25 dollars will not fetch more than $15 and oxen which Sold one year ago for 120d now sell for eighty only.
>
> The price of land has fallen more than one half–A bad time for speculators–there are many here who paid out all the money they had in first installment on land and depended on selling it before the other payments become due and as the price of land is now reduced no body will buy it at the former price. It will of course revert to the United States unless Congress does something for their relief. (p. 167)

The recession was devastating to banks all over the United States. The Bank of Edwardsville had loaned money to land speculators, and many of the loans went into foreclosure. In an ad in the *Spectator* dated May 14, 1821, Benjamin Stephenson and Ninian Edwards advertised the sale of nearly 75 lots and 28 acres of undivided land, which had been part of the John Robinson estate. The Bank of Edwardsville had loaned more than $2,000 to Robert Latham, one of its original stockholders, to purchase the property in November of 1819. Latham defaulted on the loan, and in 1821 the bank was left with the unsold lots and undivided land worth a fraction of the initial value.

The recession alone was enough to kill a number of banks in the states and territories that made up the Old Northwest; however, the Bank of Edwardsville was faced with additional problems, namely, attacks upon the bank by the rival Bank of Missouri and by the antagonistic editor of the *St. Louis Enquirer.*

The more serious attacks were launched by the Bank of Missouri. This bank was organized and funded by a number of highly influential stockholders and directors. They included Auguste Chouteau, Rufus Easton, Moses Austin, John Lucas, Robert Simpson, and Bernard Pratte. Auguste Chouteau was the most influential early settler in St. Louis and the driving force in the city's fur trade. By 1816, when the Bank of Missouri was chartered, Chouteau was 65 years old and a revered figure. Rufus Easton was still serving as a territorial representative in Congress and had been a colleague of Stephenson just two years earlier. His former cooperation with Stephenson in Congress did not extend to business, and he joined the campaign against the Bank of Edwardsville. Another of the influential charter members of the Bank of Missouri was Moses Austin. Austin was a leader of the lead-mining industry in Missouri and was both wealthy and powerful. In 1820 he sought grants from the Spanish in Texas, and his son, Steven F. Austin, founded the first American settlement in Texas. John Baptiste Charles Lucas had been a member of the House of Representatives from Pennsylvania and, after coming to Missouri, became an influential judge and a friend of Chouteau. Together, Lucas and Chouteau donated the land on which the present-day Old Courthouse in St. Louis was built. Robert Simpson was the cashier of the bank, and Bernard Pratte was an influential member of the French upper class of St. Louis. Pratte was a highly successful merchant and had married Madeline Lalumandiere, who was closely related to the French royal family. For Benjamin Stephenson, the unkindest cut of all was the fact that his old friend, William Rector, was elected one of the directors of the Bank of Missouri.

Without question, the little Bank of Edwardsville was facing a daunting set of attackers. Among the numerous schemes of the Bank of Missouri was a campaign to withdraw its capital. Holders collected large amounts of paper money issued by the Bank of Edwardsville and then presented all the bills at the bank in a lump sum; they demanded full face value for the bills redeemed in gold and silver coin. The charters of state and territorial banks required that the banks print only as much paper money as they could back with gold and silver. By redeeming all of the Bank of

Edwardsville's notes at once and demanding specie in return, the Bank of Missouri hoped to drain the Bank of Edwardsville of its gold and silver reserves and force it into bankruptcy. Initially, the Bank of Missouri was joined in this campaign by the Bank of Illinois at Shawneetown. However, the banks in Edwardsville and Shawneetown quickly came to an agreement that they would not try to redeem each other's paper for specie. Similar schemes were occasionally tried by other banks, but the attacks from the Bank of Missouri were unremitting.

These attacks indicated that the new Bank of Edwardsville had the potential to become a significant rival to the Bank of Missouri. The Bank of Missouri had earlier been designated a depository for the proceeds of land sales in the Territory of Illinois. When the Bank of Edwardsville was chartered, Ninian Edwards convinced the secretary of the treasury, William Crawford, to designate the Bank of Edwardsville a depository for land office receipts. Thus gold, silver, and notes from dozens of banks that would have previously been deposited in the Bank of Missouri began to pour instead into the Bank of Edwardsville. The Bank of Missouri was badly hurt by the loss, so it launched its series of attacks on the Bank of Edwardsville.

The Bank of Missouri was aided by newspaper attacks on the Bank of Edwardsville. The newspaper leading these attacks was the *St. Louis Enquirer.* The *Enquirer*'s attacks began within weeks of the opening of the Bank of Edwardsville. Almost every issue of the paper featured a critical article. The attacks were generally answered by Hooper Warren, editor of the *Edwardsville Spectator.* Additionally, Ninian Edwards wrote several letters to the editor of the *Enquirer* countering the newspaper's claims. Nevertheless, the attacks continued for several years. The *Enquirer* accused the Bank of Edwardsville of being illegally constituted since its principal stockholders were from Kentucky rather than Illinois. This charge was true. The territorial charter for the bank had required that the majority of stockholders be from Illinois, whereas the majority stockholders were from Kentucky. Additionally, the *Enquirer* contended that the Bank of Edwardsville could not back its paper money with gold and silver. The *Edwardsville Spectator* responded with articles indicating that audits in the years 1819 and 1820 had refuted these claims.

The attacks by the *Enquirer* were orchestrated by its editor, Thomas Hart Benton, who had a number of motives. One was a financial motive. He was a significant stockholder in the Bank of St. Louis. Although the Bank of St. Louis was not as big a competitor as the Bank of Missouri, the Bank of Edwardsville was still a threat to the Bank of St. Louis. Thus Benton had a significant financial stake in the destruction of the Edwardsville bank. His primary motive was probably not driven by financial self-interest, however; it seems instead to have been ideological. Throughout his life, Benton advocated for "hard" currency backed by gold and silver. His repeated charges that the Bank of Edwardsville had too little gold and silver to back all of the bills it issued were consistent with his honest belief in the virtue of hard currency.

What's more, Benton had a vested interest in slavery. Benton and many of the leaders of St. Louis were slaveholders. Despite its much smaller size and population, Edwardsville began to be seen by many in St. Louis as dangerous socially as well as financially. Hooper Warren, the editor of the *Edwardsville Spectator*, was an outspoken abolitionist. A number of other vociferous opponents of slavery also lived in Edwardsville, among them Edward Coles and Daniel Smith. In addition to inciting enslaved persons to rise up at Boone's Lick, as recounted in chapter 6, Smith had traveled to Sainte Genevieve to encourage revolt there as well. Edwardsville was seen by Missouri slaveholders as a nest of vipers. Anything that could destroy the leading business in Edwardsville would be welcomed by Benton. Thomas Hart Benton went on to serve as a United States senator from 1821 to 1851. Over time, he slowly changed his views and became a vocal critic of slavery. His later opposition to slavery led to his defeat in the 1851 Senate election.

Despite the recession and constant currency and newspaper attacks, the Bank of Edwardsville managed to stagger through 1819 and 1820. A significant blow came, however, when Ninian Edwards stepped down. In September 1819, Edwards wrote a spirited defense of the Bank of Edwardsville in a letter to the editor of the *Spectator*, but he concluded his letter by announcing that he was resigning from the bank's board of directors and would "withdraw from further future responsibility, of any kind whatsoever, in relation to this bank or any other." Edwards was the consummate politician, and he had aspirations for high office. The only conclusion to reach from his withdrawal from "further responsibility, of any kind whatsoever" is that he could see the handwriting on the wall and was getting out before his stake hurt his political future.

The end for the Bank of Edwardsville came in fall 1821. Before that, in mid-August, the Bank of Missouri failed and announced that it would cease to redeem its banknotes. In its August 21, 1821, issue, the *Edwardsville Spectator* reported on the repercussions:

> In consequence of the failure of the Bank of Missouri, and the consternation it produced among all classes of people in St. Louis, a run was made by every holder of a dollar of the paper of the Bank of Edwardsville, from St. Louis and St. Charles. The news of the failure of the Missouri bank arrived at this place late on Tuesday evening, and on Wednesday morning the board of directors of the Edwardsville bank caused its doors to be opened at seven o'clock, and continued them open until several hours after the usual time of closing. The same liberal course was we understand pursued during the week, and still continues.
>
> The result has been that not only have the holders had their notes redeemed with specie and every possible facility afforded them to obtain it promptly, but whatever unfounded impression had been made against the credit of the Bank of Edwardsville, from the circumstance of the failure of the Missouri bank, and the evil reports of slavers and slaveholders, has been entirely removed.

The article went on to say the run had ceased: "The solvency and resources of the Bank are unquestionable." On September 3, 1821, though, the *Spectator* ran an ad from the bank that called its solvency into question: "The Board of Directors of this institution have determined on a temporary and partial suspension of specie payment." The bank was still redeeming notes smaller than 10 dollars, but it would stop redeeming larger bills until the drain on specie reserves ended. The ad closed with an admission of uncertainty: "Whether this course of policy will prevent these drains time will determine."

The announcement that the bank would cease to redeem its larger notes with specie prompted a quick response from William Crawford. In an October 9, 1821, letter, Crawford stated:

> As, in consequence of the late resolution of the Directors of the Bank of Edwardsville not to redeem with specie its notes of ten dollars and upward, that institution no longer comes within the description of those banks whose notes you were authorized to receive. It is presumed that you have discontinued to take its paper in payment for public land.
>
> If there are in your possession any of its notes which were received by you before you were informed of the resolution above alluded to you will, if they are of a description which the Bank proposed to pay present them for payment and if they are not of that description you will deposit them in the Bank to the credit of the Treasurer . . . A bank which refuses to redeem with specie the notes of ten dollars and upward is manifestly a bank which does not discharge its note on demand in specie and the receipt of the paper of every such bank has been positively prohibited in the instructions given to the receivers by this department. No public monies are hereafter to be deposited in the Bank of Edwardsville except in the case above specified.

The drain on specie continued and, within a month, the Bank of Edwardsville closed its doors for the last time. Crawford's letter from October 9 was delivered after the closing of the bank. Ironically, it was the failure of the Bank of Missouri, not its aggressive rivalry for dominance, that was the principal cause of the failure of the Bank of Edwardsville.

For the Stephensons, the failure was a financial disaster. Not only did Benjamin Stephenson lose a great deal of money in the bank collapse, but the U.S. government also lost a large amount of land office deposits. The final account of the federal money lost in the collapse of the bank was $46,973. While Stephenson was paid a substantial salary for his job as receiver of public monies at the land office, he could never have earned enough to replace all the federal money.

Despite the collapse of the bank and the financial calamity that loomed over the fortunes of the family, life went on. On December 15, 1821, just three months after the run on the bank had precipitated the crisis, the Stephensons moved into their new brick home in upper Edwardsville. The home was built on a 182-acre parcel of land that the Stephensons had purchased from John Robinson. The two-story, southern Federal-style brick home featured a parlor and a dining room downstairs, with a master bedroom and children's bedroom on the second floor. A large, attached kitchen gave access directly to the dining room. The half-story room above the kitchen housed a number of the indentured servants and communicated directly to the children's bedroom. A log cabin, which had stood on the property before the house was built, was torn down and

The Stephenson House as it stands today. RoxAnn Raisner, "The Stephenson House," *Madison Historical: The Online Encyclopedia and Digital Archive for Madison County, Illinois*, last modified March 4, 2019. Photo by RoxAnn Raisner. https://madison-historical.siue.edu/encyclopedia/the-stephenson-house/

rebuilt close to the new house, and the free Black servants probably lived there. The home was a showplace and was by far the largest residence in town.

Whatever the fallout from the bank closure might have been, it was clear that Stephenson remained a valued and active member of the community. As his new house neared completion, he rented out the first floor of his deteriorating brick house in lower town to the clerk of the circuit court. He collected rent of $50 for a partial year in 1821 and received $120 in rent during 1822. Not only did he move into his new house and rent his old house, he and Theophilus Smith opened their subscription school the year after the bank's closure.

The achievement of statehood in 1818 had prompted the State of Illinois to begin chartering state banks, which could issue their own paper money. Despite the fact that his own bank would face competition, Stephenson had supported the development of state banks and wrote a number of letters to the newspaper supporting their creation. Authorized during the constitutional convention, state banks began issuing paper money in 1818. Like the territorial banks, the state banks were supposed to redeem their notes with specie, but the state banks were underfunded, and within a year, their notes were circulating at a worth of 50% of face value. Like the territorial Bank of Edwardsville, the state banks eventually failed.

If Stephenson's position in the community was little changed by the fallout of the bank closure, so too was his position in the land office unchanged. On February 25, 1822, the president reappointed him to the position of receiver of public monies for the District of Edwardsville for a term of four years. His reappointment letter was sent by his friend Josiah Meigs and directed him "please to qualify yourself by entering into Bond with one or more good sureties in the sum of Fifteen thousand dollars."

Since the land office job paid up to $3,000 per year in salary and commissions, Stephenson's reappointment would have been sufficient to solve his personal financial crisis. Although he would never have earned enough to refund the money lost by the federal land office to the bank collapse, there were enough deposits and other securities, like land, to satisfy a significant portion of that loss. His debts in the community were considerably less daunting. The four-year reappointment would have paid enough to satisfy all of his personal debts several times over. Nevertheless, economic disaster loomed when Stephenson became desperately ill in 1822.

The Illinois frontier was always a difficult place to live in the early 1800s. Many of the settlers, particularly those from the Northeast, found it exceedingly difficult to adjust to the summer climate. The hot mid-continent summers were difficult to endure for those raised in the Northeast. The cold, windy, and snowy winters presented an equally difficult adjustment for those who had been raised in the South and were used to mild winters where snow was a novelty.

Even for a New Englander such as Gershom Flagg, the winters were sometimes extremely difficult. Writing to his brother Artemas on March 31, 1821, Flagg related,

> We have had a very severe winter and considerable snow and this spring we have had several severe storms. Two men have been found dead in the Prairie supposed to have chilled to death by the cold weather and snow. I was one of the Jurors who examined the body of one of the men who was found dead and it appeared that after being out in the open Prairie for about 24 hours great part of which time it either Rained or snowed accompanied with a very Cold Wind he fell from his horse so benumbed with cold that he never struggled but went to sleep for the last time. (Buck, 1910, p. 168)

The hot weather in summer was also a common complaint. Flagg was initially shocked by the heat and other frontier conditions. In a letter to Artemas in 1818, he complained that horses and cattle, after doing well in the spring, began to deteriorate in June:

> They do not gain much after this being so harassed by swarms of flies which prevent their feeding any in the heat of the day. They are so bad upon horses that it is almost impossible to travel from the 15 June till the 1st Sept. unless a horse is covered with blankets. Where ever a fly lights upon

> a horse a drop of blood starts. I have seen white horses red with blood that these flies had drawn out of him. (p. 158)

Writing to John Johnson in February 1819, Flagg stated:

> The principal objection I have to this Country is its unhealthiness the months of Aug. and Sept. are generally very Sickly. I was taken sick with the fever and ague the 15 Sept. which lasted me nearly two months. I shall try it one season more and if I do not have my health better than I have the season past, I shall sell my property and leave the country. The summer past has been very hot and dry in the month of August the Thermometer stood at 98 degrees. (p. 164)

A number of physical problems confronted the settlers on the Illinois frontier. During the cold damp winters, when settlers were assailed by the strong winds that swept without interruption across the treeless prairies, lung ailments were common and frequently fatal. Severe colds, flu, pneumonia, and tuberculosis were widespread. Frequently, they were all lumped together and referred to as "winter fever." If spring was a season of starvation, then winter was a season of dying.

Mid-to-late summer, from July through August, was not much better. Aside from the oppression of heat and humidity, Flagg commented upon the sickly towns, "especially those situated contiguous to Rivers or Mill Ponds. The waters are very low and in many places covered with a green poison looking scum. The fogs arising from this stagnated waters makes the air very unwholesome." This problem affected almost every town, since the early settlers had concentrated along the rivers and streams and avoided the treeless prairies. Even the prairies, where rivers and mill ponds were rare, were frequently covered with stagnant water. The fine-grained loess soils of the prairies slowed the absorption of water, so expanses of standing water were common in spring and early summer.

Unlike the winter months, when winter fever abounded, the summers were the season of "fever and ague." *Ague* was a common term on the frontier and denoted any illness involving a high fever. Among the most common causes of ague was malaria. Today we think of malaria as a tropical disease not commonly found in the United States and almost unheard of in Illinois. That was not the case in the early 1800s. Malaria was exceedingly common in the South. Sickle cell anemia, a genetically transmitted condition, is a characteristic of Black populations in the South. Although people are debilitated or can die from sickle cell anemia, those who carry the trait from one parent, but not both parents, do not develop sickle cell and also carry an immunity to malaria. That a double-edged genetic mutation would confer advantage to some is an indication of the severity of malaria and its long history in the southern United States. Frontier Illinois was also stricken with substantial malaria. The standing waters covered with noxious green scum were prime breeding areas for the mosquitoes that carried the disease.

Stephenson had been in the Illinois Territory since 1809 and had engaged in a number of duties that took him all over the area in the spring and summer seasons, when the standing water and mosquito population were at their height. During January, February, and March of 1822, Stephenson seems to have been in fairly good health. He was still working in the land office, and he and Theophilus Smith were involved in creating the subscription school. However, by late summer or early fall, he fell ill. Dr. John Todd, the family physician, had tended to the Stephenson family for years. In 1819–1820, his total bill was $28. In 1821, his bill was $44. In the nine and a half months of 1822 before Stephenson's death, Dr. Todd's bill was $44.73. The probate records also indicate that, on September 29, 1822, the Stephensons purchased a quarter pound of yellow bark from Pogue's store. The bark, harvested in Peru, came from several species of shrubs or trees belonging to the genus *Cinchona*, the source of quinine. Quinine does not prevent or cure malaria, but it can treat its symptoms. Neither Dr. Todd's ministrations nor doses of quinine, however, proved to be effective, and on October 10, 1822, Benjamin Stephenson died. He was only 54 years old.

Two days later, on October 12, 1822, the weekly *Edwardsville Spectator* was published. Throughout its three-year existence at that point, the *Spectator* had rarely published obituaries for either local residents or well-known national figures. But the death of Benjamin Stephenson warranted not one, but two, long tributes.

The second one, published on October 19, 1822, was a poem titled "On the Death of Col. Stephenson."

The prairies spread with palls of brown,
Their summer's verdant gladness;
And autumn's leaves are fluttering down,
With rustling notes of sadness,

How fled from heaven the cheerful blue
That decks a sky unclouded!
The air puts on a dusky hue;
The earth in gloom is shrouded!

Yea, nature seems to mourn with all
Who linger, broken-hearted;
To let the tear of anguish fall
On dust of friends departed

But where is he–the just–the good–
Befriending and befriended;
Who firmly for his county stood,
And to her hall ascended.

I saw him in the summer's ray
With manly frame unbending:
But ah! behold yon corse of clay
A funeral train attending

I see their sable garbs of woe–
I hear their notes of sorrow;
Which bid the day in darkness flow,
And wean from hope the morrow

Oh! When *he* breathed his last farewell,
How wild his orphans' shrieking!
How did *her* grief, more stifled, tell
Her widow'd heart was breaking!

Insane is woe! by fits, despair
Against the blow is raving;
Or resignation, bending there,
For aid divine is craving.

And may that aid, Almighty God!
Be shed on these benighted;
And light them from this earthly sod
To where no joys are blighted.

The first tribute, in the October 12 edition of the *Spectator*, was a long obituary written by the editor, Hooper Warren. The obituary is all the more extraordinary considering Warren's adamant stance against slavery and the fact that Stephenson had been a slaveholder. The obituary states:

> DIED—In this town, on Thursday last, Col. Benjamin Stephenson, Receiver of Public Moneys for the Edwardsville Land District, in the 54th year of his age.
>
> However unavailing the tear of regret, which is shed for a deceased friend— notwithstanding the efforts of philosophy, or the just, but ineffectual dictates of sober reason—it will flow. Vain to the bereaved widow and fatherless child are all the admonitions of careful friends—who fear and mourn rather for the living than the dead.
>
> But when one who has filled the various stations of life with such pre-eminent faithfulness, as the subject of this notice, is called hence, the grief extends far beyond the precincts of the weeping relatives. All seem anxious to mingle their sorrows with the known pangs of the bereaved widow and children. Such emotions cause the present feeble attempt to sketch some of the events which have marked the life of Col. Benjamin Stephenson.

He was born on the 8th of July 1769, in the then colony of Pennsylvania–whence he emigrated, in the nineteenth year of his age, to Virginia, where he commenced his public life, and acquired the lasting esteem and approbation of all who knew him. In 1809, he removed with his family to Illinois, since which time he has filled various public offices, with such distinguished credit–so much to the satisfaction of all with, or for, whom he acted, that his eulogy is written in the hearts of more persons, perhaps, than will read this article.

During the late war he commanded a battalion under the then Governor Edwards, and a regiment under Brigadier General Howard, and in one or the other of which stations he was actively employed during nearly the whole period of danger to our exposed frontiers; and on all occasions distinguished himself so much by his vigilance, energy and intrepidity, as to secure the approbation of those under whom he acted, as well as the respect and esteem of those whom he commanded.

After the termination of his military duties, he was elected by the people of the territory to represent them in Congress. Without having become famous as a public speaker, he is acknowledged to have effected, by his prudent watchfulness, and through the esteem entertained for him, by his fellow members, as much at least as any other delegate could have done. From this high and honorable station Col. S. retired in 1816, having received the appointment of Receiver of Public Moneys in this land district. In this station he continued to retain the confidence, friendship, and esteem, it is believed, of all who knew him. As a member of the convention which formed the constitution of this state, his conduct was equally satisfactory to his constituents.

Although the writer of these lines has known and honored the deceased as a public officer, he has to state that it was in the friendly and domestic circles that the virtues of his heart shone with peculiar lustre. If the patriot mourn his death as a public loss–if friends shed a tear of sorrow over his grave–what, oh! what are the agonies of a beloved and affectionate wife—now wife, alas! no more, and of children, cherished by the kindliest sympathies of paternal love?

He alone who is the widow's God, and a Father to the fatherless, can heal the wound which His hand, in his own wise providence, has made. To Him may they look in humble confidence, and in Him may they find present and eternal consolation.

References

Index

REFERENCES

Aler, F. V. (1888). *Aler's history of Martinsburg and Berkeley County, West Virginia.* Mail Publishing Co.

Baldwin, C. R. (1986). *Captains of the wilderness: The American Revolution on the western frontiers.* Tiger Rose Publishing Co.

Bates, S. P. (1992). *History of Adams County, Pennsylvania.* Warner Beers & Co. (Original work published 1886).

Bell, R. M., & Zinsser, K. K. (1990, January). The Swearingens of southwestern Pennsylvania and the northern panhandle of West Virginia. *Keyhole, 18*(1).

Brannan, J. (Ed.) (1823). *Official letters of the military and naval officers of the United States, during the war with Great Britain in the years 1812, 13, 14, & 15.* Way & Gideon.

Brown, S. (1905). Old Kaskaskia days and ways. *Transactions of the Illinois State Historical Society, 10,* 128–144.

Buck, S. J. (1910). Pioneer letters of Gershom Flagg. *Transactions of the Illinois State Historical Society, 15,* 139–183.

Buck, S. J. (1917). *Illinois in 1818* (Vol. 1). Illinois Centennial Commission.

Bushong, M. K. (2009). *A history of Jefferson County, West Virginia [1719–1940].* Heritage Books. (Original work published 1941)

Carter, C. E. (Ed.). (1948). Papers related to the second administration of Governor Edwards, 1812–1814. In *The territorial papers of the United States* (pp. 241–452). United States Government Printing Office.

Cornelius, J. (1972). *Constitution making in Illinois, 1818–1970.* University of Illinois Press.

Dana, E. (1819). *Geographical sketches on the western county: Designed for emigrants and settlers.* Looker, Reynolds & Co.

Denny, S., & Nordhauser, E. (2011, Spring). The constitutional convention of 1818. *The Spectator: A Newsletter for the Friends of the 1820 Col. Benjamin Stephenson House.*

Dickens, C. (1842). A jaunt to the Looking-Glass Prairie and back. *American notes* (Chapter 13). Charles Dickens online. https://www.dickens-online.info/american-notes.html

Dowrie, G. W. (1913). *The development of banking in Illinois, 1817–1863* [Doctoral dissertation, University of Illinois]. HathiTrust.

Edwards, N. W. (1870). *The history of Illinois from 1778–1833: And the life and times of Ninian Edwards*. Illinois State Journal Co.

Everson, D. (2004). *A history of the National Conversation Training Center property and surrounding area*. Privately published.

Farrar, P., & Mateyka, K. (Eds.). (2011, Fall). The New Madrid earthquakes, 1811–1812. *The Spectator: A Newsletter for the Friends of the 1820 Col. Benjamin Stephenson House.*

Ferguson, G. (2012). *Illinois in the War of 1812*. University of Illinois Press.

Freeman, W. W. (1881, November 17). Obituary of Elvira Amanda Stephenson Maddox, 1809–1881. *Carlinville Democrat.*

Glatfelter, C. H., & Weaner, A. (1992). *The Manor of Maske: Its history and individual properties*. Adams County Historical Society.

Hair, J. T. (Ed.). (1866). *Gazetteer of Madison County, containing historical and descriptive sketches of Alton city, upper Alton, Edwardsville, Collinsville, Highland, Troy, Monticello, Marine, Bethalto, and other towns*. Published by author.

Halderman, J. A. (1850, August 18). Obituary of Mrs. Lucy Stephenson. *Carlinville Democrat.*

Hanser, K. (2008). *The sawmill on Cahokia Creek: Thomas Kirkpatrick's sawmill in Edwardsville around 1809* [Unpublished manuscript].

History of Madison County, Illinois: Illustrated; With biographical sketches of many prominent men and pioneers. (1882). W. R. Brink & Co.

Howard, R. P. (1972). *Illinois: A history of the Prairie State*. William B. Eerdmans Publishing Co.

James, E. J. (1901). *The territorial records of Illinois* (No. 11). Phillips Bros. State Printers.

Linn, J. B., & Egle, W. H. (Eds.). (1880). *Pennsylvania in the war of the revolution, battalions and line, 1775–1783* (Vol. 1). L. S. Hart.

McDermott, J. F. (Ed.). (1940). *Tixier's travels on the Osage prairies* (A. J. Salvan, Trans.). University of Oklahoma Press.

Meigs, W. M. (1887). *Life of Josiah Meigs*. J. P. Murphy.

Morrow, L. (2007, December). A surveyor's challenges: P. K. Robbins in Missouri. *Missouri Surveyor,* 4–16.

Nore, E., & Norrish, D. (1996). *Edwardsville, Illinois: An illustrated history*. G. Bradley Publishing.

Norton, M. C. (1934). *Illinois census returns: 1820*. Statistical Series (Vol. 3). Collections of the State Historical Society Library (Vol. 26). Illinois State Historical Library.

Norton, W. T. (Ed.). (1912). *Centennial history of Madison County, Illinois, and its people, 1812–1912* (Vol. 1). Lewis Publishing Co.

Philbrick, F. L. (Ed.). (1950). *The laws of Illinois Territory: 1808–1818*. Law Series (Vol. 5). Collections of the State Historical Library (Vol. 25). Illinois State Historical Library.

Pitch, A. S. (1998). *The burning of Washington: The British invasion of 1814*. Bluejacket Books.

Prowell, G. R. (1907). *History of York County, Pennsylvania*. J. H. Beers & Co.

Reynolds, J. (1855). *My own times, embracing also, the history of my life*. B. H. Perryman and H. L. Davison.

Riley, M. N. (1999). *Thru the years* [Unpublished manuscript]. https://familyhartroots.com/PA/Adams/Books/TTY.PDF

Rohrbough, M. (1968). *The land office business: The settlement and administration of American public lands*. Oxford University Press.

Rothbard, M. N. (2007). *The panic of 1819: Reactions and policies*. Ludwig von Mises Institute. (Original work published 1962)

Sampson, Mrs. J. R. (1922). *Kith and kin*. William Byrd Press.

Sutton, R. P. (Ed.). (1976). *The Prairie State: A documentary history of Illinois, colonial years to 1860*. William B. Eerdmans Publishing Co.

Trussell, J. B. B., Jr. (1977). *The Pennsylvania line: Regimental organization and operations, 1776–1783*. Pennsylvania Historical and Museum Commission.

Whyte, K. L. (1997). *Swearingen/Vansweringen and related families: A compilation of data on the Swearingen families in America*. Published by author.

Wood, D. C. (n.d.). *Mill Creek historic district*. National Register of Historic Places Inventory Nomination Form. Bunker Hill, West Virginia. https://wvculture.org/wp-content/uploads/2021/03/Mill-Creek-Historic-District.pdf

INDEX

SIDNEY G. DENNY (1940–2023) was the coauthor of *The Ancient Splendor of Prehistoric Cahokia* and a professor emeritus of anthropology at Southern Illinois University, Edwardsville. Professionally an archaeologist, Sid was one of the first board members of the Cahokia Mounds Museum Society, president of the Illinois Archaeological Survey, and a member of the Illinois Department of Conservation Historic Sites Advisory Board.

Sid's extensive research into the history of the 1820 Colonel Benjamin Stephenson House, probate records, and the Stephenson family was a significant contribution to the mission of the house and the success of the hands-on, living history museum it is today. A longtime supporter and volunteer, Sid served on the Friends of the Colonel Benjamin Stephenson House Board, organized archeological digs on-site, gave lectures, acted as a historical interpreter, and cochaired the 50/50 Antique and Collectible Auction for more than 20 years.